Wakefield Press

Our Mothers

In the same series

Our Fathers

Our Mothers

AS WE REMEMBER THEM

EDITED BY JUDY MACPHERSON KENT,
ANNE CRAMOND SUTCLIFFE,
ANDREW COLLETT AND BRYAN CHARLTON

Wakefield
Press

Wakefield Press
16 Rose Street
Mile End
South Australia 5031
www.wakefieldpress.com.au

First published 2015

Cover designed by Michael Deves, Wakefield Press
Edited by Julia Beaven, Wakefield Press
Text designed and typeset by Wakefield Press
Photographs compiled by Bryan Charlton
Printed in Australia by Griffin Digital, Adelaide

National Library of Australia Cataloguing-in-Publication entry

Creator:	Kent, Judy Macpherson, 1950– author, editor.
Title:	Our mothers: as we remember them / Judy Macpherson Kent, Anne Cramond Sutcliffe, Andrew Collett and Bryan Charlton.
ISBN:	978 1 74305 373 7 (paperback).
Subjects:	Linden Park Primary School (Linden Park, SA) – History.
	Mothers – Australia – Biography.
	Linden Park (SA) – History.
	Australia – Social life and customs – 1922–1945.
	Australia – Social life and customs – 1945–1965.
	Australia – History – 1922–1945.
	Australia – History – 1945–1965.
Other Creators/ Contributors:	Sutcliffe, Anne Cramond, 1950– author, editor.
	Collett, Andrew, 1950– author, editor.
	Charlton, Bryan, 1950– author, photographer.
Dewey Number:	920.720994

To our mothers, who gave us life,
opportunity and love
to the best of their abilities

Recipes included in this book

Contents

HOMEMAKERS

JUGGLING WORK and HOME

Introduction

This book was intended as a sequel to *Our Fathers*, a book which documented the lives of fathers who had chosen to settle in a new suburb of Adelaide in the 1950s and send their children to the new and reputable Linden Park Primary School. In fact we were well aware that one of the mothers, on hearing that we were writing about our fathers, wondered aloud why we weren't writing her and the other mothers' stories.

However, if it started out as a sequel, it has managed to take on a life of its own and genuinely stands alone as a sociological study of women of that era.

Many of us had thought it would be difficult to write about our mothers. They had not appeared to have lived a very exciting life – as had many of our fathers, especially during the war years. On reflection, some of us appeared not to appreciate our mothers then as much as we do now. Perhaps we saw them in the light of society's view of them as handmaidens or appendages to their husbands, our fathers. Perhaps we were unconsciously distancing ourselves from them in order to 'cut the umbilical cord' and become whole human beings in our own right. Perhaps some authors resented their mothers' perceived submissiveness, their passive aggression. It was only when we got going that the stories seemed to flow as we remembered the hardships they had suffered, their contributions to our family life and to the community, and the impact they had on our development. Some mothers are still alive and contributed to their stories; other authors interviewed aunts and uncles and many drew on sibling memories to flesh out or confirm their own.

Twenty-five of 80 of our colleagues who attended the reunion in 2012 from which the idea of *Our Fathers* emerged, chose to write their mothers' stories, the same number as for *Our Fathers*. It must be noted that there is an element of self-selection regarding our class's memories. There are no stories of infidelity or violence; that is not to say they didn't exist – perhaps they were edited out or maybe it would have appeared in some of the stories not submitted for publication. Certainly there is a degree of frustration and perhaps a lack of fulfilment felt by many of the mothers but we must be careful not to project our own feelings onto them as we struggle to understand how they reacted to their environment.

As has been described in many of the stories, our mothers' experiences in postwar Adelaide in the 1950s were characterised by a series of contradictions. Relief that the war was over, but nostalgia for the excitement and independence of the war years; the opportunity to marry and build a family confronted by the reality of their husbands' physical and mental injuries; joy of building a home but frustration at being 'chained to the kitchen'; religious bigotry and intolerance coupled with the freedom that contraception gave; individual fulfilment through sewing, knitting, craft and volunteer work coupled with these not being valued by society; and managing on one income. Some women saw the cup half full and made the most of these conditions; others took on paid work more through necessity than defiance; very few trained professionally and took up successful careers; others succumbed to their lot and suffered a decline which could only be remedied by a 'Bex, a cup of tea and a good lie down'.

The Linden Park area, or 'Mortgage Hill' as it was so often described, reflected the conservative, patriarchal values of the Menzies era. If women were given any positive reinforcement it was for the contributions they made to their menfolk and their families; and to their volunteer work with the school through the parents' and friends' associations, the Cubs, Scouts, and the Church.

In the previous decade they had willingly contributed to the war effort on the understanding that they would relinquish those jobs when the men returned. The poster: 'Our Job: To clothe the men who work and fight' made their role clear.

Some of our mothers trained as nurses to support the war effort, one escaping bombing in Darwin and Katherine. Others joined the Land Army or worked in munitions factories. Others already worked in essential services which they were not encouraged to leave. Many described their work then as stimulating and fun. They knew they were contributing in a significant way. Many made friends they would keep for life; some met their soldier husbands then.

But after the war it was assumed that they would concentrate their efforts on raising families and keeping house and indeed, many women were relieved to be able to do so. The memories of mums coping with numerous children, no car, little or no public transport, in a suburb miles away from the city and their families of origin, paint a picture of women who had no time to do much else other than feed their families and keep their houses and clothes clean. And all this with none of the technological advancements or automation we enjoy today. Many of us remember the unwieldy and dangerous wringers, the Bluo in the wash, the heavy and cumbersome meat grinders, the Fowlers Vacola, the foot-operated Singer sewing machine. But we remember most vividly what they cooked for us – the cakes and slices, the jams and preserved fruit. And how they coped with meagre resources to serve up one chop on each plate, to carefully allocate the Amscol ice-cream, to serve up the chicken at Christmas time. And no such luxury as take-away! No wonder they shooed us out of the house until teatime. No wonder they might sometimes have reflected on the freedom they had enjoyed during the war years and the missed opportunities for further study and development. For many of our mums had already been scarred by the Depression in the 1930s, having to leave school at 14 or 15 to train as typistes, stenographers, comptometristes or bookkeepers. And then once married they were legally obliged to give up their full-time work.

If many of our mothers suffered day-to-day isolation from living in a new suburb miles from the city, most of them built their lives around their families, happiest when they could share the ritual family holiday together at places like Moana, Victor Harbor, Port Willunga or up on the Murray. Here they played cards with the kids, orchestrated singalongs, listened to *Blue Hills* on the 'wireless', read the *Women's Weekly* or lapped up the sun on the beach, coping with even more adverse conditions such as ice chests, kerosene cookers, and milk from the 'milkie' in billy cans – not to mention the ubiquitous flies. And still managing to feed us. Later, after we had left home, many of our mothers were able to travel more extensively, some to revisit their birthplaces, others to see the world for the first time.

Many mothers were isolated from their families of origin, having left them in the country or interstate. At least eight of our mothers were born overseas and some of them had left their families behind. If it was difficult for the mothers to find their place in the society they had grown up in, how much more difficult was it for those women who had to learn new customs, let alone a new language – ridiculous customs such as having to wear a matching hat and gloves for a trip into town. Or bringing a 'plate' to a picnic, not realising that it was meant to be a full plate, not an empty one! And how much this affected their children, our classmates, who strongly felt their difference when they pulled their salami sandwiches from their lunchboxes or when their mothers came to visit the school.

Although we children thought we were part of a homogenous society in an upwardly aspiring middle-class suburb, our mothers had come from very different circumstances – some from country Australia, some from middle-class families who had survived the Depression, some from the 'mother country', and some escaping the horrors of war-torn Europe. These circumstances shaped our mothers as much as the society they found themselves living in. And this has in turn shaped our own destinies. It is tempting to wonder here what our children would write about us, their mothers and fathers. But that's another story.

This book would not have come to fruition had it not been for the committee which worked tirelessly to find us and organise a reunion in September 2012 – Bryan Charlton, Andrew Collett, Di Corey Skull, Rick Frolich and David Brecht. It would not have existed if Andrew had not had the idea to put together a book about *Our Fathers: Twenty-Six Everyday Heroes*, or if Bryan had not worked so hard and so professionally to edit and present the photos. But it is to the authors of each chapter, who carefully crafted their own stories and then gathered together to reflect on what they were telling us, and to Anne Cramond Sutcliffe who professionally co-edited these stories, that this book owes its life and its place in the history of Linden Park Primary School and of South Australia.

Judy Macpherson Kent, 2015

The launch in 2014 of Our Fathers, *companion to this volume, by Bill Corey. Left to right: Judy Kent, Bill Corey and Bill's daughter, Di Skull.*

The authors of Our Fathers *at the launch.*

War and its Aftermath

Marjorie Beryl BRECHT

née Illingworth

(1917–1997)

David Brecht

My mother was born Marjorie Beryl Illingworth on 3 February 1917 to Margaret Lucy Illingworth (née Maycock) and John Thomas Illingworth, both of Coventry, England. Marjorie had two older sisters, Lilian, her senior by 17 years, and Gladys, 15 years older, and a brother named John, always called Jack, who was 10 years older. Marjorie's father had been a professional soldier but a dose of German mustard gas during World War One left him with damaged lungs and no longer deemed fit for military service. He suffered greatly from respiratory ailments, particularly in England's freezing winters, and little Marjorie had severe asthma. In the harsh winter of 1918–19, a severe, often lethal influenza epidemic swept across England. Jack contracted this disease, almost died and was left debilitated and with impaired lungs. The family doctor advised John and Margaret to move to a much warmer climate for the sake of father, son and baby daughter, and John decided that Australia was where the family's future lay. Margaret was furious at the thought of leaving England and everything she knew. Her father had been a professional soldier and Margaret had lived many of her early years in India where his regiment was stationed. She had no wish to live in another 'foreign' country where one had to contend daily with oppressive heat, flies and dust, but her husband was adamant and preparations were made for the departure.

On 15 November 1919, the Illingworth family boarded the SS *Ormonde* and sailed from Tilbury Docks, bound for Adelaide, South Australia. On arrival, the family took up residence in a rented house on Magill Road and it is there that my mother's life really began since she had no memories of England at all. The Illingworths found a better rental house near Port Adelaide and began looking for a permanent residence in the area. They soon found a most suitable house in Victoria Street, Queenstown, and were very pleased to finally have a place they could call home. The family didn't own a car, so all outings were in a two-wheeled sulky pulled by a horse named Dolly who lived in a small stable in the backyard. The early years in Australia were reasonably happy despite Margaret's continuing resentment at having been taken away from her beloved homeland.

In 1923, Marjorie turned five and began attending the Alberton Primary School. Her sister Gladys was working in the city as a typiste at Goldsborough Mort where she met a man named Joseph 'Pat' Berry. They were married in March 1926 and moved to their new house at 15 Heathpool Road, Heathpool, a few doors down from the Tusmore Park. Tragically in June that same year, Marjorie's much-loved brother Jack, just 19 years old, died from complications resulting from his earlier bout of influenza. Marjorie's mother was devastated by his death, becoming more and more bitter with the passing of time. Marjorie remembered her mother often shouting abuse and wild accusations at John and hurling pots and pans down the hallway from the kitchen. With constant tension in the home, Marjorie tried to get away whenever she could. She joined the Girl Guides and went on every outing and camping trip they offered. Her father taught her to saddle the horse, fit the harness and ride.

Marjorie became a keen horsewoman and riding was her great escape. On weekends she would often disappear for most of the day, roaming the city and coastline, and, in the warmer weather, swimming Dolly in the Port River. Returning home after her extended absences, she would be subjected to a torrent of angry verbal abuse from her mother but always reckoned that a day away was more than worth it.

Marjorie left school at 15 and, following in her sister Gladys's footsteps, also became a typiste at Goldsborough Mort. Her burning ambition was to become a nurse but her mother wouldn't hear of it. A nurse's training salary was very meagre and her parents had become more and more reliant on Marjorie's income as her father's health steadily deteriorated and he was unable to work. With his future looking grim, he became increasingly depressed. One evening in 1934, 17-year-old Marjorie arrived home from work to find her father lying dead in the orchard with his service revolver in his hand. After her husband's death, Margaret became even more depressed and angry. Marjorie, now the only other person in the house, bore the worst of it for the next three years. Times were hard financially and Margaret was terrified at the thought of poverty, worrying herself to the point of physical illness.

In 1937, at the age of 20, Marjorie decided that enough was enough and it was time to get on with the life that *she* wanted. She left Goldsborough Mort and started her nurse's training at the Royal Adelaide Hospital, moving into nurses' quarters there, which was a great relief for her in getting away from her mother. Marjorie made some wonderful new friends, several of whom were to remain friends for life. She met another young trainee named Roma, and would have been very surprised if she had known at the time that this woman would be the first wife of the man she was to eventually marry – Fred Brecht, my father. Marjorie thoroughly enjoyed the training and her new life with bright, happy friends her own age. Her mother, Margaret, couldn't bear to be alone in the otherwise empty house in Queenstown and her daughter Gladys took her into her home in Heathpool. Gladys's husband Pat had a damaged heart from a faulty inoculation, given by the army before he was sent overseas in World War One, and he died suddenly of heart failure that same year.

Marjorie completed her training in 1941 and was awarded the Florence Nightingale Gold Medal for excellent results in all of her exams. By then, World War Two was in full swing. Marjorie and a number of her likewise patriotic colleagues wished to serve their country by being actively involved in the war effort. On 12 September that year, she 'signed up' with the Australian Army Nursing Service. Medical support was vital for our troops in the Pacific so Marjorie was made a member of the 2nd Australian Imperial Force and was sent to Port Moresby in New Guinea. She took care of hundreds of soldiers suffering everything from combat wounds to common ailments. The hospital was not far from a temporary US Air Force base and Marjorie could vividly recall when one young American pilot decided to show off to the nurses by 'buzzing' the hospital with his Mitchell B-25 bomber. The roar of the twin engines was deafening and caused major consternation amongst patients and staff, who thought they were under attack, not to mention the corrugated-iron sheets of the roof banging and flapping wildly and nearly tearing off in the vortex created by the sizeable aircraft. There were serious repercussions over this incident and it never happened again. The Americans had a ballroom and dance band and seemed to have a party every second evening, to which the Australian nurses had a standing invitation. Marjorie was a very attractive young lady and several of the pilots became enamoured with her to the point of proposing marriage. She had no intention of living her life in the USA and sweetly but firmly refused these impassioned overtures.

As the Japanese invasion forces began pushing further south, Marjorie and her group were moved back to relative safety in Australia where they were stationed at an army hospital in Katherine in the Northern Territory. I use the term 'relative safety' because, on 22 March 1942, Japanese bombers raided the Katherine aerodrome. Fortunately the hospital was well-removed from the area and suffered no casualties or damage. Marjorie and her nursing friend, Patsy Minhard, became acquainted with a local farmer named Bert Nixon who owned a number of horses and was happy to go riding with the two women whenever they had a day off from their duties. They would take a picnic lunch and ride out to the beautiful, picturesque Katherine Gorge. Marjorie was thrilled to be back in the saddle and those outings were by far the most pleasant times of her military service. The war ended and there were thousands of returned servicemen needing medical attention, so Marjorie was assigned to the Concord Repatriation General Hospital in Sydney where she was given the honorary rank of lieutenant. The hospital had been commissioned in 1939 as a general hospital for the Australian Army. At that time, it was the largest hospital in the Southern Hemisphere. After two very busy years there, Lieutenant Illingworth became very homesick and requested her discharge from the army. This was granted and on 9 January 1947, she was free to return to Adelaide where she took up residence with her mother and sister, Gladys, at the house in Heathpool Road.

Gladys was a wonderful, big-hearted lady whose house was always open to family, friends, neighbours and anyone in need. One of the regular visitors was a motorcycle mechanic named Fred Brecht who lived nearby. Fred had returned from overseas war service in the army to find his wife, Roma, cosily established with a *de facto* husband and Gladys had opened her doors to this divorced and lonely man. He came around for dinner one evening in January 1947 and found that the oft-mentioned but hitherto-unseen Marjorie had returned from her travels. Fred had spent some time in army hospitals and had developed a special affection for nurses. He liked English girls, especially pretty brunettes, and he had the utmost admiration for women who served in the Allied armed forces during the war – 'Our Brave Girls', he used to call them. Suddenly he was confronted with everything he admired about women all rolled into one. I don't know how long it took him to make up his mind – he may have decided on that very first evening – but pretty soon he was courting Marjorie. He owned two powerful motorbikes, a 500 cc Triumph Speed Twin and a 500 cc single-cylinder Norton ES2, and he taught Marjorie to ride them. She had a natural skill with the motorbikes and she and Fred were out somewhere most weekends, racing through the hills and countryside and having a wonderful time. Fred soon began proposing to her whenever the opportunity presented itself and they were married within the year. Their first home together was a rental flat just around the corner from Heathpool Road in Northumberland Street, Tusmore. A daughter, Helen, arrived in 1948 and was followed by a son, myself, in 1950.

The family transport was the Triumph, now with a sidecar fitted, but, when I arrived, Dad decided we needed a car. The Norton was sold and Dad purchased a rather neglected Standard 12 which was the best he could afford at the time. It was a typical English sedan of that era – heavy and underpowered. The engine, gearbox and front end needed a complete rebuild. Dad worked on the car after work at night and on the weekends, stripping the major components down to separate pieces. Mum used to go out to the garage and look at the dismantled car and wonder if it would ever run again. But Dad was a 'trooper' and he restored the Standard to excellent working order and it was our family car for years. Mum drove it during the week, shopping and driving Helen and me to school when it was raining, and on weekends we went on family picnics at the beach, in national parks or elsewhere in the Hills, or somewhere along the River Murray. We named the car 'Stanny', and, during the school breaks, it faithfully took us on holidays to Port Victoria, Victor Harbor and Narrung on Lake Albert where Dad's sister Bessie lived with her farmer husband and six children.

As soon as they were married, Mum and Dad had applied for a War Services Home Loan, which was duly granted. Mum wanted to choose the location for their house and Dad agreed, so she spent the early part of 1950 looking for an affordable block of land in a nice eastern suburb. She had unpleasant memories of the rather squalid aspects of Queenstown and was determined that her children would grow up in a much better environment. She wanted a nice house in a lovely tree-lined street in a safe neighbourhood near a park, just like her sister Gladys had. Mum had also inspected the new Linden Park Primary School and decided that it would be eminently suitable for educating her young daughter and baby son when the time came. Because of the shortage and resulting rationing of building materials, combined with the procrastination of an obstinate old builder, the Brecht house took two long years to complete, but in 1952 we were finally able to move into our very own home at 4 Seaton Avenue, Hazelwood Park.

Dad loved his garden and planted fruit trees, grape vines and many different types of vegetables, so we always had plenty of fresh food to supplement the bought goods. He planted a special little garden for Mum with parsley, mint, chives and various other herbs to use in her cooking. Mum was an excellent cook, and, as well as delectable main courses, she produced a wide variety of mouth-watering desserts and cakes, scones and a very tasty home-made ice-cream. I remember the apple pies and lemon meringue tarts and a delicious pudding called Pittencrieff, a real treat served with Mum's rich yellow custard. Every so often she would buy a packet of Rice Bubbles and make a batch of chocolate crackles and they never lasted long. She also made different types of jam and a superb marmalade. In the warmer weather, Sunday night was Pancake Night and we would cover the big round pancakes with Golden Syrup or lemon juice and sugar before rolling them up and devouring them voraciously. The apples, apricots, peaches, pears and cherries were harvested each year from our trees and any not eaten immediately were preserved by Mum so that we had fruit readily available for desserts all year round. Nobody left the table hungry.

During those first 10 years, we had many happy family times and some of my favourite memories are of the cold, rainy Sundays in winter. The family would spend the afternoon in the lounge room, basking in the cheery warmth of the log fire. We would play Scrabble or listen to the radio or sometimes just chat. Mum and Dad would tell their childhood and war stories and, even though my sister and I had heard them all before, we would listen with rapt attention. When it was time for dinner, Mum would disappear down to the kitchen for an hour and return with the wooden tray-mobile loaded with toasted sandwiches, a fresh batch of scones, hot chips and other treats. There was something really lovely about us all being together, snug and warm inside on those wet, icy nights. On hot summer nights, we'd sit outside on the back lawn and chat quietly and watch the skies. We saw many shooting stars, sometimes up to six a night, and during the evenings of October 1957, we would see a tiny moving star that was the Russian satellite Sputnik 1 – the first space vehicle to orbit the earth. We tuned our AM valve radio to the publicised frequency and thrilled to the sound of Sputnik's beeping transmitter, which grew louder as it approached and then faded away as the tiny speck disappeared over the horizon.

We had many outings and one of our favourite destinations was the town of Milang on Lake Alexandrina. My sister Helen and I were keen swimmers and would spend the day diving off the old wooden jetty and frolicking around in the water, only stopping briefly at around midday to hungrily consume one of Mum's delicious picnic lunches. Mum contributed to the family finances by working part-time. She found a job nursing a wealthy elderly lady and also joined the District and Bush Nursing Society – later to be renamed the Royal District Nursing Service – which provided home-nursing for outpatients. The DBNS provided Mum with an FJ Holden to make her rounds and she marvelled at the power of the six-cylinder engine compared to the heavy old Standard's smaller four cylinders. In the late 1950s, Stanny was replaced by another English car, a Jowett Javelin, which was lighter, handled better, had twin carburettors and was a virtual Ferrari by comparison.

In 1962, the bubble burst. Mum became chronically depressed, which led to an emotional breakdown. She spent six weeks in bed and we had to creep around the house so as not to disturb her. Dad was very frustrated by this problem he could not fix and was prone to losing his temper, so Helen and I had to be very careful about what we said in front of him. During those grey days, we escaped to the nearby Hazelwood Park whenever we could, very relieved to get away but always nervous about what we might walk into when we went home again. We were very concerned about Mum and wondered if we would ever return to the life we had previously taken for granted and now so sorely missed. Mum eventually came back to us but the dark cloud over her head took some time to disperse and left its mark. Helen and I both had radios in our bedrooms and we listened exclusively to the Adelaide stations 5KA and 5AD, which played pop music continuously. Although we always had to keep the volume low during Mum's illness, she somehow heard and remembered a bestselling song from those days. It was called 'Wolverton Mountain' and Mum came to associate it with that dreadful time in her life. For years after, Helen and I were not allowed to sing the song within her earshot and, if it came on the radio when she was there, it had to be turned off immediately. The opening line of the song went, 'They say don't go on Wolverton Mountain if you're looking for a wife', and I would think to myself, 'They say don't go on Hazelwood Mountain if you're trying to have a life', but we all moved on.

Later that year, Helen, a chubby 14-year-old, suddenly put herself on to a strict regimen of diet and exercise and transformed into a real beauty. She became extremely fashion conscious and Mum, an excellent dressmaker, began making beautiful clothes for her. Helen would find photographs of dresses in magazines and, where possible and practical, Mum would replicate them. She made clothes for herself as well and I remember a very smart trouser suit which she made, complete with a matching waistcoat. She also made seat covers for the family cars and reupholstered the lounge-room sofa and armchairs. Mum was the eternal economist and was proud of how much money she saved with her sewing. She made extra money by decorating wedding cakes professionally and each one was a work of art. Dad was happy to let her handle the family finances and handed over most of his pay packet each week. Mum had a drawer full of little screw-top jars labelled Gas, Electricity, Telephone,

Insurance, etc. in one of the bedroom wardrobes. She would regularly allocate certain amounts to each jar and, when the bill arrived, there was always enough money in the relevant jar to pay it. We were not wealthy by any means, but Mum's wonderful management of the money meant that we were always well-dressed, well-fed and had whatever we really needed, and there was always enough for Christmas and birthday presents and a few treats along the way.

In early 1971, my girlfriend Jan announced that she was pregnant and we moved into a little maisonette just off Norwood Parade. We were there for several months and then my mother offered to take us in so that she could look after Jan while I was at work and help when the baby came. Jan was rather anaemic but Mum fed us highly nutritious meals, gave Jan vitamin supplements and she positively bloomed. Jan was quite petite but our son Adrian, born on 7 October, was a healthy, happy baby of over eight pounds. We stayed with my parents for a year, during which time Jan and I made the decision to get married, and then found another place of our own in Magill. Mum and Dad were always wonderfully supportive and when Adrian turned four, they took him and my sister's daughter Amanda, aged six, for the first of a number of caravan holidays at Victor Harbor. The children loved these holidays and still remember them vividly many years later. Mum used to say that she felt as if she had Helen and me back again as little children.

After Dad retired in 1975, he and Mum began taking holidays away, exploring Central Australia and going to Sydney to visit Helen and her family. They took a long road trip up the eastern coast to Townsville in the early 90s. It was to be the first of many such trips but Mum became very ill and spent most of the return journey lying on the back seat of the car. From then on, her health steadily declined. She was diagnosed with several heart diseases, chronic inflammation of the central nervous system and the onset of emphysema although she had never been a smoker. By the beginning of 1995 she was bedridden. She wanted to be in her own home so Dad and I took care of her with daily visits from nurses and regular visits by the doctor.

On the evening of 1 April 1997, Dad was sitting by Mum's bedside holding her hand. He thought she was asleep, but, just before eight o'clock, she gently squeezed his hand and slipped away. Her gifts to me were many and varied. She fostered in me a strong sense of morality and responsibility, an appreciation for classical music, English literature and a host of other things. I learned to cook, iron and sew by watching her. Both she and Dad taught me that a job is not finished until it is done properly. I came to appreciate her more as I grew older. I also began to understand how her own childhood, and the things she endured, had shaped her into the complex person that she was. Adding it all up at the end of the day, I know that I was lucky to have her. She still lives in my heart.

Marjorie's Lemon Meringue Tart

Pastry

225 grams (1½ cups) plain flour
2 tablespoons icing sugar
125 grams butter, chilled, coarsely chopped
2½ tablespoons iced water

Filling

50 grams (⅓ cup) cornflour
125 mL (½ cup) water
250 mL (1 cup) fresh lemon juice
430 grams (2 cups) caster sugar
60 grams butter, coarsely chopped
4 eggs, separated

Sift the flour and icing sugar into a large bowl. Use your fingertips to rub the butter into the flour mixture until it resembles fine breadcrumbs.

Add the water and use a round-bladed knife to stir until a dough forms. Use your hands to bring the dough together in the bowl. Turn onto a sheet of non-stick baking paper and roll out to a 5 mm-thick disc. Use the pastry to line a 23 cm (base measurement) pie dish.

Trim excess pastry. Cover the pastry with baking paper. Place in the fridge for 30 minutes to rest.

Preheat oven to 180°C. Fill the lined dish with pastry weights or rice. Bake in oven for 15 minutes. Remove the paper and pastry weights or rice. Bake for a further 15–20 minutes or until crisp and golden. Set aside to cool completely.

Meanwhile, to make the lemon filling, combine the cornflour, water, lemon juice and half the sugar in a saucepan. Use a balloon whisk to stir over medium heat for 4 minutes or until the mixture boils and thickens. Continue to cook, stirring constantly, for a further minute. Remove from heat. Whisk in butter and egg yolks. Transfer to a bowl. Cover with plastic wrap and place in the fridge for 3 hours or until cooled completely.

Preheat oven to 190°C. Use an electric beater to beat the egg whites in a clean, dry bowl until soft peaks form. Gradually add the remaining sugar, 1 tablespoonful at a time, until the mixture is thick and glossy.

Spread the filling over the base of the pastry case. Spoon over the meringue mixture and spread to the edge of the pastry. Use the back of a spoon to create peaks. Bake in oven for 5 minutes or until the meringue peaks are light golden. Set aside to cool completely. Serve.

David Brecht

David Gordon Brecht was born in Toorak Gardens, Adelaide, on 24 January 1950 to Marjorie and Fred Brecht. He was their second child. A sister, Helen, was 17 months older. David received his primary education at the Linden Park Primary School and then moved to Norwood High. In January 1969, he joined the then Department of Civil Aviation as a clerical officer and spent the next 23 years working in a number of positions and locations, helping to ensure the safety of civil and commercial aircraft operations in the South

Australia/Northern Territory region. During this time, he was married twice and the second union produced a son, Adrian, born in 1971. David was a keen surfer and motorcyclist and had a passion for writing and producing his own pop songs on multi-track recorders. He was mostly a 'one-man band' and played guitar, piano, keyboards and drums and sang lead and backing vocals. He became adept at building electronic audio devices and built much of the equipment used in his recordings. In 1991, the aviation department was subjected to a 56 per cent staff cut and David's entire section was made redundant, along with many others. David left the department in 1992 and spent the next two years taking care of his girlfriend who suffered a long illness. Then he helped his father to take of care of Marjorie who was bedridden for the last two-and-a-half years of her life. Following her death in 1997, David looked after his father for the next six years until Fred's death in 2003. These days, David spends his time with friends, hobbies and a large collection of favourite books, movies and music.

Fay Elaine FUSS

née Pitchers

(1925–2015)

Kym Fuss

Fay was born in 1925 at Woodside, a small Adelaide Hills village in those days, about 16 miles (26 kilometres) as any crow or magpie, or even a black-faced cuckoo shrike, flies from Adelaide. She was an only child born to Kathleen May Pitchers.

We, five sons, no daughters, have never found out much of her very early life there, because Mum was never very forthcoming about those years. It is possibly because her dad was caught in the 'grip of the hop', there not being much in the way of grape varieties of alcohol to be in the grip of way back then.

Life wasn't all that easy for women in my grandmother's day (and I will hear cries of 'What's changed?') but having an alcoholic husband without a job couldn't have made things easy for Kathleen ... we heard many times about what it had been like.

As it transpired, Kathleen's husband (my maternal grandfather) rode into the side of a train on his way home from 'somewhere' one night and that was his ending! This actually happened some years after they had separated because of his 'hopping' problem!

I think they divorced at some stage, because Mum told me that he 'ran away with the maid', and she was somehow a part of the Tessiere family who went on to be the original owners of Harris Scarfe Pty Ltd. But just quietly, it seems that his appointment with the train was the divorce, and again, just quietly, I think that it was around the time that Mum turned 17. My maternal grandfather is now at rest in the Cheltenham cemetery in an unmarked grave, and we just can't find out where he is!

Fay's early years up until about the age of 17 were spent in Woodside where she lived with her mother, Kathleen. It sounds like it was a typical Victorian time in Woodside back then, and that there was a tight rein on young girls, much to their chagrin. Her father sounds like he had quite a controlling grip on her as well, because she at times spoke of just how strict he was and how she was never allowed to go out with boys. Fay made many friends in Woodside, and it has only been quite recently that she hadn't been able to maintain contact with some of them.

One of them was Margaret Baker, who in her working life was 'Aunty Margaret' at 5KA. I think it may have been her familiarity with Fay that enabled me, Kym Fuss, to win an ice-cream birthday cake in a quiz on 5KA, but I prefer to believe that it was simply my knowledge that secured the prize for 'Who can tell me what this sound is?'. Believe it or not, when Aunty Margaret had been at our place for dinner just the Sunday before the night this question came over the air, she 'sort of' talked about it, knowing that during that week I would be turning eight and possibly listening to the wireless.

Fay's mother Kathleen, Nan as we knew her, was left with no income after her husband Cecil Preston Pitcher's railway accident, and it had been meagre before. She was poring through the *Argus* looking for employment when she saw an advertisement for a live-in housekeeper for a gentleman at an 80 acre (okay, 32 hectares) grape and fruit tree property at Langhorne Creek, a small community about 75 kilometres south-east of Adelaide past Strathalbyn.

Langhorne Creek is the home of a very early South Australian wine-making company, Bleasdale's Wine Company, owned by the Potts family. Ownership of the wine entity has since passed on, but it is still employing some of the Potts family.

I can remember my mother recounting stories of her times helping to harvest the grapes, trying to avoid the redback and orb-weaver spiders that made their homes in the vine rows, and trying to avoid stepping on the many red-bellied black and tiger snakes that slithered their ways from the adjacent property's swamp on Step Road. Step Road was a right-angled road, which stepped its way from the little hamlet of Langhorne Creek down to the main road between Strathalbyn and Milang on the 'coast' of Lake Alexandrina.

The property that Fay Pitchers ended up living on for some years was on Step Road on the north-eastern side of the fifth corner from Langhorne Creek. There was on the property, close to the road, a huge pine tree hedge, much of which still remains. The climate at Langhorne Creek was at times quite diabolical, some days being very calm but others suffering from westerly winds of some magnitude … and often very strong northerly winds which scorched the vines at the worst time. Under these bulky pine trees Fay at times had to space out Japanese and butternut pumpkins that she harvested from the adjacent vegetable patch to age quietly out of the sun.

Fay's and her mother Kathleen's lives at the property were at times quite trying. Fay had gone as far as was possible in her education given her locality, and so was made to carry out 'farm assistance duties', having to walk some miles to neighbouring property houses to clean them … even as far as four miles to Langhorne Creek to help clean the house of the Potts family. The gentleman (Horace John Taverner) who owned the property where my mother and her mother were assistants was quite a gentleman indeed … however, he was a very steadfast opinionated person. 'What I say is what will be, and what will happen.' We all called him 'Tav', and it wasn't until I actually asked the question when I was about nine that I discovered that he wasn't my mother's father.

My mother recounted times of Tav saying 'I won't be paying for an electricity supply to be connected to this property' changing to 'I am so glad that I decided to have "the electric" put on'. It had been, however, quite a struggle for it to happen. And that wasn't until around 1956. Even after 'the electric' had been connected, Mum still had to walk about one kilometre to 'the swamp' to collect what fallen wood she could find to use in the beautiful green-and-cream enamelled Metters wood-burning stove, so that the electricity bill wouldn't be too much. Even in 1974 when the property was finally sold to one of the neighbours, there wasn't a hot-water service in the house. The bath (yes, there was a bath) was filled with water heated in two very large kettles that seemed to be permanently heating on the wood stove.

How I wish I had had the forethought back then to save that stove for installation in the backyard of the home that I would have many years later … a better and more attractive wood-fired pizza oven would be hard to find. I still have at home a painted steel candle-holder which I used to find my way to my bed when on holidays there even after power was connected. Fay has told of the numerous times that she almost trod on snakes at night when she had to go to the toilet, which was about 25 metres from the house's back door, out a gate, next to the ubiquitous country house rubbish heap where all of the used tins and bottles were dumped – a perfect residence for rats and mice and therefore snakes too.

We stayed as a family, then of five, at the property during the 1956 flood, arriving at night and walking through swirling floodwater by the light of kerosene lanterns. Well, Fay and Doug were walking, I was carried on Fay's shoulders because of the depth of the water. The next morning, the door into the sloping short passageway that was between the main part of the house and the kitchen was opened to find two black snakes seeking firm ground there, as the floodwater was still quite high. The house had been built in the knowledge that the area flooded regularly and needed to be elevated from the surrounding plains. Fay quickly shut the door, loaded a .410 shotgun (both barrels) and dispatched the reptiles when the door was again opened. Not only could she sing!

Fay had to live with the hope that she would one day marry Tav's son Rex and help him to carry on ownership of this property, despite the fact that Rex was very much an uneducated country fellow and simply not the man that Mum would have countenanced partnering. I can remember my grandmother abusing Rex for entering the kitchen for lunch without taking off his boots. It needs to be taken into account that the kitchen was the only room in the house that Rex was allowed to step foot into. The poor sod would have been working in the heat for about six hours at that time with no sustenance, and I'm sure that a 'Come in, Rex, have some lunch out of the sun' would have gone down a lot better than the usual greeting.

My mother, Fay, grew up nonetheless to be an extremely accepting and calm person.

I'm trying to set the scene of the environment that Fay lived in. It was for her at times extremely stressful, but it seems that it was at times not all so bad. Mum was one for singing, and she did have a remarkable mellifluous singing voice … she used to sing while washing the dishes of an evening and became known as 'The Nightingale of Langhorne Creek', and it has been told to me by some of the older neighbours in later years that they loved hearing her voice lilting across the vineyards to their houses, in some cases about two kilometres away. The sound did carry a long way across those areas, and I can really say that I was at times, when staying with Nan, scared witless by the sounds rolling our way from the nearby swamp, a kilometre from the house. The local foxes did have a very particular penetrating and haunting cry which at times was scary for a small boy.

Every night, be it raining or 108°F, Mum would have to take a three-pint billy can to the start of a neighbour's driveway and hang it on a wire bracket, and every morning before the sun rose she had to retrieve it, by then full of very creamy and warm fresh milk.

While resident at Langhorne Creek, Fay had to go with her mother on visits to Strathalbyn to have 'tea' with her mother's friends, but only on a Sunday which seemed to be the only day in the week that one could leave Langhorne Creek and visit Strathalbyn. One of them was a very upright lady named Connie Joy … I have never found out if Joy was her last name, or whether she even had a last name. There was never a man in sight, but that doesn't necessarily indicate joy either. There were many times that I holidayed at Langhorne Creek with my grandmother and had to accompany her to afternoon tea with Connie Joy … I must admit I enjoyed it, but can't really say that I knew why. It seems to me that the character of Connie Joy somehow permeated that of my mother. Fay at all times presented as a calm person, which to all of her children (in later life) was remarkable. More about that later.

Fay's late teens and early 20s were spent in somewhat forced reclusion … the only glimpses of the outside world that she was able to experience were when she was conveyed to Strathalbyn. There she was able to encounter (but only when her mother was otherwise engaged) people from outside Strathalbyn. Strathalbyn had at the end of World War Two become a base for repatriated and discharged soldiers.

One of the soldiers, who somehow caught her eye at a local dance at a hall at an even tinier community called Belvidere, at the junction of the main road from Strathalbyn to Langhorne Creek and Milang, was one Douglas Gray Fuss. He had seen action with the 2/43rd Battalion in the Middle East at El Alamein, Tripoli and some other places which escape my memory, and in New Guinea on the Kokoda Trail as well and so I can only guess at what his demeanour was at that time. I was told by my grandmother, of course, that 'Douglas would stroll, nay prance, up and down the street outside of Connie Joy's stropping his flanks with his short whip' as if he was, well, I don't know what, because I was never told!

He was also a man of great foot dexterity, that is, he could bloody well dance and very well at that. Mum, with her ability to sing so very mellifluously, must have thought, 'Well, here's the perfect follow-on for Ginger Rogers and Fred Astaire' …. except of course that neither of the aforementioned could sing well, if at all. Although Fred *did* try.

Needless to say, Fay married Doug in 1945 at a quiet ceremony at a church on a corner of Railway Terrace near the intersection of Greenhill Road and Railway Terrace at Wayville. It was obvious that Kathleen wasn't at all happy at the fact that her only child was spirited away from her at the tender age of 20 years, and this is understandable when it is taken into account that Nan would, after the wedding, have to catch the bus back to Langhorne Creek to a place that became a nightmare to her.

I'm extremely embarrassed to say that my father's life should have figured with others in the book *Our Fathers* and because of my tardiness in producing script for his side of things there will be snippets in this story of his life as well.

After their marriage, Doug and Fay Fuss lived with Doug's mother and father, Francis and Lillian, at 86 Leader Street, Forestville, next door to where Francis Gray Fuss was born, yes, born in the house at 84 Leader Street ... unfortunately for posterity neither of these houses still stands, thanks to 'progress'. Even then life wasn't a lot of fun, especially given that even in 1966 when I had to stay for some months with my grandfather and aunt at Forestville, the only source of heat for a shower was a chip-heater fed with tightly screwed-up *Advertiser* pages ... again a digression from what I should be writing. Showers were taken very quickly.

Fay and Doug then did something that most at the time considered to be madness ... they purchased a house being built in the near country, at a place without a name but which later was called Sunnyside, and eventually Beaumont. Most knew it then as 'Mortgage Hill'. The house, at 7 Thirkell Avenue, Beaumont, still stands basically in an unaltered state from back then. I go past it every Saturday on my way home from golf, and every time a memory or two floods back.

Fay's first child, a son Colin, was born not long before the move to the new house occurred, and her second son Barry was born 18 months after the move. The nearest public transport to the city at the time was at the terminus at what became Burnside Town Hall, some two-and-a-half miles from home. But the two-and-a-half miles was by way of a sinuous earth track which meandered through acres of olive trees planted years before. Some would say that it may well have been a pleasant stroll to go to catch the bus, but with two small children in the one pram plus whatever groceries had been purchased it was no pleasant stroll.

The child-control situation was exacerbated in 1950 by the happening along of one Kym Francis Fuss, and what I mean by that is that a trip through the olives then was with Colin, now five, walking but getting lost often, and Barry and Kym now in the pram, with the groceries. I will never understand just how Mum coped with it. I certainly couldn't envisage a young, 25-year-old modern mum doing anything near to what Fay did. Furthermore, all of the walking which had to be done just to get food on the table, helped Mum to stay extremely fit without having to go to Goodlife gym at the top of Greenhill Road, which was just as well because it didn't exist then!

Fay was, as most women had to be in her day, a housewife. There were already several other houses in Thirkell Avenue, and Mum very soon became friends with all of the neighbours. Fay had been brought up a Christian, and she wanted us to be Christian, so we were told that we had to walk to Sunday school in Glenunga every week. But that didn't necessarily mean we had to actually go in. I think that we grew up as agnostic Christians, being extremely good people but not calling ourselves Christian.

Fay and husband Douglas eventually set up a vegetable stall in the Central Market. There was also a cold store, which she and Doug maintained for storage of the vegetables at the (now demolished) East End Market, the main source of the vegetables for the stall. We often had to, as a family, get dragged out of bed at an ungodly hour, something like 3.30 am, and bundled into the utility that was our family transport of the time. The quickest two children would be lucky, because they were able to sit inside the cabin with Mum and Dad. The slowest of the three boys ended up in the tray of the utility, but there was always a supply of thick hessian bags that one could lie on and pull over oneself to try to stay warm and out of the wind. The purpose of this early foray was so that we could get out to the numerous vegetable growers near Virginia, most of whom were Italian. Our task was to plunge our hands into almost freezing water to wash the dirt off potatoes to take to the market, and even after doing this for some years, Fay's hands were still soft and comforting. Except when we misbehaved, needless to say, and then they weren't so soft or comforting. It was actually our father who administered punishment more than Mum ... she was always too soft, but we loved her for it!

Another part of the business was a vegetable shop at the Gepps Cross Migrant Camp, a collection of Nissen huts near the corner of Grand Junction Road and Main North Road. The shop was exceedingly hot in the summertime, often quite unbearable. Fay, who by then had a car, a Morris 10, often went and opened the shop at 8 am while Doug was loading up the utility with vegetables at Virginia, and the two of them would unload and carry the wooden cases and crates of produce into the shop. Some of them were heavy, and Fay was slight, however everything got done. She would leave Doug to man the shop while she drove to pick up us three kids from school.

During our primary school years at Linden Park, Fay would often come and pick us up. We would stop on the way home at the local Beaumont shops and in winter months get a six-pack ... of Golden Crumpets. Mum would almost soak them in butter after toasting them as a treat for us. Then she had to start getting dinner ready for when the man of the house returned, as well as making sure that the kids had clean shirts for the following day.

I mentioned earlier that Douglas was often distant and not totally with us in mind. He was one of the many men who witnessed terrible scenes during the war, had to wield a .303 with a bayonet at the end, and it seemed that he relived some of this when he punished us. No, he didn't stab or shoot us. Fay had a magical effect on Doug, and was able to get him back to a calm demeanour easily. She really was the strength of the family, and I think her early country years were instrumental in creating the person she was. Having had to do many things that city girls would have baulked at, created in her a strength that kept our family going, even when Doug's business partner in the vegetable stall and Gepps Cross shop drained the business bank account and retreated to England. This forced us into bankruptcy. I believe that had that person stayed in Australia, Fay would have found him and done him in. It was just as well that he fled. Even through *this* crisis Mum kept everything going.

Sons number four (Anthony) and five (Robin) arrived in 1957 and 1963. Fay was often at her wit's end with five of us at home, plus the big kid Douglas, but still she held the proceedings of family life together. Mum was one of those people who would almost lay down her life to help someone. There was one time around 1959 when Doug, Fay, me and one smaller son Tony were driving at night coming back from Langhorne Creek having visited Nan. Just below Eagle on the Hill we were first on the scene of a van having struck a tree. The occupants were cut and bleeding; Dad got the woman into our car somehow and left Fay (at her insistence) back at the crash scene with the man while he raced off to the city to alert the ambulance brigade of the need for them to attend. We were advised some weeks later that Fay's having stayed with the man had been honourable but foolhardy since they had found out some things about his past.

A year after the bankruptcy Doug got a job as a country traveller for Hoadley's Chocolates. This kept him away from home from Sunday afternoon to Thursday night, and of course keeping everything going was 100 per cent Fay's requirement. She had by this time found five-and-a-half days a week work at the local Beaumont vegetable shop. It was at this stage that I started to get meals ready for when she got home tired, as she often did. Once all us five kids were off her hands, Mum and Dad took several trips by sea and a motoring trip in New Zealand. Dad had had to take early retirement having had a massive heart attack and subsequent triple bypass, and then not long after that a knee replacement. Fay was the only person who could look after him, and so still she had no rest from daily toil.

Fay and Doug realised, after having lived at Beaumont for nearly 40 years, that the block, around 1040 square metres, was just too big for them to manage. Doug by this stage had to use a walking-frame, and if he needed to go anywhere Fay was his chauffeur and nurse. They sold the Beaumont house and moved to a retirement unit at Clarence Gardens. They were the first people to move into the complex of 13 units, and the manager gave Fay the job of setting up collection of maintenance contributions, which gave her purpose. She busied herself doing much more than that, as well acting as chauffeur for the majority of those occupants of the complex who had no ready transport.

They had a yappy little wire-haired terrier called Charlie whilst living at Beaumont, and being the first to move into a unit, they were able to negotiate having Charlie there with them. He used to get upset at the noise of aircraft for some reason, and even when the distant rumble of jets taking off from Adelaide Airport could be heard, he would bark until he couldn't hear the noise any longer – which of course was well after we couldn't hear it. He just continued barking for what seemed like forever. Fay loved him immensely, and when he died she kept his registration and nametags on a small chain, which hung on the key rack in the unit.

Douglas had unfortunately been infected with golden staph during his bypass operation and started having to endure long stints in hospital having antibiotics dripped directly into his knee joint. Fay was at his bedside for more than a few hours every day. She nursed him as well as she could when he was discharged from hospital after about eight months, after amputation of the lower part of his right leg, but the task became too much for her and she had to face the decision to place him in a nursing home. He eventually had his left leg amputated (also due to gangrene) and spent his last 12 months in an unhappy state, curled in a fetal position but lying on his back. Dad passed away in 2000.

Fay stayed in the unit until she could no longer manage, but it was also quite obvious that a slightly demented state was at times hovering. She would sometimes wake her neighbour at three in the morning to invite her in for a scotch and water, or wake her and ask, 'Do you know where I am?' Her world fell apart after she was involved in a motor accident having misjudged the speed of an oncoming vehicle when attempting to turn across traffic, and her car was wrecked. The police advised her that it was time for her to relinquish her licence, her only means of occasional escape from the retirement complex.

Fay was in a nursing home where, of course, if one person gets a viral infection it courses through everyone. In early March 2015, a respiratory infection spread through the nursing home, as it had a year earlier. Mum, stronger then, had defeated it. This time, however, she was significantly weaker and finally left this world on Sunday 15 March 2015. Heaven is now a better place with her looking after it. RIP Fay Elaine Fuss.

Kym Francis Fuss

Kym is the middle of five boys who all attended Linden Park Primary School, as it was then known. He often borrowed someone else's bicycle and rode home for lunch. He then attended, and also sometimes studied, at Adelaide Technical High School, now Glenunga International High School, until the end of 1968.

His first job was working in the order office at Cooper's Brewery at Leabrook, studying accountancy part-time for an extremely short while. He then worked as an observer in a light plane carrying out radiometric recording of outback areas, effectively seeking out radioactivity indicative of mineable uranium oxide deposits.

In 1972 he successfully applied to gain entry to pilot training with the RAAF and became the first civilian from South Australia in nine years to do so, however, an injury sustained in a motorcycle accident in 1969 finally put paid to that. He then commenced a series of jobs in the construction industry, culminating in his now running a construction cost consultancy practice in Adelaide.

Kym married for the first time in 1974, and was divorced 10 years later. He remarried in 2002 having found a new partner, Natalia, an engineer in Sydney, who had migrated with her husband from Russia to Australia in 1993 but divorced soon after that. She has a son who is in his final year of medicine at Adelaide University.

He has lived in Frewville since 1978, on the block where an old friend from church youth group used to live. Kym somehow inveigled the guy's girlfriend away from him many years ago. Kym will be living in Frewville until carried out. He has made a promise that Charlie's tags will be placed in Fay's coffin at her funeral when she passes away. It is her wish to be cremated and her ashes scattered partly in Wittunga National Park with her mum's ashes, and partly at the church in Woodside where she used to go where some of her mum's ashes have been scattered too.

Fay's five sons will retain some as well.

Pamela Anne GOLDNEY

(1926–1989)

Frances Goldney Nilson

Pamela Goldney was my mother and also my best friend. It is often a sad fact that when we are finally ready to know more about our parents' lives, the opportunity to ask them has gone. This is the case for me as I began to realise how little I knew about my mother's early years. The combination of both our parents' journeys as children, as husbands and wives, as parents, and as grandparents, is so important in shaping who we are, their children. And yet the opportunity can be so easily lost.

It is therefore with the help of my mother's younger sister, Janet, 85 years old and living in England, that some of my mother and her family's story can still be revealed. Janet, my godmother, tells of her memories when she and my mother were children, living in London at the beginning of World War Two.

Janet writes:

Pamela was born in Ealing, London, England in 1926, the oldest daughter of four children.

Our mother, Eileen, had 4 children under the age of 13, and lived in fear of what might happen to us all. You have to remember that when war broke out in September 1939 we did not know that we were going to 'win the war', and at one stage, we feared the invasion of England by Germany. In fact England had nothing more than Winston Churchill and the 'fight-to-the-end spirit'!

I remember WW2 very well. Anyone who has lived through it will never forget it, but we have all tried to move on. There was fear that war would be declared for several months beforehand and so our father, Hamish, had arranged for a builder to come and build an air raid shelter in the garden, far away from the house under a very large Christmas tree.

On the day that war was to be declared and broadcasted on the radio by the Prime Minister, Neville Chamberlain, at 11am September 3rd, 1939, we all went into the hall and sat on the stairs. This included Father, Mother, Pam, sister Anne, the builder, Cliff the boyfriend of our cousin Margot, and myself. Following the announcement Father stood up and said: "Well, we had better get on and finish the air raid shelter." Mother looked on the verge of tears and gave us each our new gas masks tied with a string thread so we could hang them around our shoulders. There wasn't one for our baby brother Richard, which added to Mother's distress, but he was later issued with a special helmet designed for babies.

Hamish (my grandfather) was an electrical engineer and journalist, and worked as a departmental manager of publicity for General Electric Company (GEC) in Birmingham. During World War Two, GEC was involved in heavy industry supplying power, and was a major supplier to the military of electrical and engineering products. The company made significant contributions to the war effort that included the development in 1940 of the cavity magnetron for radar at the University of Birmingham, and advances in communications technology. Hamish was of Scottish and Viking descent, an imposing figure of six foot four inches and considered very tall in his time. I owe him my height of five foot eleven inches, via my mother who was also tall, and I must admit that I have been known to claim to be a particularly proud Viking woman, mainly at parties and after a few drinks.

For about a year it was a bit of a phony war and nothing much changed. Mother, Eileen, joined the W.V.S. (Women's Voluntary Service) and would not be called up as she had children and a baby. Father was in a reserve occupation but was soon drafted into the Home Guard. He worked during the day at GEC and at night in the Home Guard. Eventually he was made a Major and later became the Commanding Officer of the Ack Ack Division which was responsible for all aspects of ground warfare against the Luftwaffe, using heavy guns, light guns, rockets and search-lights. He had ATS (Auxiliary Territorial Service) girls and the Home Guard to defend Birmingham!

The Birmingham Blitz was the heavy bombing by the Nazi German Luftwaffe of Birmingham and surrounding towns, between 1940 and 1943. Birmingham, England's second largest city after London, is an important industrial and manufacturing location which made it a strategically important target for the Germans. Birmingham became the third most heavily bombed city in the United Kingdom in World War Two, behind only London and Liverpool. Reports of the bombing were kept quiet as wartime censorship meant that Birmingham was not mentioned by name in news reports, being referred to as a 'Midland Town' to keep the outcomes of the raids from the Germans. Approximately 9000 people were either killed or injured, and 12,391 houses, 302 factories and 239 other buildings were destroyed, with many more damaged.

We spent many nights sleeping in the air raid shelter at the end of the garden. The bombing of Coventry, seventeen miles away, was just terrifying. The raids continued night after night and when they had finished bombing Coventry, Birmingham, six miles away, was next. Coventry was burnt to the ground. Somehow people became more determined. The King and Queen came and visited us, and so did Winston Churchill. Without him I don't think we would have won the war, his speeches spurred us on.

Every man, woman and child fought in whatever way they could. Mother collected any type of iron and various metals for the war effort and I remember Pam out in the courtyard with a hammer and chisel knocking holes in the items so no one else could use them. She made a very good job of it, and Mother said at the time, I think Pamela is going to take the Germans on single-handed!

Mother made everything she could out of the vegetables and the fruit we grew. We had a greenhouse where Father grew tomatoes, peaches and figs. We were more fortunate than people who lived in towns, we had fresh produce and eggs. However we had very little meat as all the meat produce was sent to London and other large towns. We had to rely on rabbit and fish, if we could get it. On one very memorable occasion, the local coal merchant turned the coalbunkers into pig sties as he had little use for them with fuel in short supply, and everyone in the village bought part of a pig. We all came together and enjoyed suckling pig, roasted on a spit and shared whatever food we had. A veritable feast, no less.

As the War continued food became more and more scarce and rationing became tighter. Hitler's U-Boats had caused chaos to food supplies from America and the country feared it would be starved out. Father bought nine pullets (young female egg-laying hens) and my job was to look after them, as well as looking after the peach tree. Pamela, being the oldest, always named the pets. The four Black Leghorns were Brigit, Meagan, Sheila, and Mona. The five Rhode Island Reds were Fiona, Morag, Shauna, Iona, and Brenda. You can see that they all had Gaelic names except for Brenda. We thought one chook should have an English name. Brenda, she was the best layer.

Prior to the war Pam commenced school at the age of four years at a little primary school nearby and was a very bright child. She could already read having been taught by her grandmother. At eleven years-of-age she won a scholarship to Litchfield Friary School, Warwickshire. However, with war being declared peoples' lives changed dramatically and with it, their priorities. Many teachers were either called up into the armed services, or escorted some of the 3.5 million children who were evacuated from the cities considered to be most in danger. The education of children became secondary to the war effort, and to survival. Consequently Pam had other ideas rather than schoolwork. She heard that they were calling for volunteers to fill sands bags at Sutton Park and she felt that this was her war effort. She was only 13. I know that she was in trouble at school for taking time out to do this, and the train journey from Sutton to Litchfield was quite long and full of troops. I remember my parents being concerned about her safety.

Not surprisingly your mother Pam left school the summer after she turned 14 and got a job in Birmingham as a trainee window dresser, much to our father's disappointment. His hopes for her were to be a newscaster with the BBC as her speaking voice and vocabulary were excellent. She was also nobody's 'yes' girl, and could argue extremely well! He was very proud of her.

By 1943 England was on the point of starvation, and the call went out for girls to join the Land Army. They took girls as young as 17 and included girls who were hairdressers, shop girls, and office clerks, none of whom had ever worked on the land before. They were city girls and most had never seen a cow, never mind milk one, these unsung heroines.

On her 17th birthday, in April 1943, Pam, after biding her time until she was old enough, came home and announced that she had joined the Women's Land Army. This was quite a shock to the family. One could hardly blame her for grabbing the opportunity to get away from the endless nights spent in the family air raid shelter, while also helping to replace one of the 10,000 farmers who were away at war.

The Land Army girls were involved in all aspects of farm work, including milking and dairy work, poultry, general farm work, transport driving, outside gardening and glasshouse work, and pest destruction. In 2012, Neil Storey and Molly Housego, wrote in *The Women's Land Army*: 'Despite some of the old prejudices against women to "do the work of a man" that still existed, many became skilled and proficient in farm work.' However, initially 'the sheer ineptitude of some city girls led to many funny tales and cartoons in local and national newspapers, but the farmers found their antics both frustrating and costly. Some damaged tractors and machinery, while others even confused male and female livestock, with unfortunate results'. This resulted in a four-to-six week training program being introduced, before the girls were placed on farms.

My mother's family tells of a funny incident when she became very ill with a very serious case of rheumatic fever in 1946. When they worriedly tried to contact my mother and asked for 'Pamela', they were told that they had no one by that name. They did however have a 'Roberta' with the same surname, causing some initial confusion. It seems that my mother had decided that the opportunity 'to get away from it all' also included the opportunity to change her name to one that was much more to her liking. Since remembering this story I suddenly wondered if I have unwittingly inherited this quirky trait from my mother. Given the right circumstances of being unknown, I admit that I have shamefully introduced myself as 'Francesca', a name that is so much more exciting than 'Frances' to my way of thinking. Fortunately, some of my more tolerant friends indulge me.

My mother was invalided out from the Women's Land Army and, following a lengthy convalescence, went to live in London. She began a sales assistant traineeship at the famous Harrods Department Store in London's Knightsbridge. During World War Two, the store had transformed itself from selling luxury goods to making uniforms, parachutes and parts for Lancaster bombers.

Following the war, however, it returned to its former reputation of selling world-class luxury and exotic items. While at Harrods she involved herself in their amateur theatre club and was in many shows. She loved London and went to all the musicals, her favourite stars being Danny Kaye and Frank Sinatra. She worked at Harrods for two years until 1949, the year the world-famous store celebrated its centenary, and left the week before she married my father.

My parents met on a train travelling to St Ives in Cornwall. She was on her way to stay with friends for a holiday. He was an Australian amateur artist on his way to paint, as he had heard that there is a special quality of light in Cornwall that makes it unique and attracts many artists. I don't know how much time my father devoted to painting pictures with the presence of my mother as a distraction, but they obviously spent enough time together to fall in love. They married in 1949 in Penzance, and lived their first year of married life in beautiful Cornwall, which they both loved. My father worked as a chartered accountant for a company that made mead, an alcoholic beverage created by fermenting honey, hops and water. It sounds like the perfect honeymoon. My parents lived in a small rural village just out of Penzance and were free to take romantic walks along the country lanes, coves and beaches, enjoy the quaint, cosy smugglers' inns, and of course, the mead, the 'honeymoon drink'. I was conceived and born nine months later in Penzance.

Due to unforeseen circumstances their ideal lifestyle came to an abrupt end when they received news that my father's mother (my grandmother) in Adelaide was very ill and they immediately set sail for the six-week journey back to Australia. My mother had previously been corresponding with her new mother-in-law, and was looking forward to meeting her but, sadly, my grandmother died before they docked in Adelaide.

When my mother arrived after a long ship voyage from England to Port Adelaide in 1951, with only her husband for support, and me as young infant, she must have had mixed feelings of excitement and trepidation. Her family was convinced that she was travelling to a wild, hot, barbaric country where facilities were basic, schools were conducted in tin sheds, and kangaroos hopped down the main street! There must have been times when my mother questioned her decision to marry an Australian man with an 'odd' strine accent, to leave her family and friends, and to travel to the other side of the world. She could hardly fly back home for a quick visit like we do today. There were no computers, no Skype, nor mobile phones for texting, and the decision to phone England was a stilted, expensive affair that required booking in advance. Calls were disrupted by time lags and loud whooshing noises that sounded like waves crashing on to the telephone wires, and consequently happened only on rare occasions like Christmas. Letter writing was an option for many but as neither my mother nor her family were good at corresponding this was not a source of comfort for her either. Hers was a decision for life and it would be another 12 years before my mother, her husband and five children, would sail back to England on a six-month trip of a lifetime to see her family. In this she was fortunate, as many postwar migrants and refugees never had the opportunity or the luxury of returning to see their families or homelands again. I never heard her express any regrets about the decision to move to Australia and I felt that she really accepted Australia as her home following the trip to England in 1962.

I know that my mother was lonely and homesick at times in those early years. I vividly remember one occasion as an eight-year-old child feeling the helplessness of hearing my mother crying on the phone to her friend, Marjorie Cooper, my father's second cousin (of Coopers Brewery). Her distress was palpable and something I've never forgotten without feeling sad. My father had just been readmitted to the Dawes Road Repatriation Hospital with post-traumatic stress disorder symptoms following his wartime experience, she had five young children under the age of eight years, and had recently been diagnosed with insulin-dependent diabetes or type 1 diabetes. She was 31 years of age and type 1 diabetes is usually considered a disease of childhood or adolescence. At the time of her diagnosis it was a disease where management of the condition was crude and it was often difficult to control. It meant twice-daily injections of very unstable insulin, not like those of today, a low carbohydrate diet that had to be carefully measured and regular urine testing; and it manifested in extreme fluctuations of high and low blood sugar levels causing faintness, tiredness, and a propensity for coma. There was little understanding of this condition amongst the medical fraternity at that time, and, unlike today where there is an abundance of information, she learnt to manage this complex condition on her own. However, on this particular occasion, when I witnessed my mother weeping on the phone I was grateful that the person who had befriended her from the time of her arrival in Australia with her kindness and generosity of spirit, was there to listen to her. Marjorie Cooper, a wonderful, fun-loving lady who I secretly looked upon as a surrogate grandmother. She became our extended family in those early years.

However, my mother was not one to complain. She was a strong, stoic and determined women with a sense of adventure, and I think these traits stood her in good stead. The family she missed in England she created here in Australia and she devoted her efforts to developing a strong sense of family with her husband and children. She was the glue to our family and our lives were dependent upon and revolved around her. Not only was she an excellent cook, especially cake making, but generous to a fault, and everything she made and did for us was full of love. I recall her icing a cake while sitting up in bed with a severe case of the mumps. You can't keep a good woman down.

My mother embraced motherhood, and threw herself into all that it entailed. In class I would study the carefully covered schoolbooks, labelled pencils and clothing, year in and out, and these small but significant acts would say to me, 'I am with you'. This included preparing costumes for school plays and dress-up days, ferrying us around for our school sporting team events on Saturdays, and frequently cooking for the copious number of trading tables that were a regular feature of any fundraising event or fete day. Mothers were the backbone of the school community and provided many hours of voluntary and valuable service to schools, something that is often missing these days with so many mothers working in the paid workforce.

When I was eight years old I took my turn cleaning the inkwells as the inkwell monitor, a messy and dirty job. I had placed my new birthday wristwatch into my top shirt pocket but it accidentally fell out into the ink-filled trough. My new watch was ink-stained and completely ruined. My parents had always been very fair, and as in the case of my watch, understood that it was an accident and nothing more was said about it. This was an era when it wasn't unusual for misbehaving children to be caned or 'given the stick/ ruler' as punishment at school, or belted with a strap, hit with the wooden spoon, or 'given a thrashing' by parents at home. We were therefore pretty lucky regarding discipline, although I did get a well-deserved slap on a few occasions as a younger child. I remember my father trying a couple of times but I think his gentle taps hurt him more than me. A far more effective punishment for me was being sent to my room to dust my considerable collection of ornaments arranged in shadow boxes on my walls and shelves. Now that was torture and took me ages to complete. If my mother was cross she had that certain narrowed-eye, tight-lipped, set of a determined jaw 'look' (that my sons say I have also adopted) that meant business, and we all knew, including my father, not to push the boundaries.

A fierce lioness at times, she demonstrated total loyalty by supporting and protecting those she loved. On a few rare occasions when I felt unfairly treated at school, my mother took up my cause and discussed her concerns with Mr Sexton, a stern but kind principal. Although she was not a demonstrative person, her trust and belief in me never faltered and I loved her dearly for it. She was my security and kept me safe, my staunch advocate if others ever doubted me, and her belief in me, her child, was everything.

She had a wonderful sense of fun about her and enthusiastically joined the Mothers' Club at the Linden Park Infant School. Like many women of her era she didn't work outside the home and gradually made many friends through these mothers' activities at school. Her love of amateur drama encouraged her to partake in performing various skits on the school stage. On one particularly enjoyable and very successful occasion, she played the part of Peter Sellers as an Indian doctor, and mimed the song *Boom boody-boom boody-boom boody-boom, Goodness Gracious Me* with another woman playing the part of Sophia Loren. She was decked out in dark brown body paint, dark wig, white coat and a stethoscope around her neck. Apparently it brought the house down and I still laugh when I hear that song today.

Christmas was a magical time for my mother. She loved it. The preparations would start in October each year when she would prepare the Christmas cake mixture for her family and Marjorie Cooper. It was a serious affair where we would stir this wonderful-smelling mixture full of fruit soaked in sherry and spices three times, without touching the bottom of the bowl, before making a wish. Once cooked, these delicious-smelling cakes were carefully basted with rum every second day for 12 days, rotated, and eventually wrapped and sealed for maturing until the week before Christmas. She would then cover the cakes with a marzipan undercoat before the final application of royal icing and decorations, and firm instructions to her children 'not to touch' until Christmas Day. At the end of the school year, all five of us would present our teacher with a thank-you gift, a plate of freshly baked shortbread tied with a tartan ribbon. It was always well received.

My mother gradually began working outside the home when I was about 17 years of age. She began cooking and selling cakes for the *Captain's Cabin*, a homemade-cake shop in Tusmore. The friendship of the other women who also baked, the sense of satisfaction from creating a demand for her specialty cakes, and the additional income and independence it generated was very satisfying for her. The kitchen would be overflowing with chocolate cakes, lemon curd tartlets, ginger gems filled with cream, and jam-filled shortcakes, to name a few. Prior to this time, my father had had her undivided attention since they married and he didn't take too kindly to this new demand upon her time. He worked from home as a chartered accountant, and due to his postwar insomnia, did most of his accountancy work late at night and into the early hours before going to bed. My mother would wake him around eleven o'clock in the morning with a cup of tea and a slice of freshly baked cake, which of course he loved. However, the increasing demands upon her time meant that this ritual went by the wayside, much to my father's bitter disappointment. To make matters worse, I completely misread the situation and excitedly surprised him with the latest, whiz-bang tea-maker-alarm clock for his birthday, thinking that this would solve his problem. What I hadn't realised as an 18-year-old who still had a lot to learn, was that it was the pleasure of having my mother bring him his tea that he enjoyed and missed. The automated tea-maker's arrival had added salt to his already raw wound and was promptly returned to the store.

In later years when I had my own children my relationship with my mother developed into a friendship that included her in so much that we did together as a family. My husband, Ric, was generous in accepting that his mother-in-law would be a constant presence in our lives and never once complained. I think he realised he was on a good thing, enjoying her cakes too much for it to be a problem. My mother would babysit our children regularly, travel with us on our trips to the Flinders Ranges, the Grampian Ranges, Victoria and New South Wales, and was often a regular guest at weekend barbeques with friends. Our sons adored her and she them, and she would indulge them with all the treats and liberties that are only extended to grandmothers. She would delight in their naughty, cheeky ways, mimicking their funny sayings and wondering why I sometimes had trouble sharing in her mirth as I rushed around trying to multi-task all the chores that needed to be done before work or bedtime.

My mother had spent her teenage years, normally a time of transition from childhood to adulthood, experiencing the trauma and disruption of World War Two. Her education was rudely interrupted and she was robbed of the usual pleasures of discovering the world around her as teenagers usually do. The war years did take their toll on her and her health in later years.

But one has to keep everything in context. Very few people around the world came out of World War Two unscathed. Thousands of people lost their lives, both soldiers and civilians, millions were injured and rendered homeless, and others suffered terrible atrocities at the hands of others. Families were torn apart and children shipped to the other side of the world, some of whom never recovered from the separation, and suffered at the hands of people who were meant to provide shelter and safety for them. I don't think anyone wins wars.

My mother was mindful of all of this, considered herself lucky, and lived a rich, full life. She and my father provided their children with so many opportunities that she herself had missed as a teenager. My life as a child was full of swimming, tennis, ballet, eurhythmics, sewing classes, Brownies and Girl Guides, basketball, dancing lessons, carefree adventures and holidays to Victor Harbor, food for the asking, peaceful nights in a warm bed, and the list goes on.

She died suddenly at the age of 63 years after a two-week illness, a complication of type 1 diabetes.

I am forever in her debt, and I miss her so.

If you want to understand any woman you must first ask about her mother and then listen carefully. Anita Diamant, *The Red Tent*, (1998)

Pamela's Chocolate Cake

Cake

4½ ounces (130 grams) butter

3 level tablespoons cocoa

1½ cups self-raising flour

1½ cups caster sugar

¾ cup milk

3 eggs

½ teaspoon vanilla essence

Icing

4 ounces (120 grams) milk chocolate
¼ cup of cream
Rollo chocolates or flaked almonds
(Double the icing ingredients if serving as two single cakes.)

Heat oven to moderate temperature – 180°C (approximately) for a conventional oven. Line two round 18 cm cake tins with tin foil. Melt butter over a slow heat and leave to one side. Sift all dry ingredients into a bowl.

Beat eggs, milk and vanilla essence together and add gradually to the dry ingredients. Pour in melted butter to mixture and beat well. Divide into the two cake tins and bake in a moderate oven for 20–25 minutes until the centre springs back to touch. Leave to cool on rack.

To make the icing, gently mix chocolate and cream in a bowl over water and heat. Turn cake(s) over and ice bottom of cake if a smooth finish preferred.

Cakes can be iced separately as single cakes, or served as one cake with whipped cream between. Decorate as desired.

Frances Goldney Nilson

Frances is the oldest of five children all of whom attended Linden Park Primary School from Grade 1 through to Grade 7. As the eldest child she tended to take her responsibilities a little too seriously and it wasn't until she left school, studied to be a Registered Nurse at the Royal Adelaide Hospital in 1968 and headed overseas that she learnt to have fun – something she excelled in. She studied midwifery in London, nursed in Paris and travelled widely for three years before heading home. She completed a BEd (Nursing) and has alternated between nursing and nurse education

for 46 years. Her goal is to celebrate 50 years of nursing in 2018, if her body and mind will last the distance. Frances lives in Brisbane with her wonderful husband Ric and two beautiful sons, and the memory of her mother comforts and sustains her. Her mother's legacy is 'a love of family and all its rich gifts'.

Lorna Clarice HARRISON

née Byrnes

(1923–2001)

Sandra Harrison Mikelsons

My mother was born on 25 June 1923 in Marrickville, New South Wales, the first of two daughters to Arthur and Emma Byrnes. Her entry to life was dramatic, as she was not expected to live due to breathing difficulties and a lack of medical assistance at the time. Suffice to say, the staff must have done miracles because she survived and went on to live 78 years, passing away in November 2001, with her five children by her side.

She and her sister Shirley lived idyllic childhoods, being given opportunities not often afforded others of their day. Their father was the general manager of Winchcombe Carsons Wool Company (I believe they were eventually taken over by Elders), where he worked his way up from sweeping the wool floors to classing wool, then onwards to travel the world as an agent for the company and eventually becoming the general manager. He was also the great-great-grandson of Peter Hibbs, seaman on the flagship *Sirius* of the

First Fleet and later the master of the *Norfolk*, part of the Bass and Flinders expedition around Tasmania which provided proof that Tasmania was a separate island from the mainland. The family were members of the First Fleet Association and because of this, they were afforded the honour of being invited on board an official boat used at the opening of the Sydney Harbour Bridge in 1932.

Lorna and Shirley had wonderful trips with their parents, often going to visit sheep properties; Mum loved to watch the shearers at work. She would often tell me about the shearing sheds and how amazing the shearers were! Mum suffered from warts on her hands and found that wrapping her hands in newly clipped greasy wool made the warts disappear!

She loved to go on voyages up and down the east coast of Australia, stopping in Brisbane, Newcastle and often down south to Hobart. The ships were merchant ships transporting wool. Her father would spend time on the bridge with the captain, having become good friends with different captains over the years and at times his girls were allowed to accompany him. Mum would often talk about the fantastic fun she and her sister had on board.

There was one time, when some containers of sweets, which were meant as treats for the girls, all fell out of their containers on to the floor and of course the girls grabbed the opportunity and helped themselves. The girls had a ball! The crew member who was responsible for the containers was hopelessly seasick due to very rough seas there being no stabilisers in those days. The girls and their parents weren't seasick but many others were, including the doctor and the captain! Grandpa was called upon to render assistance to many of the crew including the captain.

Mum lived her early years in Marrickville and was made aware of the troubles of people living through the Great Depression. The family would often go to the seaside to give food and clothing and cash to people living in makeshift shelters. She would tell me how sad it made her feel that she had a home and car and food! She felt privileged as her father had a job that was very secure in a time of great insecurity.

She lived in Marrickville until her teens when the family moved to Beverly Hills – to a much bigger home, in what was a developing suburb. Grandpa had bought a new car and it was unusual for homes to have their own garages, so he had to park in a garage shared by others in the street.

Mum's interests were reading, embroidery and painting; she wasn't much of a sportswoman but did enjoy swimming and played vigoro at school. (Vigoro was a combination of cricket and tennis but is now similar to a combination of cricket and baseball.) Mum's mother was an accomplished seamstress but would never allow the girls anywhere near her sewing machine. She employed a maid who did most of the housework and cooking and, therefore, the girls never had much opportunity to learn about domestic duties.

Mum was an average scholar but she had beautiful penmanship and following the end of high school, she got a position as a 'ticket card writer' and window dresser in Farmers' department store in Sydney. She loved her time at Farmers' and enjoyed a social life that included spending time with her friends and taking in the nightlife of Sydney. She told me that she sometimes went dancing in a club called The Trocadero, where servicemen would take their rest and recreation leave. Mum loved to sing and she said she often did so at this club.

Mum dated American sailors who were billeted in Sydney during the war. She would talk about how the sailors would give girls nylons (stockings) as they were in such short supply. Apparently if there weren't any stockings around, girls would paint a seam up the back of their legs to make fake stockings. Mum dated at least two sailors during her time at Farmers', in fact she became engaged to them both (neither knew about the other!). They were from different ships. One of these men was from Mexico and the other was from California. Mum was Protestant and they were both Catholic and these denominations rarely married. Inter-denominational relationships were not a common phenomenon for many years; in fact, my dad's mother was disowned by her Catholic parents for marrying a Protestant.

After Australia entered World War Two, Mum's job of being a ticket card writer was deemed by the government as 'unessential to the war effort' and she was advised that she would have to either work in a factory or join the services. Her father was horrified! No daughter of his was going to work in a factory or join in the services; he thought he could have control over what she did but Mum told him there was no choice, everyone had to do their bit for the country. She enlisted behind his back! Her parents had refused to let her marry either of the sailors and now her father was furious – ranting and raving that she had enlisted! All the while Grandma kept silent as Grandpa very much called the shots; autocracy was a common state in marriages of the time.

Mum was sent to Ingleburn in New South Wales to do her training and on the day she left, there was quite a scene at the railway station – Grandpa apparently could be heard yelling down the platform. How embarrassing! He realised he was losing his control and he didn't like it.

Mum was to do a nursing training course along with basic army training. This was quite a culture shock for her. Early morning wake-up calls, cold showers, exercises, uniform and accommodation block checks, followed by classes in general nursing care. I talked to Mum about her experiences when I went nursing some years later. She said she was so embarrassed when she had to wash a man for the first time – I believe her educator told her to 'just make out you're washing your doll and try to ignore any lewd comments the men might make'. Not so easy but I guess she accomplished the job.

Once her training was completed, Mum found she was to be posted to Adelaide. She didn't know anything about Adelaide but looked on this move as an adventure. Her father again made a scene but he had no influence on the Australian Army! When her group arrived in Adelaide, they were to have further education at the Royal Adelaide Hospital and once completed, they were to relocate to the Repatriation Hospital. Mum was very excited to find out that she was to be accommodated at Government

House – what an honour! This accommodation was certainly much grander than at the Repat, where the nurses were to have their quarters in Nissen huts.

Mum settled in to her new life at the Repat but it was about to change again when she became aware of a young soldier whistling at her on her way to her quarters. He would often be doing electrical repairs around the hospital as part of his recovery from wounds he received in New Guinea. She said he could often be found 'up a pole', calling down to 'Nugget' (the nickname given to Mum because she dyed her hair red-brown, a similar colour to a shoe polish brand named Nugget). So began the romance!

The courtship was brief; Dad didn't have much to offer but Mum loved going for rides in the sidecar of his motorbike, having outings to cheap or free movies put on for servicemen, and eating out at the pie-cart in the city because they had special deals for soldiers.

They went to Sydney to be married and honeymooned in the Blue Mountains. Not long after their marriage, Mum and Dad started to clash; they realised they didn't have a lot in common. Mum wanted to leave the marriage but she found she was having a baby (my brother Ian born in 1946), so she reached out for help from her mother but was met with no support; in fact her mother said, 'You made your bed, now lie in it!' Very harsh but not an uncommon comment in those days I believe!

Her mother-in-law Hannah was particularly cold and hard, having had to rear her nine children on her own after being widowed quite young – Mum was told that she was spoilt and must have been 'born with a silver spoon in her mouth'. So she had to pull herself together and do the best she could to survive.

Mum and Dad unfortunately had to live with Hannah in a small cramped room. Mum spent hours in the bedroom, hiding from Hannah as much as possible. Mum told me that baby Ian would spend the day in a play-pen on top of the bed! If he was unsettled or crying Hannah would yell at Mum, belittling her frequently. It was a miserable life. Thankfully, Dad realised that they needed to be in their own home if their marriage had any chance of success.

There was never a plan to have more children but when Mum and Dad moved to a brand-new home in Camden, and they started to make a new life and new friends, a decision to have another baby was made and I was born in 1950.

Mum loved living in Camden; it was a new housing development with everyone starting out together. The closeness and fellowship of the area was wonderful for Mum and she revelled in the new and happy life she was now living. This was to be short-lived as Dad wanted to move to improve his employment status. His plan was to move to the eastern suburbs as he had now started working for ETSA (Electricity Service of SA) in a much better job so Mum had to leave behind her many friends with the move to Glenunga in 1955.

At first it was exciting, setting up another home, this one an older established house with a bigger garden and potential for expansion. It met Dad's needs more than Mum's because Dad was keen to do all his own handyman work. Mum did help with ideas such as having Dad build a large bird aviary; a built-in barbeque and an extra room above the house. Some years later, about 1966, she was instrumental in our family attaining a backyard pool. It was at a time when above-ground pools were becoming popular. Mum often asked Dad if we could get one but he always answered with, 'If I ever get a pool it will be a conventional in-ground pool!' – he thought that would be the end of it but Mum had other ideas! One day Dad came home from work to find Mum and children digging a rather large hole in the backyard, and after his initial shock and anger, he gave in and we got our pool!

Mum missed her friends from Camden and found it difficult to keep in touch because she didn't drive, and neither did they. There was no phone at home, so all calls were made from the closest pay phone-box or (in emergencies) from a neighbour's phone. We had a phone service until about 1962 but it was removed because Dad thought we would abuse the privilege! It was some years before the service was reconnected.

Dad attempted to teach Mum to drive but this was fraught with disaster. My brother Ian and I were disruptive in the back of the car.

Poor Mum was driving all over the road and a passer-by reported her to the police as a drunk driver! She never got to drive but always paid for her licence, just in case she ever learned.

In 1957 my brother Nigel was born, followed three years later by my sisters, twins Verity and Gaynor. So now Mum's life was very full. Having five children of varying ages was a challenge and maintaining a home kept her very busy.

Mum wasn't one to join in school mothers' groups so it was a rare occasion that she would come to Linden Park School. I do remember one visit though, when my sisters were babies and Mum brought them in their pram to observe the school sports day – I was so excited to show off my little sisters!

The arrival of television in 1959 was exciting for Mum. Now she could indulge her love of movies and musicals and especially the daytime television serials. Before we got a television set, Mum would take us to an electrical store on Portrush Road to sit outside their window and watch programs! This was a lot of fun and very common at the time.

Eventually we got a television and it wasn't long before she indulged herself in daytime serials – we would never be surprised to see her watching *Days of our Lives* when we came home for lunch! She was a dreamer and would fantasise about travelling to the USA to visit the places she knew from the movies and she was thrilled when she got to do this in 1976 and again in 1978. She often broke out into songs made famous in movies – we children would groan and make fun of her but actually she could hold a tune quite well.

She was a collector/hoarder and when she travelled she would bring home an assortment of items: decorative packs of matches; flags were a particular favourite; paper serviettes; soaps; every kind of pamphlet known to man; quirky souvenirs of all kinds – Dad would baulk but had no control over this. She kept her memories alive by making colourful displays utilising her collectibles.

Mum also loved to make plant and flower arrangements and would spend hours working on these. She would collect cactus, pine cones, small tree branches, driftwood, leaves etc. and paint them and make wonderful displays, decorating many an empty spot in the home.

Along with inanimate objects, Mum was a lover of small creatures. She encouraged a love of pets – at one point we had 13 cats! In fact, she had to act as midwife to one cat when it was in trouble giving birth to a kitten in the breech position – the cat, kitten and Mum survived this ordeal; there were hens; many budgies and finches; a galah; rabbits; tortoises; the occasional dog; lizards and goldfish. It was a labour of love caring for all of these.

School holidays were often spent at home; Mum would take us on bus outings or we would make our own fun, however, for some of our Christmas holidays we would go to Sydney and stay with our grandparents. Mum loved to show us around where she grew up, it was during these trips that a love of family history began.

As her parents aged, she would try to get to Sydney as often as possible to make sure they were managing. I did a couple of trips with her and spent a lot of time cleaning their house. During one trip, Mum and I had the opportunity to go to a cabaret in the city and hear Robert Goulet sing – it was a great experience to share with her. It was terrific bonding – as was a trip to Victoria in 1964 during which Mum and I had the opportunity of seeing Judy Garland perform. I thoroughly enjoyed these experiences with Mum and got a wonderful appreciation for the music of the 40s and 50s.

When my grandparents moved to Adelaide to live out their days, they lived near Mum on Portrush Road until their health deteriorated and they went into nursing homes, where Mum would volunteer regularly. She would have loved to get a paid job but Dad had always been against this idea; he believed a wife's place was in the home. Mum was frustrated and not at all keen on being a full time housewife but there was no way around this.

She did get a job once, but it only lasted a very short time because Dad expected her to give him her earnings to manage and she didn't want to. This would mean he would cut out her housekeeping money. Some years later, she did do volunteer work in opportunity shops, where her flair and creativity blossomed! She would rearrange and decorate the shops, however, she often brought home many clothing items! Shoes. Handbags. Dresses. Jewellery. Everything had to be colour-coordinated! I lost count of how many bangles she had.

She loved her working days at Goodwill Norwood. She did this for many years and finally had a feeling of fulfilment, particularly once her parents were gone and we children had moved on with our lives. Dad didn't mind her volunteer work – he even drove her to Norwood occasionally.

When it came to cooking, Mum wasn't the best of cooks but she tried. The school lunches were 'interesting' – the sandwich fillings: fritz, cheese and tomato sauce, cold spaghetti, cold baked beans to name a few. In 1968, Mum contributed to a recipe book published by the 1st Glenunga Scout Group Mothers' Club – Heavenly Tart was my favourite!

Heavenly Tart

Base

1 cup self-raising flour

1 tablespoon butter

1 tablespoon sugar

1 egg

Rub shortening into flour and sugar, mix with egg and roll out thinly. Line a tart dish and bake until crisp.

Filling

2 firm bananas

1½ cups water

Juice of 1 orange and 1 lemon

1 cup sugar

2 tablespoons custard powder

1 tablespoon butter

Put everything except the bananas into a saucepan and cook slowly till mixture boils, stirring constantly. While still hot, pour half the mixture into the baked pastry shell. Slice the bananas over the top. Pour on the rest of the mixture. Refrigerate until ready to use. Slice and serve with a dollop of cream.

Food shopping changed by the early 60s – prior to this, Mum would have almost all groceries, meat and vegetables delivered by the grocer, butcher and fruiterer – each would leave specials leaflets one day and wait for the order Mum would ring in from the local phone-box. The orders would be delivered a couple of days later, brought inside personally – and paid for in cash – not a credit card in sight! Interestingly, home deliveries are now very much back in vogue.

When we went shopping in the city, Mum would never use an escalator – she was frightened that she would get her feet caught. So we always had to use the elevators. This issue was overcome in 1976 when after many sessions practising getting on and off escalators, Mum was cured of her fear. She had to be, because she was going for a holiday to the USA and we told her she would never get out of the airport if she didn't master the escalators.

I think Mum made the best out of life that she could. Taking trips was always high on her agenda. I have already mentioned overseas trips but she did many within Australia, sometimes with Dad but many times with different children or with friends. One fun trip was when she was 70 and my children and I took her to visit my sister in Canberra and during this visit we took her to the snow. She was enthralled and had a ride on a toboggan! It was a gutsy thing for a woman of her age.

As the years progressed, Mum became more involved with helping collate the family tree which was subsequently published in 1995 as *Sailing on ....the Hibbs Line*. She was fascinated with her ancestry to the point that she visited the old cemetery in Windsor, New South Wales, and located Peter Hibbs' gravesite. She was so fascinated that she asked that her ashes be scattered there when she passed on.

In 1997 Dad passed away and Mum subsequently sold our house

in Glenunga. This was a sad day for me and my siblings. We filmed the last days of 93 Allinga Avenue for posterity. Unfortunately in the July of 1998 Mum became ill with multiple myeloma and spent very little time in her new home – there were hospital admissions, some time living with me and my family and some time in a retirement home and then in a hospice until she passed away in November 2001.

My siblings and I were able to gather around her in the hospice and be with her when she passed away and we all agreed to honour her wish to spread her ashes. We all flew to Sydney, hired a small commuter bus and drove to Windsor, where we were able to fulfil her wishes – we scattered them and then spent some time reflecting on the history around us along the banks of the Hawkesbury River. My siblings and I will always remember her as a woman who did her best to love life against adversity. She wasn't perfect and probably if she were living in this generation, would have left her marriage and pursued her own goals and ambitions.

We loved her and miss her today and remember her often; I particularly do as I am ageing and I see her in the mirror every day!

Sandra Harrison Mikelsons

Sandra is the second eldest of five children, all of whom attended Linden Park Primary School from Grade 1 to Grade 7. After leaving high school, she followed a clerical path, working as a secretary and typist with the Commonwealth Bank for four years then with a secretarial agency for three years. She married Juris (bank officer) at the age of 18 and at 25 decided to have a complete change of working career and began her general nurse training at the Queen Elizabeth Hospital. This was to be one of the best decisions of her life. She finished her general training,

then after a short time completed her midwifery. After a short break to start a family, she completed her Neonatology Certificate and her Bachelor of Nursing Studies. Her career fully focused on the care of sick and premature babies and she is still working in this area today at the Women's and Children's Hospital in Adelaide. Her husband and her parents fully supported her career. They were always there to help with her two children and were very proud of her achievements. A career in nursing was also followed by three of her siblings, and the other is an ambulance officer. Her children also have health-related careers: her daughter is a dietitian and her son is a laboratory technician. Her interests are travelling, gardening, theatre and walking for exercise.

Juliet HIATT

née Cobbin

(1928–1978)

Jane Hiatt

My mother's name was Juliet, a romantic and symbolic name that suited her entire self. Like the Shakespearean heroine, my mother was innocently attractive, even beautiful in a gamin manner, idealistic and a victim of unlucky fate.

Whilst the adversities in Juliet's life were not of her own making, she was capable of huge resilience, mischief and courage and was definitely the poised and decisive mistress of her own life. She made necessary sacrifices but had the integrity to remain herself, and to quietly and diligently achieve what was important. Juliet possessed a kind of nobility and kindness, often manifested to neighbours, friends and close family. We don't use the epithet 'sweet' now, it has gone out of fashion, but it suited my mother's temperament and gave Juliet a mentor's power to inspire others with her example.

The rest of Juliet's given names were Mary and Cobbin, more banal and ordinary, although there seem to be few Cobbins presently in Adelaide; the family had migrated from England in the

1850s with the romantic profession of 'musician' written on the shipping inventory for the original two brothers, Robert and William, who arrived together in Adelaide.

Juliet was born on 24 December 1928 in Gawler at a time when Gawler was a completely separate country town, a thriving wheat and sheep community on the fringes of the Barossa Valley. She lived next door to Brenton Langbein, the famous violinist, who left tickets for her at the reception desk of the various auditoria in South Australia when he performed. Friendships in Gawler were like that – generous, serious and for life. Juliet and her sister Patricia's friendships were lifelong commitments and several of their girlfriends were a major part of my sister's and my life as we grew up. Gawler was a confident, if sleepy, community on the banks of the Para River, and most of the houses were solid limestone or bluestone, with surround verandahs and underground tanks. Juliet lived in just such a house on the Lyndoch Road, reasonably well off as the daughter of a regional manager of the South Australian Electric Company.

Given the date of her birthday, Juliet was rarely given two sets of presents. It amazed me as a child that she did not resent this misfortune. I would have! Somehow this privation did not ever worry her and said much about the era and her country upbringing.

Juliet attended Gawler High School, also on the Lyndoch Road, and was very popular. She had an engaging manner, was very pretty and affectionate to her friends. She was head prefect and seemed to have a hopeful future ahead of her when she won a job in Adelaide as a stenographer. Her father would drop her off and pick her up from the train at Salisbury.

One of the horribly formative experiences of my mother's childhood was the presence of tuberculosis. Her mother, Edith May née Cooney, was a quietly charismatic, lovely and able woman with a strong will and self-denial that must have had a powerful influence on my mother. Whilst content with her housewife's role, Edith had had nursing training and that was very useful in the family battle with tuberculosis or consumption. Very little was known about the causes of this disease but it was known that a dry climate, bed rest and anti-infection strategies such as carbolic soap and hot water, could be therapeutic. Edith was convinced that careful medical nursing could eliminate the spread of this disease. When her husband William's siblings began to succumb to tuberculosis, Edith was determined that they would not be neglected or sent away. This was a time when much stigma was attached to tuberculosis sufferers, and they were often shipped away to so-called sanitoria, rarely to return alive to their families. Edith resolved to take them in.

Jack the footballer was the first to die after puncturing his lung. My grandmother nursed his two sisters when they also fell ill, and she took them into her home. Juliet and Patricia were under strict orders not to touch food or dishes that the patients had eaten from, to destroy any gifts, and to wash their hands each and every time they entered the patients' bedrooms. Neither of the girls was affected even though their aunts endured a lingering death with disintegrating lungs. My mother gave me a jet and gold ring that had been given to her by her aunt Jess with her name inscribed on it by her loving fiancé. This was a touching memorial of a young woman whose life ended too soon.

When Edith began to exhibit symptoms of tuberculosis, her husband was prepared to bankrupt himself to save her life. He absolutely adored her. By then the 40s had arrived and although antibiotics had not reached the back-blocks of South Australia, William did have Edith operated on by a famous surgeon who did a radical rib and lung removal. It saved her life even though Edith was an invalid for years and walked with a downward slope on her right side and pressure on her heart.

Tragically William contracted tuberculosis too but kept it a secret as long as he could. Edith was his salvation and the money, in an era when Medicare did not exist, was too far diminished. William practised an early form of meditation and psychological control based on self-help books he had sent to him. He lived painfully for a couple of years and died eventually in Gladstone where he was still regional manager of the South Australian Electric Company. He was only 42 but had saved his family. I wish I had known him.

Juliet's character, values and destiny were determined by the awfulness of this ghastly disease and its aftermath. For the rest of her life she treated her mother as precious and vulnerable and cared for her with discretion and devotion as well as running her own home. She missed her father acutely as he had been a devoted friend. Yet this tragedy reinforced her unshakeable knowledge that compassion for those who suffer is essential, and self-denial and self-knowledge important values. The war did affect Juliet but only incidentally. Her older sister, Patricia, was engaged to an Australian Air Force pilot whose missions were mainly in New Guinea. I still have lovely photographs of the church wedding with the beautiful chestnut-haired bride and my lovely mother resplendent in a filmy bridesmaid's outfit made from cretonne curtains. She looked gorgeous with her olive skin, large blue eyes and high cheekbones, an inheritance from her father and her mother's Irish background.

Pat conceived my cousin John quickly, and it was an unspeakable tragedy when Bob Gordon, her husband, disappeared whilst flying in New Guinea. The plane was never found and she gave birth without her husband. She fell in love eventually with another soldier, Ron Jordan, who pursued her resolutely. They married and Pat had more children. They left South Australia when Ron obtained a job in Muswellbrook as a meat inspector. Juliet was separated from her sister and the care of Edith fell to her alone.

Juliet continued working and enjoying the humorous antics of her friends. Her albums are swollen with photos of beaus, and clans of her Gawler friends in scarves and clinging skirts at the beach or in the bush for picnics.

The 30s and 40s were decades with few options for entertainment. We forget how important the radio and episodic comedies were in those days. There was privation, even poverty, illness that could strike any time, and much unemployment in the 30s.

After the Armistice the atmosphere lightened and many of

Juliet's friends began to marry and move to the city. In 1946 Juliet and her close family and friends became addicted to *The Mackackie Mansions*, a radio comedy which regularly entertained Australians who admired Mo Rene's rather 'blue' humour, never abusive but always superbly timed and full of innuendo. Mo had been born in Adelaide, a Jew with a black-and-white clown's face and a sense of vaudeville. His distinctly Australian sense of understatement really appealed to radio audiences and Juliet and her family used to go into paroxysms of laughter about the carryings-on of the characters created by this comedian. The family gave themselves nicknames from *The Mackackie Mansions* that lasted their whole lives. Juliet became 'Chowgi', one of her best friends became 'Aggie', and her mother Edith became Mo or Mowee, which is what I called my grandmother all her days.

I am not sure how my mother met my father. I do know he was besotted with her and graffitied the railway bridge outside Gawler with their names entwined inside a heart. They married in 1948 and Juliet used to say that, despite the difficulties of living with my father who suffered insomnia and post-traumatic stress, she chose him so she would never be bored, and she never was.

I was born in 1950 and was a small baby. Mum used to say she was teased about whether she was giving birth to a rabbit! Apparently I was almost a month overdue and Dad used to drive the Austin with Mum aboard repeatedly over railway tracks. It had no effect. I came in my own sweet time, on 10 October, at the Unley Park Private Hospital.

Whilst awaiting the construction of their postwar brick home at 20 Highfield Avenue, St Georges, Juliet, Syd and I lived at 20 Kennaway Street, Tusmore, with Mowee my grandmother, and Alice Maud Sare, my great-grandmother. I adored this house for many reasons. I became very close to my great-grandmother with whom I shared a special bond. She was also a lovely woman physically even in her 70s, with a quiet and fey approach, and a desire to play with me, unlike other adults. Another reason I loved Kennaway Street was because it backed onto Tusmore Park with its mysterious creeks that went through drains under the road, and it backed onto other people's properties where you could filch fruit and overhear their conversations. There were endless trees to climb and long adventures to be had. I think we must have kept returning to Kennaway Street because we moved to St Georges before I went to school. I also remember the wonderful furniture and china and wooden animals that Alice had in the house and which I used to farewell every night before bed. There was the elephant, the tortoise, the glass swan, the alligator (a favourite, in brass, a nut cracker with snapping jaws). The grandfather clock would need to bong the hour before I would move to bed! These delaying tactics were very successful.

It was a privilege to have four generations in the same house and a great way to connect with your heritage and understand different age groups and their needs. You don't forget the experiences and inhabitants of early childhood.

In Highfield Avenue I think my mother must have missed her family. She did visit Mowee every day when she moved to Dulwich after Alice's death, but there were long hours when Dad was at work and I was at school and all she had were domestic chores. Juliet was not a natural homemaker and probably resented having to leave her job when she married. The domestic routine was unremitting and labour-saving devices were only recently being introduced. On Monday the washing was done. Mum would light the copper, add the Bluo and Lux to the water, and the clothes would be washed in strict order. Delicates had already been handwashed and wrung separately. Bed linen was near the end, followed by handkerchiefs, then the water was let out and the rinsing water put in the trough, the clothes agitated by hand and put through the hand-turned wringer. Improvements did happen over the years, and the washing machine halved the labour, but the early 50s were very labour intensive for women.

Mum hated cooking and rebelled against the tedium of her allotted domestic role in this respect. Mum's meals were usually grilled or baked and she had the amazing skill of incinerating nearly every dish she made. The kitchen was the realm where she did use the new labour-saving meals, such as Deb instant mashed potatoes and Surprise dehydrated peas and carrots. Steak and chops always curled their edges in contempt at the hungry family. Casseroles were less inedible with small sachets of herbs and stock shaken out of boxes. Mum's pièce de resistance was roast lamb with potatoes, pumpkin and fresh beans. I loved Mum's roast and she always gave me the shank, which I still love. At the end, before dish washing, Mum would save the fat which would be reused during the week, sometimes in sandwiches and also for other cooking. Mum's years of privation as a child, and her training, also meant that she ironed brown paper and re-used it along with fragments of string rolled into a ball.

Juliet was a wonderful female and an inspiration to me in ways I only half realised at the time. However, she was not an instinctive child-minder. I can remember the boring hours traipsing after her whilst she did domestic tasks, correcting her vacuuming, handing her pegs and listening to ABC radio's Kindergarten of the Air. That is where I first heard Doris Day sing *Que sera, sera*. One boring day I recall trying to impress her with my latest skill learnt at kindy, stuttering! The effect was dynamic, even hysterical. Very satisfying.

Juliet was rather bewildered by unpleasant or abusive people. For some reason they brought out the competitive side of me, and my passion for justice overpowered me, often ultimately with her support. She loved and supported me, but also seemed to enjoy my rebellions. One example occurred at Linden Park Primary when I was immersed in my tomboy phase. I engaged in a ruler fight on the desks with a fellow musketeer now forgotten. It was fun and Mr Button was not in the room. Then he entered, and in modern parlance, *freaked*! Suspensions didn't happen so my mother was summoned and gave Mr Button a dressing-down about the harmlessness of my activity and the ridiculous over-reaction that had taken her from her busy home. I never heard more about the incident. Another example occurred in Leaving French at Unley High School when my French teacher Mrs Harbich, she of the scary bun and battle-axe persona, forbade me to go on an excursion to see *The Canterbury Tales* because I was too talkative. I loudly refuted her right to so decide and my mother came into school like a polite banshee and also endorsed my right to go on the excursion. I went to *The Canterbury Tales* and got an A for English in revenge!

My mother always did her duty as a mother, but did not really warm to the role as it seemed to her a trap which might rob a female of individuality. She always said she wanted to be a pilot. The freedom and speed of the upper stratosphere appealed to her. What my mother found natural was sincere and utter love. She also understood love in its purest form – forgiveness. I remember a time when I was 18 and determined to go away with my boyfriend on an unchaperoned holiday. She was appalled, and refused to talk to me for weeks. Then one afternoon, she held out her arms to me in the street and hugged me to her. We were as one again. An example of her consideration was when my second cousin was killed in a car accident and she delayed telling me until after I had completed an exam a day later.

As we grew up, Mum enjoyed the cats we owned – briefly, because Highfield Avenue was very busy and families did not lock up their cats at night so quite a few met a violent death on the night road. She also loved our dogs, one a mutt of questionable breeding that she christened Spoofendyke. Her sense of humour was a life-saving attribute. She often reverted to crass phrases from her Irish grandmother, which made little sense to us but were hilarious in context, expressions like 'She's got as much class as Paddy's pigs'. Mum absolutely adored the Labrador–collie cross dog that I brought home and whom we christened 'Goldie'. We didn't choose him, he chose us, and he crossed very busy roads often in his pursuit of bitches on heat. He was only hit once but by then we would pay anything to save his life despite a fractured skull and a triple-broken leg. Goldie was naughty, noble, loyal and a devoted fun seeker. When he moved out with me in my 20s, I dropped him off every day to Mum to dog-sit during the days so much did they love each other's company. When he got stomach cancer I was distraught and she organised to have him put to sleep during the day as I was so unable to let Goldie go. She sublimated her own grief for his sake and mine.

My parents' marriage was a firm one, but my father was an often eccentric, insecure and unwell man who slept little. This put pressure on Juliet and she took sleeping tablets to get some sleep at night. Juliet was also a smoker, smoking dreadful Craven A with the black cat on the packet, and Ardath in a green-and-gold packet. These were cork tipped, not even legal today, and one always seemed to be burning beside the stove, discolouring the curtains and ceiling. I am not sure when she took up this habit but my father smoked and so did her dear friend Aggie who often visited. Smoking seemed a sophisticated custom for women in those days and little was known of the health risks.

Juliet also suffered excruciating headaches and frequently took Bex, a powdered analgesic popular in the day, often in combination with a 'ciggy'. Possibly partly because of the smoking, but also as a lasting residue from her childhood exposure to tuberculosis, Juliet used to be bedridden periodically with pneumonia. I was very worried and my sister and I tried to tend to her as she lay delirious in bed.

Time passed and I became more and more admiring of and devoted to my mother. She was so wise and lovable, always attentive to my sister's and my needs, able to listen and give to us. She never missed a netball match or my sister's athletics training. As a family we had a wonderful camping holiday to Ayers Rock and Alice Springs, one of my father's ideas, and a real adventure in 1967 when no roads were paved north of Port Augusta. Juliet had courage too, and when our Holden shore through its engine mountings, she and I hitchhiked with miners to Coober Pedy to get parts and hitchhiked back to the stranded car and my father and sister.

Another memorable family holiday was to New Zealand and we did risky things like driving around hairpin bends to Skippers' Canyon. By then we had almost inured Juliet to fear, so she was quite philosophical when my sister and I climbed as far as we could up Mount Cook and were driven back by a roaring landslide. She loved holidaying with us and when I could drive my sister and I used to take her away, to Burra, Victor Harbor and Milang. Sadly, she and Dad only had one overseas holiday but she appreciated it with gusto, and in the spirit of adventure that had always attracted her to Dad they went to wild and unusual places like the Orkneys and Iceland.

My darling mother had a sudden brain haemorrhage one morning in late July 1978. She just dropped as she was cleaning her teeth. Her neurosurgeon said she had a congenital aneurysm in a brain artery. With her typical fortitude she refused to give up despite brain injury and coma and sadly, after a long battle, she died less than an hour after I said goodbye to her. It was 14 October.

The sheer unfairness of her death and the suffering she endured were sufficiently earth shattering to shake our family's faith. How could such an entirely beautiful person as Juliet die so prematurely at the age of 50, and leave us all at a time when she deserved some peace and happiness? It was impossible to discern a meaning. My opera-singing uncle sang the 23rd psalm unaccompanied over her grave, an awesome experience that truly recreated the Valley of the Shadow of Death. At her funeral, in which she was buried not cremated, we put her favourite flowers, red-hot pokers from the road verges near Gawler, on the coffin. Her headstone is Tanunda granite and inscribed on it are the words 'A True Fighter' and the words from Wordsworth's *Tintern Abbey*, about 'a sense sublime of something far more deeply interfused, a spirit that rolls through the rocks, the trees and the mind of man'. Juliet seemed to me to be in touch with pure spirit, truly in another sphere.

When I remember Juliet now I am overjoyed that she was my mother. I feel blessed, as her early death gave me a knowledge of what love means and I have used that lesson as an inspiration, a pattern for my own life ever since. Before this loss I was selfish and superficial and she made me determined to make my life count, to give to others as she had lived. Juliet was not a victim of fate. She was a vital and decisive person who personified self-sacrifice in love.

Leg of Spring Lamb

Ingredients

A leg of lamb, preferably spring lamb, of approximately 2 pounds (I kilogram), with shank bone attached. (Mr Addison on Greenhill Road can advise as to quality.)

Large cup of dripping with plentiful meat essences from earlier roasts

Salt and pepper to taste

2 pounds of assorted potatoes and pumpkin, peeled, washed and cut into large cubes

Gravox or other similar meat stock for gravy

Mint leaves from the bush in the garden

1 cup Seppelt white wine vinegar

Materials

A large Sunbeam frypan

Eggslice (heavy duty) for separating the crisp potato skins from hot pan without rupturing, and for turning meat

Glass jug for mint sauce

Lard the leg of lamb liberally with the dripping making sure the tasty meat essences at the bottom are used. Place leg in pre-heated frypan heated to 350°F and cover the pan after liberally applying salt and pepper to taste. Allow meat to cook undisturbed for 45 minutes. The success of this dish is all about timing and method.

Remove frypan lid and you will observe that the lamb has been steaming as well as baking. Turn the meat carefully, scraping up the meat fragments that may stick. Pause to inhale the sumptuous smells and deflect hungry kids who are keenly awaiting the dishing up and generally lurking. Add pepper and salt to this side and replace lid. Cook for 30 minutes.

Remove lid again and add the potatoes cut side down. Place pumpkin on top of potatoes. replace lid and cook for 30 minutes having reduced heat to 200°F.

Remove lid, take out pumpkin, scrape potatoes carefully off frypan base and turn. Tuck pumpkin into available gaps between meat and potatoes as the pumpkin will caramelise when in contact with meat juices. Remove the meat and check for doneness by sticking the carving fork into it. A very little pink juice is acceptable but if the meat is too underdone, return to pan and continue to cook. When done, rest the meat on the carving dish with prongs for holding the leg in place.

Increase heat and fry the potatoes and pumpkin on high, eg 300–400°F for 20 minutes. Remove and drain potatoes and pumpkin. Meanwhile slice the washed mint and add to the vinegar with a little sugar and salt. Put in your pretty jug and place on checked tablecloth with table settings ready. Seat rabid children.

Pour excess fat out of the frypan. Add Gravox or meat stock and flour, add sufficient water to make a roux, and gently heat until thicker. Correct seasonings. Place in a bowl or jug and put on table. Cut off shank bone and give to eldest daughter who prizes this cut above all others as it is chewy and glutinous and keeps her out of the kitchen for a while. Arrange potatoes and pumpkin around the joint and give to husband to carve at table with drama, conversation, and enormous sense of culinary privilege.

Place boiled peas or French beans, sliced, on table and serve first with the insistence that the greens are eaten first. Place lamb slices on plates, less for eldest daughter who has eaten the whole shank. Allow all to serve their own potatoes, pumpkin, gravy, and mint sauce.

The cook should enjoy the enormous accolades from the grateful family.

Linden Park School, which the contributors to *Our Mothers* attended, and below, the catchment area.

LINDEN PARK GRADE 6 CLASS – 1961

Back Row: **Anne Cramond**, Julie Shields, Andrea Barlow, Helen Tregilgas, Leonie Stenhouse, Sue Millard, Margaret Holden, Christine Curnow.

Third Row: Robert Malcolm, Laurie Cousin, Don Cranwell, David Leonie, Peter Conway, **David Brecht**, Stuart Main, Brian Bateup, Jane Ridyard.

Second Row: **Rick Frolich**, David George, Rodney Duke, **Andrew Collett**, John Church, Craig Dreyer, Kenton Lillicrapp, Darryl Brewer, David Turner.

Front Row: **Bryan Charlton**, **George Adler**, Warren George, Ula Potchies, Diana White, Lucille Wotton, Beverly Johns, **Judy Macpherson**, Esther Bennett, Tait Koldits, Arthur Lemon.

(all names left to right, contributors' names in bold)

Mothers come first! Greg Perkin's mother Muriel behind the signboard in her own class photo for Colonel Light Gardens school in 1929.

GRADE 6 GIRLS – 1961

Back Row: Ann Green, **Sandra Harrison**, Christine Ware, Roslyn Knight, Sandra Hunter, Sue Bertram, Judith Blake, Judith Lewis, Elizabeth Hassold.

Third Row: Christine Newcombe, Jane Greacon, Barbara Keats, Jennifer Barton, Margaret Rowland, **Helene Sarap**, Kay Smith, **Teresa Mitchell**, Susan Duance.

Second Row: Jennifer Muxlow, **Julie Gillies**, Susan Brewster, Kathryn Bagshaw, Jennifer Cheney, **Judith Hasse**, **Jane Hiatt**, **Frances Goldney**, Anna Segers, Janet Cox, Mardi Ward.

Front Row: Julie Walter, Virginia Heath, **Dianne Corey**, Barbara Grimm, Margaret Boylan, Christine Mudge, Maria Sergi, Margaret Gregg, Margaret Laws, Susan Dyson.

(all names left to right, contributors' names in bold)

Marching into class.

Lorna Harrison, nurse.

Sandra Harrison, nurse.

Lorna Harrison at her daughter Sandra's wedding, 18 January 1969.

Edna Macpherson steps out, left, and Edna with daughter Judy on holidays.

Edna Jean Speirs marries Ross Macpherson, 26 June 1943, at Hawthorn Presbyterian Church. Bill and Ailsa Speirs are best man and bridesmaid.

Bertine Cramond with daughter Anne.

Bertine and Bill Cramond with their children Anne and Stephen in Aden *en route* to Australia in May 1961. The ship is the *Himalaya*.

Della Joyner in her kitchen, and below, with son Steve on his 21st birthday in 1971.

Meta Sarap with baby daughter Helene.

Meta Sarap in a relaxed mood.

Greta Frolich.

The Hasse's home at 21 Rothesay Avenue, Hazelwood Park.

Juliet and Jane Hiatt outside their home in 1952.

Peg Mitchell with baby daughter Terri.

Peg Mitchell fashionably dressed for an outing.

Edna Macpherson, Judy Kent's mother, posing with her bike in 1942.

Iris Corey holding daughter Di at a Christmas party at Hazelwood Park. The present she is holding is an Alice in Wonderland Tea Set.

Iris Corey dressed to impress, probably for the local dance at the Druid's Hall, Collinswood, where she met her husband-to-be Bill after the war.

Merle Higgins and son Phil, 1951.

Garrie and Ronda Hisco
outside their family home of over 60 years in Linden Avenue.

Renna Gillies.

Kym Fuss with a portrait of his mother, Fay.

Nancy Swanson in Papua New Guinea during World War Two.

Bryan Charlton accompanying his mum across Portrush Road in 2015,
a crossing they both knew well.

The Toms family ready for a holiday.

Gordon and Ruth Rinder on their wedding day. Ruth (*née* Iverson) composed the words and music for the Linden Park School song.

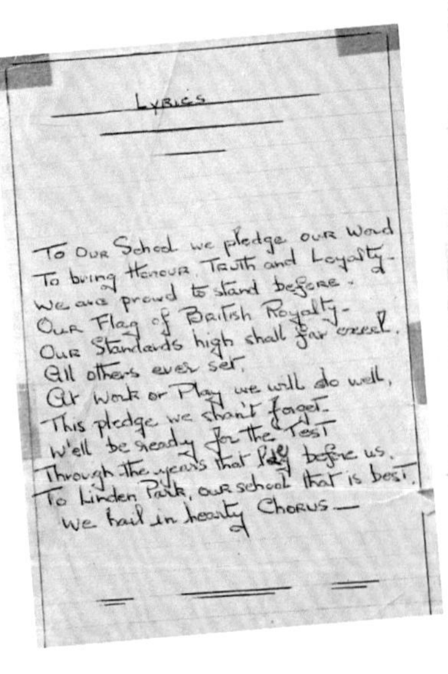

Lyrics

To Our School we pledge our Word
To bring Honour Truth and Loyalty
We are proud to stand before
Our Flag of British Royalty
Our Standards high shall far excel
All others ever set,
At Work or Play we will do well,
This pledge we shan't forget.
We'll be ready for the Test
Through the years that lay before us.
To Linden Park, our school that is best,
We hail in hearty Chorus —

Jane Hiatt

Jane Goodwin Hiatt was born at Unley Private Hospital, now a wing of Walford Anglican School for Girls, on 10 October 1950. She was particularly thrilled to achieve the auspicious birthday of 10/10/2010 two years ago. It was a disappointment that she did not win a lottery, and no apocalypse occurred.

Jane was the elder of two daughters born to Juliet Mary nee Cobbin, and Sidney Goodwin Hiatt. Her sister Cathryn Mary Hiatt was born on 13 January 1954. Shortly before she attended kindergarten, Jane moved to 20 Highfield Avenue, St Georges. She began attending Linden Park Primary School in 1955, and went home for lunch most days missing out on the gorgeous pies and pasties that more fortunate children ate in the shelter sheds.

Jane rode her reconditioned green bicycle to Unley High School in 1963 and loved the expanded world. She remembers NOT being allowed to go the Adelaide airport to greet the Beatles in 1964. The box pleats on her tunic occupied a lot of her time as did hitching up the hem over a tight belt. Her favourite subjects at school were English, Latin and French. In 1967 she completed Matriculation. She completed an Honours degree in 1971, focusing on Spanish and English, a Diploma of Education in 1972, and began teaching in 1973. She qualified as an English Senior in 1978 whilst at Glengowrie High School. In 1981 she took up a student counselling position at Thebarton, Mitcham Girls' High School, and transferred to Christies Beach High School as Student Counsellor in 1993. She retired after 19 years of service at that school in December 2012.

Jane married Syd Harrex in 1984, and they live together on 20 acres on the outskirts of Adelaide. She has travelled widely in Latin America and Asia. Jane gave birth in 1989 to her beloved only son Jaime Nathaniel, on the day the Berlin Wall came down. Jane loves life and is excited about all the possibilities in her future.

Ronda Evelyn HISCO

née Venus

(1924–)

Garrie Hisco

My mother, Ronda Evelyn Venus, was born in 1924 to parents Alice (née Sampson) and Wilfried Venus. She lived at 4 Alma Road, Fullarton, with her brother Maxwell and stepsister Olive, attending Glen Osmond Primary, then Adelaide Girls' High School before enrolling at Muirden's Business College. She later enlisted in the Australian Women's Auxiliary Services (AWAS) and served in South Australia and Seymour in Victoria. Her then boyfriend, Philip Hisco, was posted overseas to Borneo for the duration of World War Two. He returned and they were married in Scots Church, North Terrace, Adelaide, in 1947. In 1948 they started a family. First born was Peter Philip Hisco and in 1950 came Garrie Clarence Hisco.

Childhood for Ronda was fun with many family gatherings and parties, big Christmas celebrations, and visits to the movies. Judy Garland, Mickey Rooney, and the Glenn Miller Orchestra were among her favourites.

Her father was a representative for a tobacco company. He travelled extensively around the countryside whilst Alice her mother, ran the family home. She still keeps contact with those remaining school friends from the Glen Osmond Primary School. My mother speaks of her father as a gentle soul who never raised his voice and who treated her and her siblings like prince and princesses! She still laments his early passing.

Life in Fullarton was very pleasant; home was warm and immaculate with a large concrete fishpond out front. My own memories of that home were the hanging pictures of scenes from World War One as it happened in the Middle East featuring rows of tents neatly pitched in the middle of the desert. There were glass-fired tiles around the coke fireplace and a walk-in pantry with a meat safe (blocks of ice inside a cooler) and a copper in the laundry. There were almond trees and chooks in the very long back garden.

After the war in 1947 the newlyweds built their own home in the paddocks of the new development called Hazelwood Park Estate in the village of Burnside. The big Tudor home is still standing and Philip and Ronda chose a triple-fronted style of building that was in vogue at the time.

Mum had several jobs; she was first and foremost a mum, and treasurer of the Parents' Club at Linden Park School. She also worked as a nurse/receptionist for Drs Bateman and Ligeti at their Marryatville surgery. She would shop in that precinct and on one occasion became a photo model for Lyndon Stacy Photography, which was seeking a pic of someone choosing breakfast cereals!

She aided and abetted my father by throwing numerous parties and social events at the time.

Business friends, birthdays, national holidays were always an excuse for her to cook large spreads with cakes and all kinds of delicacies.

I always remember her talking into a long brass jardiniere to obtain the right echoes, imitating the voice of the Queen, 'My husband and I etc., etc.', very funny for us kids at the time. That was her party trick! My parents were a fun couple and hopefully their sense of sharing joy with others has passed to both me and my brother. After work and in the evenings the rumble of the Mini Cooper S could be heard travelling along Tusmore Avenue, heading for Linden Avenue. Ronda still lives at that address, number 68 Linden Avenue. She is now in her 90th year. She achieved over 60 years of marriage to my recently deceased father, Philip Hisco.

She was an enthusiastic world traveller and made a number of tours of Europe and Asia with Philip, whilst taking herself away with girlfriends from time to time. She adored England and remains a staunch monarchist. History was a fascination for her, and the beauty and architecture of Europe still drives her to subscribe to a number of English and European country life magazines. An enthusiastic reader of some five novels a month (regularly delivered by the Burnside Library direct to her door) she enjoys her afternoons reading all manner of fiction. She is fit, lucid and independent. As a mother of two boys, Ronda was in a household where there were many colleagues calling on my father, and school friends calling on Peter and Garrie. I remember her saying that she took up interests of us three males in order to *feel part of the action*! She has always had a good sense of humour and would make an attempt to be 'one of the boys' on most occasions.

I was always interested in vintage and exotic cars and it was something that my mother participated in by way of owning a couple of quite collectable cars along the way. At 89, she still talks about the fun she had in the Mini Coopers that she drove in the late 60s. Prior to that she had a Morris Minor convertible, 1954 model. We boys all learnt to drive in that car. Despite our youthful attempts at destroying it by using it as some kind of racing car, it never missed a beat. She would have been annoyed if she knew what mischief we got up to in that defenceless little car! Prior to that she had a very early VW sedan oval window model and after the Morris Mini Cooper S she drove a Morris 1100S. Later she purchased a 1978 Toyota Corolla Liftback, which she parted with 32 years later for a sports car!

In 2011 she purchased a 1978 Mercedes Benz 450 SL, and a red one at that! At 87, I think this may be some kind of record! The thinking was that the boot space would easily accommodate her push trolley and her shopping bags and still close!

Whilst she stopped driving some 20 years ago, she still enjoys the comfort of a nice car and is happy to play along with the fun as I drive her to and fro in the big red Mercedes! I often, to this day, take her with me on interstate and local country trips as she enjoys motoring.

It would be fair to say that she is very much a woman of her time, reflecting conservative values and caution in her affairs. She has always won my respect and admiration as a very fair, honest and generous parent. I could say the same for my father and am extremely grateful for the fun, trouble-free, safe, and supportive existence they constructed for myself and my brother through their hard work, thrift and the good friendships they made. I would say they were perfect role models for us both to follow.

I believe that should my mother have her time again she would have been in the vanguard of feminism – debating, waving banners and enjoying the hard-won freedoms that young women of today enjoy. I believe her quick wit, intelligence, sense of history and fair play would have led her to a career as a legal expert at the very least.

Librans are like that!

Garrie Hisco

Garrie's background since schooldays has been in a range of areas, but always to do with art and design. He studied at the South Australian School of Art on leaving Adelaide Technical High School. He also qualified as a high school teacher in the specialist field of Design. He spent seven years teaching Design in schools before being appointed as a Design Education Lecturer to Torrens College of Advanced Education (later known as the University of South Australia).

He worked in the School of Design and School of Education for over 20 years teaching various areas of study from Product Design, Philosophy of Design, Art and Design History, Graphic Design and clinical in-school teacher training, as well as studio subjects like Drawing and Computer-aided Design.

It was a long and enjoyable career from which he resigned in 1998 to begin his own business. He chose to develop a Japanese Ryokan in Adelaide. For 11 years it held a five-star rating and was known as Allessandro Maandini's Ryokan. It was a lot of fun and many interesting people, celebrities and business groups were entertained there.

Garrie has written two books: one published and the other still in process, with a third book underway. His big passion in life has been exotic sports, vintage and racing cars.

Since 1986 he has been a world traveller/adventurer. Many tours of Europe, Asia, the Middle East and the USA have taken him to the world's most fascinating places. Garrie lives in the Adelaide Hills with his collection of motor vehicles and his cat.

He still owns the Ryokan, which is now leased to corporate groups.

Muriel Loraine PERKIN

née Coombe

(1923–2000)

Greg Perkin

My mum, Muriel Loraine Coombe, always known as 'Mim', was born in Moonta Mines (part of Australia's Little Cornwall) on 5 August 1923. She was the first child of Joseph Pensilva Coombe (Joe) and Amelia Gertrude Coombe (Gert, née Eden) both of Cornish descent. Joe's parents and older sisters had emigrated from Pensilva, Cornwall, to Lithgow and then Lucknow, New South Wales, where Joe was born. Times were hard on the New South Wales gold fields so Joe's father returned to mining in the US where he had worked previously and where he had come across Billy the Kid, a notorious gunslinger of his time. The Coombe forebears had allegedly arrived in Britain with William the Conqueror, which suggests that this family had Scandinavian roots. Mum's mother's family, the Edens, on the other hand, were the original settlers of the Agery area south of Moonta on Yorke Peninsula where they cleared the bush and established the family farm. The original farm is still in the hands of Mum's cousin. With this background it was little wonder that we children were well aware of our Cornish ancestry, the family farming tradition and the fact that we were related to half the people then living in Moonta!

Mum's first home was attached to the Moonta Mines Post Office where her father was the postmaster. This was located opposite the Moonta Mines Primary School and from her vantage point on the top step of the Post Office, Mum would watch the children go to and from school and dream of the time she could join them.

From this early age Mum had a yearning to learn and as a result put a high value on education. When Mum was three, the young family moved to Adelaide, initially living in Goodwood with Joe's older sister Annie while the family's new house was being built in Adelaide's garden city suburb of Colonel Light Gardens. This was Mum's first, but not last, experience of living in a new suburb of young families setting up new lives. From this new home and suburb Mum attended Colonel Light Gardens Primary School, Unley High School and Muirden's Business College. Mum really wanted to be a nurse, however, during her Intermediate year she won a scholarship to Business College. This meant that her parents would be saved from paying her education costs but her career would take a different path from that she had dreamed of. Mum chose to reduce the financial burden on her parents, which was pretty much the character of Mum – always thinking of others and putting their needs above hers. With her newfound secretarial skills Mum gained employment with the Australian Army at Keswick HQ where she met my father Pearce. During the war when Dad was posted to Melbourne, Mum became secretary to the Postmaster General in Adelaide, a key role during wartime.

At the end of the war, Mim and Pearce married and established their first home in two rooms at the rear of Dad's parents' home in Tait Street, North Croydon. My older sister Dianne was born in 1948 and in 1950 when I was born my parents bought a block of land in St Georges. Dad spent his spare time over the next two-and-a-half years building our new home thus leaving Mum to spend many hours alone with her two young children and her in-laws in an unfamiliar part of town. In 1952 our young family moved to 52 Highfield Ave, St Georges, another suburb of new families. This house was Mum's castle and she often joked that she would only leave it in a wooden box. Unfortunately that proved to be too true.

Mum was always there for us, she was the cornerstone of our family. As a young child I remember we had a car, however, over time this was sold and our family was pretty much marooned in our suburb. My two younger brothers, Kym and Bruce, were born after we moved to Highfield Avenue meaning Mum had four of us to raise on a single income. During school holidays I remember a real escape was to catch the bus with Mum, my sister and brothers, to Tusmore Park where we would spend the day playing in the creek. The real thrill was to sit in the front seat on the upper deck of the double-decker bus as it slapped its way through the branches of trees overhanging Stirling Street and Northumberland Avenue, Tusmore.

Buses had another part to play in our family's history. One day in 1958 Mum had taken all four of us kids to town with our youngest brother Bruce in a pram and second-youngest brother Kym a bit of a tearaway. Rundle Street was frantic with traffic and pedestrians when Mum saw a bus coming with a 'B…' destination displayed and started to fold the pram and organise all four of us to get on the bus. Mum was not able to load the pram and Kym and Bruce before the bus moved off so told Dianne and me, who were on the bus, to wait for her at the terminus and she would catch the next bus. As it turned out Dianne and I were on the B for Burnside bus and not the B for Beaumont bus which became obvious to us when the bus started travelling up Kensington Road. After we had travelled up Kensington Road for a few stops we decided to get off the bus but then had to decide what to do next. The decision was taken to follow the trolley-bus wires back to Fullarton Road and then follow the Beaumont trolley-bus wires. We put this plan into action and were finally found at the bottom of Devereux Road, Linden Park. As a kid of around eight at that time I was pretty much tuckered out by this stage, but this skill of being able to 'read' the city may have foretold my future career as a town planner/city manager.

While our family was not religious, each Sunday we religiously attended Sunday school, firstly at the Baptist church in Kennaway Street, Tusmore (just down the road from my Adelaide house), and then the Beaumont Methodist church just around the corner from home. Dianne, the neighbourhood kids and I were taken to the Baptist church by Mr Groves in the back of his 1950s Vanguard utility. I believe the regular attendance at Sunday school was one way of achieving respite for Mum who tended to slave morning, noon and night every other day.

Mum was very houseproud and cleaned the house to within an inch of its life. There were regular chores that we kids had to undertake including cleaning out the ashes from the wood fire, bringing in new supplies of wood, dusting the skirting boards and polishing the backyard sink and front doorstep. Yes, I kid you not, the backyard sink and front doorstep were polished with dark brown Kiwi shoe polish until the lucky kid with that chore could see their face in the reflection.

Meals were also prepared to a high standard. Mum believed in serving the best quality food she could afford. We NEVER ate mincemeat from the shop. If a recipe called for mince, Mum would buy the best quality meat and mince it herself. I remember the traditional meat and three veg meals, however, in the 1960s there must have been a menu revolution as the mornay made a welcome appearance with ingredients such as tuna and sweetcorn topped with cheese and breadcrumbs. Then came spaghetti bolognese, sweet-and-sour pork with pineapple, and traditional staples such as stew, vegetable soup and wiener schnitzel. The pride of place had to be taken by the Cornish pasty which never had peas in it, the meat was skirt, and the vegetable swede not turnip. The pasty was eaten with home-made tomato sauce. Dessert often included home-bottled fruit from the peach and apricot trees in the backyard, with home-made apricot jam and marmalade also being in ready supply.

Mum was very cautious if not suspicious of new technology;

she insisted on a hand-wringer on her washing machine long after spin-dry was the fashion and continued to have milk ladled from the milk can into our billy years after bottled milk became available. Mum's cautious nature also ensured that while she had an open licence and could have driven a semitrailer she did not have the gumption to drive a car on the public road.

A couple of unique aspects of our suburb during the 50s and 60s was that milk was delivered by a horse-drawn float and vegetables delivered by Mr Hounslow in a large walk-in truck. His market garden, which is now covered with houses, was in Sturdee Street, Linden Park.

The horse-drawn milk float played a part in putting me off strawberries. One morning on my way to school, I came across Mrs Symonds shovelling the horse droppings off Highfield Avenue. With a glint in her eye she told me that she was putting the droppings on her strawberries 'because it was better than cream'!

With my younger brothers growing up and becoming more independent, Mum became a regular volunteer at the Unley High School canteen. She really enjoyed these times when she had the opportunity to talk with other mothers including Mrs Mugge (Phil and Andrew's mother) and Mrs Lee (Neville's mum).This gave Mum some independent time and a life of her own, which she had put on hold while raising her family.

One issue that I found really odd as a young kid was that Mum was addressed as Mrs Pearce Perkin. I could not understand how someone called Mim did not have that as part of her name. That was just the way it was in those days but as the 60s progressed 'Mim' Perkin began to emerge. The 60s social revolution did not just belong to the teenager after all!

I had mentioned earlier that Mum was keen on education. Mum regularly came to Linden Park Primary School to check on my progress. Mum wanted me to become a doctor and thereby vicariously fulfil her missed dreams of becoming a nurse. I usually finished in the top three in primary school so Mum was content that I was tracking in the right direction.

At high school I was keen to study art and geography but Mum required me to stay in the A stream and study science and Latin, prerequisites for studying medicine or law a second best. I did not really take to high school, studying subjects I had no interest in, being lost in a first-year class of over 60 students and at a school where intimidation and corporal punishment were the order of the day. School became a place of punishment and boredom rather than of enlightenment and learning. As a result I trudged through high school not achieving the results that would lead me to medicine or law, and despite completing matric was lucky to be accepted into tertiary study on my fourth year's results. I was fortunate that my younger brothers were taking Mum's attention at this time and she reluctantly accepted that I would not become Dr Perkin.

My saving grace is that I did study at university and mirrored Mum's success by gaining a scholarship to cover my fees and, despite not studying geography at high school, for which Mum achieved 100 per cent at Intermediate level, I achieved the first distinction in that subject at the South Australian Institute of Technology (now consumed by University of South Australia).

Perhaps the best indication of Mum's priority on education came when I had an accident in the schoolyard. I had been running around for some time and ran around a corner panting with my tongue out and crashed into Roger Springthorpe. The result was I bit my tongue off with it literally hanging by the skin of my teeth. The teacher on yard duty offered no help so I went home to Mum. Unfortunately, Mum was not home but when she returned from town I had to write a note to explain my predicament. My note read 'I have bitten off my tung'. Without hesitation Mum first corrected the spelling of 'tongue' and only then proceeded to deal with my injury.

I don't believe Roger ever knew of his role in our family history but it was clearly not his fault. It is rather ironic that in my office, when City Manager of Port Augusta, was a photo of the main street in earlier times showing a lad standing under a sign that read 'Walk round corners'!

Mum had a great passion for her extended family and knew all of her aunties, uncles, cousins, nieces and nephews in the Moonta area and Adelaide, and kept in regular contact. Mum knew the family history and had a wealth of family information that has unfortunately been lost with her passing.

Luckily Mum was able to travel overseas and visit Cornwall and places in Europe she had read about and was keen to see in real life. She was proud that all four of her children went to university and completed postgraduate studies, married and produced 10 grandchildren who were the apples of her eye.

Mum passed away on Dad's birthday in 2000. Our family is much poorer from the loss but we are determined to keep a strong and connected family to honour Mum's vision. We know how thrilled she would have been to know her seven great-grandchildren. We are relieved, however, that she did not have to comprehend the 11 September attacks on the US, the bombings of London, the jailing of refugee children in Australia, and beheading of people in the name of religion.

Mum deserved to live in those better times.

Nut Loaf

A favourite recipe from Mim Perkin's cookbook

1 large cup boiling water

1 level teaspoon carb soda

1 cup dates and sultanas (chopped)

1 teaspoon butter

Put all ingredients in a basin and allow to cool. When cool add:

1 beaten egg

1 cup plain flour

1 cup self-raising flour

½ cup chopped walnuts

Place contents in greased cake tins and cook in an electric oven for approximately 45 minutes at 400°F.

Greg Perkin

Greg has recently retired after a career of over 40 years working as a town planner and city manager. This involved working and living in Adelaide, New Zealand, regional South Australia and undertaking a project in Vietnam. During an overseas sister city relationship visit Greg had the daunting task of presenting a speech in Japanese to a very formal Japanese Council meeting.

The most rewarding parts of Greg's career have been to work with the late Joy Baluch, a remarkable woman and irreplaceable mayor of Port Augusta, and the Aboriginal people in Port Augusta. The heartfelt thanks given to Greg by the Aboriginal Community on his retirement was both humbling and priceless and more than compensated for the otherwise ordinary experiences in local government.

Greg has been married to Raelene for 42 years with three daughters, Kylie, Rebecca and Emily, who also attended Linden Park Primary School. In his spare time Greg enjoys bike riding, camping and kayaking and visiting his three grandsons, Max, Harlowe and Phoenix, in country New South Wales.

Alice Joan HASSE

née Bryan

(1924–)

Jules Hasse

Alice Joan Bryan was only five months old when she migrated in May 1925 to Australia with her parents from West Bromwich, England, where she was born in November 1924. They were assisted passengers on the ship the SS *Baradine* and were to be allocated a soldier settlement farm after World War One. Her parents were Samuel and Gladys Bryan. They were escapees from a cold and industrial area of Birmingham in England. Sam Bryan has a legendary status and is still an icon for progressive politics for my family. He was in the Medical Corps at Gallipoli and was then posted to India. His imagination, insights and standards were formidable … but that's another story. It is enough to say that Alice Joan Bryan (hence referred to as Joan) inherited notions of justice, caring and social equity more deeply felt than even she would care to admit. She and her sister May would follow their father into landscape painting with talent and observation of natural colours, distilled from growing up on the land. Joan favoured semi-abstract art – selling to galleries locally and around the world.

Sam worked at his trade as a toolmaker in Sydney until the allocation of his farm in Griffith, in New South Wales, the following year. They travelled to Beelbangera ('place of High Winds') near Griffith by train and then to the Red Cross Training Farm and a private fruit orchard where they were grateful for Mr Pride's practical expertise and tutelage. The pioneers were allocated a block in the Riverina, New South Wales: an irrigated fruit orchard where Sam threw his whole heart and soul into being a good farmer. It meant hard work on Farm 1242. Italian workers joined neighbours and friends who had magical evenings on the farm. During fruit picking, workers like the Bisigos, a family who liked opera, sang among the trees. At other times, Sam and Gladys invited friends from the Fruit Co-op, or from town. Their parties left a lasting impression on Joan who was sent to bed with music filtering to her through many nights.

The group were in awe of Miss Marr, an independent woman who sang and played the piano, leading the musical evening. Joan loved the baritone voice of Mr Mallinson, from a neighbouring orchard. His voice was beautiful. They seemed to lean on Sam to organise and determine a social and farm calendar. Sam listened to people and encompassed their stories in his politics.

Sam grew peas and Gladys made butter, and apricots were dried with sulphur and the sun. Sam owned plough horses, and valued his radio. Joan and her siblings rode one pony to school until their first bicycle was purchased. Sam focused on Joan's education and her intense seven years of classical piano tuition. Sam was ambitious for Joan, his eldest, to be a lawyer. Sam was passionate about politics and economics including the Douglas Credit Movement, and read widely with regular magazines sent from Europe to fuel debate. They believed they could change the world. Interminable conversations after hours ensued. Sam was a Labor then an Independent candidate for Griffith. Joan did not share her views later with her family.

Joan's mother, Gladys Bryan (née Harper), had never been outside the Birmingham town area where her father ran a tavern in

West Bromwich. She wore clothes well and seemed to like the city life. She had to adjust to Australian heat, flies, dirt roads, wood fires and hard work.

Joan grew up on the farm and did her schooling in Griffith. In 1939 the family moved to Adelaide. Sam arranged work in the city with the help of former workmates, who were then managers of Ackles & Pollock in England. As the war in Europe ignited tensions, Joan finished her education to Leaving standard in 1940 at Adelaide Girls High School. Sam was working with British Tube Mills, and Joan went to family picnics sponsored by this company. Joan was used to country life and found it difficult changing to South Australian schooling, catching public transport and adapting to her young friends' social world. She was just 15 years old.

The University of Adelaide Public Examinations Board shows Alice Joan Bryan passed six subjects in her Leaving Certificate: English Literature, Latin (with credit), French (including oral), Mathematics I and II, and Modern History.

Sam was disgusted with Joan because she'd only learnt classical music until she came to Adelaide and it wasn't easy to share in singalongs or adapt to the rhythms for dancing. Her friends weren't musical people. Her future husband Ray later bought sheet music of his favourite up-to-date tune. Joan could sight-read any piece. Everywhere Joan went, she took music – 'Oh you can play …' –and they shared years singing around Joan's piano. On reflection, she realised she was missing out at parties, on conversations, on the fun, and left it to others. Ray encouraged Joan who still plays for him. Rachmaninoff was a favourite and Joan played his music for years in her home. A visit to Edvard Grieg's home in Bergen in Norway was a highlight of their trip. Joan loved to play Grieg's 'To the Spring' and cried while listening to his music in his home during the 1970s. Joan's music album *100 World Masterpieces* was well-used!

Joan left school and obtained work as a clerk at Temperance & General Insurance (T&G) for six months, much to her dad's displeasure. Sam was 'livid'! Joan made friends with Joan Lampe, her neighbour at Beatrice Street, Prospect, whose mother sewed new clothes for both girls to go dancing. A bunch of girls cycled to Aldgate, Norton Summit, and Belair for picnics. Joan played hockey competitively for the Brown Owls, a city team. She was an 'inner' and it helped her to adjust and get over her shyness. Abruptly, Joan applied under her own steam to get onto the list of candidates for the Metrology Laboratory, Islington Workshop. With trepidation, she skipped work at T&G to go to the interview. Joan then worked at Islington in a unit with 16 girls until 1945. (The *Advertiser* article at the end of this chapter was published following a reporter's visit to the Metrology Laboratory. The contents of this article would have been vetted and censored by the government of the day!)

Joan and her metrology workmates were very diligent and enjoyed the professionalism of their job for four years in a top industrial hub at Islington. In 1942–1943 when the Japanese invasion was threatening, the girls had regular drill sessions to react to the warning sirens. Trenches were dug, sandbags filled and the order was to quickly pack and store the gauges and equipment in a safe place. At this time, emergency shelters were being identified and built throughout Adelaide in backyards and institutions where bombing was feared. Joan was 17 or 18 years old. Her memories of digging trenches outside the front of the metrology building at Islington include the following.

> Joan: 'We were asked to volunteer to fill sandbags in our lunchtime and we were paid tenpence a bag. The idea was to use a lot of bags! We all got the bright idea of dying our white uniforms all colours so that we would look like flowers while we were in the trenches: brown, orange, yellow, pastels so that we were camouflaged … The bombers would think we were flowers.'
>
> Ray quipped: 'So they would not look like intellectuals.'
>
> Joan: 'We knew very little of the progress of the war, the Japanese in Northern Australia or the Pacific. War news was somewhat restricted.'

Movietone News kept the girls up to date on overseas events if nothing else. It was an essential service. In 1941 Joan went to see Charlie Chaplin's *The Great Dictator* with Joan Lampe, her friend. At least some perspective was presented in a humorous light. Ray happened to be working there at The Yorke Theatre in his office at that time. Events in Europe seemed not to panic Ray or Joan's families and yet both were affected within a short period of time.

The girls regularly worked overtime till 10 pm. They started at 8.30 am. The supervisor gave guidance to work out the method to measure each individual gauge. For even a screw to be evaluated it was projected, enlarged onto a screen. Mathematics was used and measurements were recorded in minutiae to conform to the specifications. Patience, exquisite patience, was required to confirm that these items could indeed be used.

Bill Crowe was always there! He sat with the girls giving the impression of a calm, competent man. Howard Brown, the manager, was always in the office ... very serious, with his door closed with the only phone in the establishment. Joan recalls being advised there was a call for her in his office and going in to pick up the phone. Ray was calling her and she mumbled something about 'not being able to go out tonight; can't talk, goodbye' ... (imagine a blushing apology to Howard, an inscrutable look from over his reading glasses and a hurried manoeuvre by Joan out the glass door of his office). As Joan says, 'You don't remember all these details if it didn't affect you! When one lady got the phone call to say her husband had been wounded in the Middle East, in Tobruk, she would have had to take the call in that office with Howard listening in.'

As Joan says, 'These women about 26 years old were living on a precipice.' Joan says these were very rewarding years. When so many males were away at the war, the girls formed lasting friendships. Those left are still meeting regularly. They wrote letters continuously to the boys; some girls continued studies. Joan fitted in night school to study shorthand and typing to set herself up for a job after the war. They recall having great evenings together. Five girls played the piano so there was always music, singing and great suppers. There were dances at The Embassy, Palladium and the Palais, and they gathered at National Fitness Camps.

During the early period of the war, Ray Hasse was across town: a junior clerk at Waterman Brothers' Theatres in Adelaide, and doing turns at live shows, making a 'bob' in a vaudeville role as a stooge in the audience. He went to ballroom dance classes on North Terrace at the Grosvenor Hotel basement, and met Joan there. The room was blacked out because of the war and Ray was sent sprinting for the Majestic Theatre afterwards to make it onto stage. The girls left in the dark. In the war years, windows were covered all over Adelaide and no streetlights were shining, making it very hard for the girls to ride home at night from Islington to Nailsworth where Joan's family had moved. The bush in the paddock was scary. Mona, Joan's co-worker, walked by Joan's bike, lit only by a hooded lamp (which was permitted) shining on the bike tyre. Then Mona would leave to catch her tram and Joan proceeded to cycle up her street towards her home.

Frugality was the order of the day. The Austerity Sponge Cake recipe was often used by Joan.

Because of rationing during World War Two, Joan used a special sponge recipe for her friends that was economical and also used a minimum of eggs and butter. It was always open house at home in Nailsworth, and Joan and her sister May felt free to have friends for tea on Sunday nights. Salad, cold meats and chocolate cake were prepared by Joan and May, followed by singing around the piano. Here's my friend's mother's recipe for chocolate sponge.

Wartime Austerity Sponge

1½ cups self-raising flour

2 tablespoons cocoa

½ teaspoon carb soda

1 cup sugar

1 egg

1 tablespoon vinegar

1 cup milk
½ cup melted butter

Sift dry ingredients into a basin. In another basin beat the egg, then add vinegar, milk and melted butter. Mix dry and wet ingredients. Pour into two sandwich tins and bake in moderate oven for 20 minutes. Join the two sponges together with cream made from butter, beaten with a little boiling water as needed until creamy.

'Not only was food rationed, clothing and shoes were too. For long dance frocks, we bought mosquito netting, dyed it various colours and made lovely gowns. For shoes, we silver frosted over white shoes (or gold paint). Stockings were unavailable so we painted our legs with a darker seam line down the back.'

When Joan was 19 years old, a new brother was added. The Bryan household was 'in the money' at this time with Sam working regularly and highly regarded at British Tube Mills while Joan's sister May and brother Bob were at school, doing well. Ray didn't even know Joan could cook until he married her. However, their many family picnics cycling up to the hills or to the beach must have given him a hint.

Ray enlisted in the army at 18 years of age in 1942. He served in the Australian Imperial Force (AIF) in the 24th Heavy Anti-Aircraft Battery in Papua New Guinea. He returned from Newcastle on discharge in New South Wales in May 1946. Joan had the AIF Badge from Ray, fashioned with 'JOAN' imprinted on it (as guys did to give to their girlfriend or their mother). They got engaged in June and Ray was back at work with Watermans' (to become Hoyts Ozone Theatres). Once the war ended and girls were no longer employed, marriage and children followed from around 1946 on. Cynthia and Joan travelled by train to Kapunda to attend Mona's wedding and stay overnight, and Ray and Joan plotted to tell Sam they wanted to get married. The Movie Ball was the big annual event. Ray cycled over to pick up Joan at her home, but got a flat tyre and was therefore late. Sam lent him his car, a Ford Prefect, and Ray retrieved the corsage intact, and made the best of it. A great time was had by all and then followed a remarkable series of fundraisers every year – the Movie Ball – to put money into a Provident Fund, which is still looking after cinema staff and ex-employees who need it.

Raymond Trevor Hasse and Joan Bryan were married in September 1946 and Pamela Joan arrived in September ... the following year. This is a perpetual family joke, funny in the retelling. Judith (nicknamed 'Jude', now known as Jules) was born in 1950, an easy quick event when the future manager of 5KA, Ross Parham, was in the right place at the right time to drive Joan to hospital in his car with minutes to spare before her second daughter was born near the Prospect Hospital entrance. By this time Ray and Joan had a two-bedroom house they built at 21 Rothesay Avenue, Hazelwood Park, opposite Wood Park and the Mothers' and Babies' centre. The family's social calendar in Adelaide had expanded to include get-togethers of the 'girls' from Joan's Metrology days. This occurred every two to three months. Then there were the 'do's' with Ray's army buddies and their wives. Joan's parents, Samuel and Gladys, with Joan's sister and brothers had left her in 1946 – their job done – to go home to the farm near Griffith. Joan was in shock. In the ensuing years, she didn't ever let her family feel neglected or without love and a bed! Joan still recalls the loneliness and the adjustments that she had to make. Joan cooks beautifully with the fresh vegetables and fruit from her own garden. At the time, though, Joan and other neighbours seemed to be isolated in suburbia. With the taboos of the time Joan did not 'work' for the next 25 years. Joan: 'I think a lot of men felt inadequate if their wife went to work – as though they couldn't support them.'

Joan was catapulted into a new life. She had glamour, at times, accompanying Ray to premieres of the latest blockbusters in cinemas all over Adelaide and beyond. There were singalongs and sewing and holidays back at her siblings' farms in the Riverina of New South Wales. In fact, today, many Christmas cards – sent and received annually – are testament to all the love felt by a wide, diverse community of artists, scrubbers and old friends from before the war!

Joan earned her moniker, 'Doctor Hasse'. Joan kept the family healthy in line with her own philosophy. Sam's adage to only pay your doctor when you remain healthy, not to be charged a fee when you fall sick, was consistent with Joan's preventative strategies. When Jude did break her leg at school (a compound fracture), the solution in the Children's Hospital as well as at home was good rest, simple food, homemade beef broth, salads and spaghetti bolognaise and quiet time for reading … 'feed the cold and starve the fever'! For the three months she was in hospital, Joan came in every day to feed her daughter as well as the Italian boy in the next bed and other lonely kids in the ward who didn't have many visitors. The Aboriginal boy with chalk bones from the north of South Australia was a regular favourite. It was assumed children were naturally strong and resilient. When measles and mumps occurred, students stayed at home so the bugs were not passed on to others at school. Pam, on the other hand, had her appendix and adenoids removed very early and this was traumatic.

It was Joan who chose eurhythmics Movement to Music Saturday classes for Jude to strengthen her leg. Joan thought the attitude and creative purpose was 'beautiful'! The presence of relaxed teachers and mothers and classical dance was enjoyable. This German school with voice classes with Morna Jones set up a template for free-wheeling expressive storytelling that was and is successful. Speech training and articulation is increasingly relevant today so young and old can enjoy clear diction and interpretative dance.

Events: beach day memories include sleeping over in a tram carriage at Hallett Cove and beach cricket with our cousins of similar age and disposition. At home, Joan played the piano and Ray sang at the top of his voice with gusto renditions of 'I'll Walk with God', 'Three Coins in a Fountain' … and hundreds of others. Chopin rang out each morning with Pam practising. It resonated throughout the house. Dr Zhivago's 'Somewhere my Love' was a popular song. The Russian book classic and the Metro-Goldwyn-Mayer movie were overwhelming: with the balalaika playing as the gold curtain opened slowly in the cinema in Hindley Street,

Adelaide. The sweeping grass tundra was revealed and history with epic snow scenes and epic theatre created sensual awakenings. Jude played the theme tune over and over but gave up lessons from her strict classical teacher on Highfield Avenue, choosing Joan to coach her instead.

The drive-in picture theatres gave Joan some reprieve. With Pam and Jude already in pyjamas, Ray would do his rounds with his daughters and be on duty at Hoyts Ozone Concessionaires sites for over four hours around the suburbs of Adelaide. Thus Ray would spend his nights out four times a week (a rotten job for wives who commiserated together!). In those days, chicken Maryland was a treat. Ray's manageresses would serve it up hot and fresh to customers who could eat in comfort with families sharing the counter at the drive-ins – a full dining experience. Australian film-making and distributors and exhibitors created an industry with new jobs from the 1960s. With every new Hoyts release, Ray and Joan were always involved in the charity premieres. Entertaining celebrities who came to town to market these events created photo opportunities in *MOVIE NEWS*. The press and everyone got excited. Joan dressed elegantly like a movie goddess; the women all in gowns and the men in bow-ties. They were heady days! Joan had ideas for her own dressmaking and millinery and flower-arranging endeavours followed. Joan's English rose complexion also came out in the choice of subtle hues when she took up china painting. She successfully made gifts and sold heaps of an ever-expanding collection of teapots, plates and jewellery built up and fired many times to achieve the gold and the beautiful!

Joan's musicality assisted in presentations at Tusmore Methodist Sunday School and the Youth Choir with modern arrangements and musicians. The guitar and drums featured in a hootenanny choir and Jude toured locally with the same choir with a repertoire of jazzed-up sacred music pieces. Pam and Jude made their own fun, putting on puppet plays with shadows and sheets. The Linden Park group of playground buddies seemed to attract the 'Js' – Jude, Jenny, Julie, Julie, Judy, Jane, Joanne, with Diane and Frances and

Margaret ... so the list goes on. Some of the parents lived near Hazelwood Park or Tusmore and so Joan engaged in social activities and school fundraising or child-minding at home and card playing with a circle of friends. Costume parties each year were held by Linden Park Primary School at Burnside Town Hall and mothers created many of the outfits. The girls were variously a horse, a chocolate wrap, a Japanese girl or a gypsy.

The big end-of-year extravaganza that was rehearsed for months in 1962 was a 2000 voice choir of combined schools. Joan helped rehearsals in the background and referred to the music sheets to assist Jude with lyrics and tunes. It rained at Elder Park on the night although the spectacle and singing went precisely as rehearsed. The exit from the portable staging was not as accomplished! It threatened to bring the house down – literally. The parents saved the day. Pam was doing well and was organised in school so well that Joan and Ray took a punt and enrolled both girls at Presbyterian Girls' College. Joan judged it to be too far for her daughters to ride each day to Unley High School. They wanted for their girls the comforts and opportunities they'd delayed for themselves during the frugal years, especially the Depression in Australia.

The girls' high school years changed attitudes at home markedly. Joan cemented her friendships during a time of upheaval. Then Pam later got married to Graeme after a stint as a teacher in the South East of South Australia. Jude got a Commonwealth Scholarship to go into teaching training. Nursing or secretarial work were the only other options ... or get married! Ray was offered a promotion in Victoria, covering South Australia and Tasmania as well, so Joan and Ray sold their house in Hazelwood Park. When Joan departed for Melbourne to live in 1969, the Canasta girls gave her a tribute, a 'small remembrance' from Josie Fradd, Fay Anderson, Laurel Bassham, Joy Jones, Edith Benger, Joyce Sargeant, Mary Tregilgas, Maria Walkons, Kath Webber, Brenda Thomas, Doris Nadge, Margaret Casey, Thel Lyon, Vera Fluit and Kath Taylor. Joan still has the beautiful pearl bar brooch with a special card today. Helen Tregilgas and Brenda Rinder also attended Linden Park Primary School.

Joan and Ray played the old tunes and Joan's classical repertoire over the next half a century with Ray and the family singing around Mum's piano and Ray's tenor voice over the top setting the tone of passion and gusto. They retired to Aldinga Beach and the Scrub, but still ingratiated themselves into their avant-garde community of artists, architects and driftwood! Grandchildren love these memories and will think of these times where they felt at home. Joan and Ray have remained loving and true to their family, an exemplary model of a couple with passion and commitment through difficult as well as exciting transitions, a result of 50 tumultuous years of technological change in the 20th century.

Advertiser, 1943

TESTING MUNITION GAUGES

Work of Small Group of Women

By A Staff Reporter

Sixteen young women, working quietly in a sandbagged building at a munitions works near Adelaide are playing important parts in this country's war effort. They wear no uniform, and belong to no other army than the great and unknown army of plain men and women of this country, whose work on the production and planning front is keeping our fighting men in the field.

A year or two ago and in some cases a few months ago, these girls were completing college or university careers with a view to taking their place in the commercial or professional life of this community.

Most of them had passed the Leaving Examination; some are still studying at the University in their spare time; all had shown a flair for Mathematics.

Today they staff the metrology section of the munitions production in South Australia and Western Australia. No shell can be filled, no barrel can be rifled unless these young girls give the 'all clear' on the gauges with which munitions of all sorts are measured.

There are only three of these metrology sections in the whole of the Commonwealth and the Chief Mechanical Engineer said yesterday that the girls were doing the work so expertly and with such enthusiasm that the staff were to be doubled at an early date. The gauges by this time are so near perfection that no human eye can detect a flaw.

Intricate Machines

Intricate machines in the metrology section, however, can find discrepancies that measure as little as one five-millionth of an inch.

Much of the machinery could not be replaced. Some of it was made in Switzerland, and was cleared from Genoa only a few days before Italy entered the War.

Two girls make gauge tests on an imported machine that could not be bought for less than about 3000 pounds at present, but it is considered that replacement would be most difficult if not impossible. This is the master measuring machine and is used for the most intricate work. It is housed in a special room which has a fixed temperature.

Even minor variations in temperature affect the size of very small gauges, and the engineer in charge of the metrology section (Mr H.A. Brown) pointed out that the heat of one's hand may swell a hard steel instrument. Mr Brown placed his hands around a seven-inch piece of steel on an electrical comparator, and within a minute and a half the needle above it registered an increase in size of 1000th of an inch. Factory operators of these small gauges are asked not to handle them unnecessarily or to subject them to much heat.

All gauges in South Australia and Western Australia pass through the metrology section. On passing the tests they are sent to factories in other parts of Australia and New Zealand.

The additional staff will be selected from girls 17 and over with knowledge of Mathematics. The highest paid girls at present receive 257 pounds a year, but the rates for beginners run from 95 pounds a year for girls under 17.

Jules Hasse

I seem to be returning to my 12-year-old mindset of Grade 7 vintage. My identity, values and thinking I can remember beginning at this age, knowing self-consciously I'm me. Life in Adelaide in 1962 was expanding and so was I. No preconceived ideas … I could quietly just try it on. Socially naïve, we headed for high school ill prepared for competition but I was curious and felt that I had to get to Matriculation, and maths and science should be included. My role models were girls in sport and my heroes came from books … all male. Then, in addition, girls in theatre and music and academic ambitions appeared at our all-girls' school.

So it led to my evolution to be the best I could be: to teach at the best school system for adolescents developed in Darwin; a producer for one of the best original theatre companies that was brave and local in Adelaide, with themes of historical significance and the environment and politics and the personal power of the imagination. I learnt to be in a team focused on clear deadlines and trust. Then finances and real fears surfaced overseas. I was vulnerable and I could have disappeared in a blink of an eye. I returned to Australia sick and needed to refocus, once again retiring to Mum and Dad's home for care and recuperation. The Northern Territory beckoned. Back to teaching and I fell into a relationship of a lifetime, two children and a creative, scary but adventurous audiovisual business following my partner's ethic of excellence and dedication.

Immigrants

Trudy Neufeld ADLER

née Neufeld

(1912–1991)

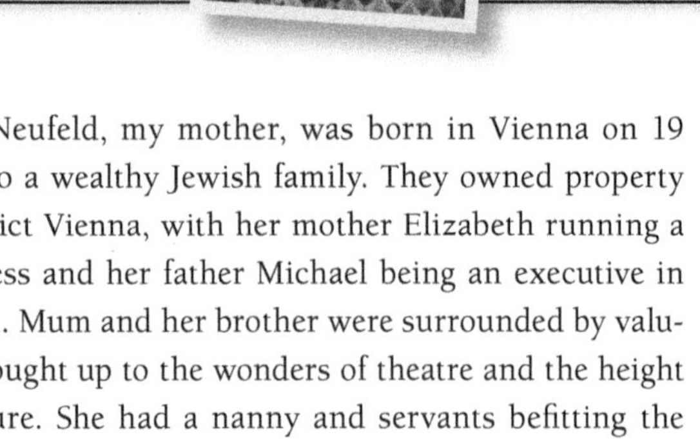

George Adler

Gertrude Mary Neufeld, my mother, was born in Vienna on 19 December 1912 to a wealthy Jewish family. They owned property in the third district Vienna, with her mother Elizabeth running a successful business and her father Michael being an executive in British Petroleum. Mum and her brother were surrounded by valuable antiques, brought up to the wonders of theatre and the height of Austrian culture. She had a nanny and servants befitting the family's status in Viennese society.

As she grew into womanhood, she was naïve but had a drive to be at the forefront of women's advances and applied to study medicine. She was courted by a man 20 years her elder with the title of Von Trojan. He came from a long line of nobility but was short of cash. She had money but no title. The families would join with both sides gaining from the union. For the marriage to proceed she would officially have to convert to Roman Catholicism and as the family Neufeld were more interested in status than religion the wedding went ahead.

Sadly, like many arranged marriages, love was somewhat absent and with the rise of Nazism in Austria being married to an ex-Jew was not so becoming to a man of title. Also at this time Jews were excluded from universities and this was extended to include Mother even though she had been officially christened. So ended her hope to complete medicine and her desire to be one of the first female doctors in Vienna.

In 1938 she gave birth to her first son, Kurt. He was baptised and was officially Roman Catholic. By this time the Nazi regime was persecuting Jews on a daily basis, removing more rights every day and with regular bashings and vandalism against Jewish properties. At this time her parents decided to flee Vienna and chose Australia. They used Mother's documents and her title to ship their considerable wealth out as for most Jews escape meant abandoning everything they owned.

War erupted and the Nazi regime took hold in Austria building on the country's anti-Semitism. Jews were being deported, their property confiscated and those who resisted, murdered. In the face of this, Mother would stand on the street-side ridiculing in public the anti-Jewish propaganda and decrees posted by the Brownshirts. She was either very brave or very stupid. It brought her to the attention of the Gestapo who arrested her.

Whilst she was in their tender care it was discovered that her parents had moved their wealth using her documents, and the Gestapo set about torturing her for a confession of conspiracy to defraud the Nazi regime. For many days and nights she was tortured with sleep deprivation between beatings. She was at this time pregnant with her second child and miscarried as a result of Nazi 'justice'. Half dead and without having confessed she was dumped in the gutter outside Gestapo Headquarters. Most likely it was only her title that had saved her from a bullet in the back of the neck.

As she lay dying in the street she was found by some nuns who carried her back to their convent and nursed her back to physical health. I believe that she was never mentally the same woman again. She had lost her innocence, no longer trusted individuals, and had to meld into the populace. At least her title kept her from having to wear the yellow Star of David and from deportation to the death camps. Her husband would no longer walk on the same side of the street as she did; being born a Jew meant that no amount of baptism water could cleanse her.

Now, abandoned by her husband except for her marital duties of providing him sex, she was pregnant again. She would have to hide from him the little food she could obtain by standing for hours in the ration queues or by swapping jewellery so she could feed her son and the baby growing within. She told me of how her husband would steal any food she had not hidden well enough because by now being married to a converted Jew with half-bastard Jewish children and no Jewish wealth had no benefits.

The bombings of Vienna by the Allied air forces began in earnest with daily raids by the US during the day and the RAF by night. She told of the wailing sirens, the rush to get her toddler son and babe-in-arms to the shelter, the horrifying whine of the bombs as they fell, and the concussion of the explosions. She vividly retold how, on emerging from the shelters, she would see the destruction, the fires, the gaping holes where buildings once stood, the pieces of humanity that had been blown apart and now hung as decorations from what was left of trees. Her eyes twinkled as she recounted how, out of this horror, she would find bits of dead horse, or cats, dogs and even rats that she could salvage for food. She was proud of being a good mum and doing what had to be done to protect her children.

As the war reached its last days, having survived torture, humiliation and starvation, she and her young family nearly lost their lives when the Russian Army invaded. She was in a country farmhouse, having sought refuge from the bombings of Vienna, when drunken Russian soldiers burst into her home, firing their submachine guns. She threw her eldest boy out of the window and dived after him as machine-gun bullets peppered the wall just above their heads. The youngest, Eric, still a baby, was left in his cot. After the soldiers had left she returned to find the bullet holes just above him. It had been a close shave but God had been with them.

After liberation her sector of Vienna was handed from the Russians to the US and she was declared a stateless person. She was malnourished and very ill and was placed into a refugee camp for many months as they tried to find her family in Australia. At this time she divorced her estranged husband as he had all but abandoned her in her hours of need.

In 1947, after two years living in poverty in the camp, she gained permission to join her parents in Melbourne. On leaving the camp she had agreed to a sham marriage to a Jewish refugee so that he could migrate to Australia. She said it was just a paper marriage with no love or intimacy. In years to come her willingness to aid this individual would cause endless heartache.

After a period living in Melbourne with her parents and two sons she answered an advert in the Jewish paper from a man from Adelaide looking for a wife. She thus met my father, Leo. He was a small man by stature, nearly deaf from the beatings by the Nazis, and came from a background very different from her own. Whilst she had grown up in wealth, surrounded by antiques and culture, looked after by servants and nannies, he had come from a poor rural part of Austria, the son of a rural overseer. He had little money but did come from a family with strong ties. He was a very hard worker and would accept her with her younger son. She elected not to tell him of the older boy lest he might find taking on a son who had been raised in his early days in the Hitler Youth, as all good Aryan Austrians were, would be too much. She would tell him later.

Against her family's advice and with the threat that she would be disinherited, she moved to Adelaide and married Leo in 1948. She was told that should she move to Adelaide she would be on her own and that she would not be welcomed back should the relationship fail. At first she lived with Leo in the Adlers' North Adelaide boarding house and by the time I was born in 1950 the family had pooled their resources to buy a property for my parents at Parkside.

My birth nearly cost my mother her life. She was taken to a third-grade hospital, the Quamby in South Terrace. There she nearly bled out due to complications. To save her life a Viennese doctor performed an emergency hysterectomy taking her ovaries as well. This meant she could have no more children and also lost her libido. These added extra pressures to a marriage based not on love but on mutual loneliness.

My mother was meticulous as a housewife. Even though she had grown up with servants she made sure that the home was spotless. You could have eaten off the floor. As we children grew she entertained us by playing the piano. She was gifted with perfect pitch and could play any music by ear. We spoke German at home but she took to English like she did to the other four languages she spoke fluently.

When our family purchased a bed-and-breakfast boarding house at Glenelg, she took on the roles of cook, cleaner, washerwoman, supervisor of staff and public relations manager. She worked day and night at this and at being a mum. The early summers without air-conditioning were most cruel to her and she would seek shelter by sleeping in the musty cellar below to gain some relief. As a young child I still remember the perspiration streaming off her as she toiled in the kitchen or over the hot copper and ironing.

As our family became more affluent she undertook less hands-on work in the business and settled in more to the duties of home-maker. Sadly for us children the war had changed her. She found it hard to impart warmth to us or to give love to Leo. Our family home was beset with daily fights between our parents, hysterical outbursts, and Leo being put down as just an uncultured peasant.

In 1956 she persuaded Father to buy a property at Beaumont as she preferred the hills to being at the seaside and hence I was enrolled at Linden Park School. My mother found Australia harsh and whereas my father had embraced it with a passion, her passion lay in the cool green fields of Europe and in the snow-covered European Alps. Mother found only a few spots in Australia that she enjoyed; Mount Buffalo in Victoria with its chalet and mountain trails was one of her favourites. The other, near the end of her life, was the property I live on with my wife at Yankalilla.

When I was seven, Mother took me on the only holiday that was exclusively with her. We boarded the MV *Kanimbla*, a converted World War Two naval vessel, for a cruise from Melbourne to Cairns. Despite my being constantly seasick, I have wonderful memories of this adventure. We visited the Taronga Park Zoo in Sydney in the company of Roma Mitchell (who would later become Dame Roma), visited a rain forest outside Cairns, were awed by the Great Barrier Reef, dressed up together for fancy dress and fancy hat parties on board, and were the closest we had been and have been since.

As soon as the family had enough spare funds she was off to Europe by herself for six months at a time. She would spend her time in Switzerland till the money ran out then return for our summer. Whilst on these yearly excursions she would live very frugally as if she felt guilty enjoying herself. She would enter a world of make-believe and would live her life as the visiting professor or some other important person she had longed to be.

These early escapes to Europe were made by sea on the impressive ocean liners of the day. She would return home with a suitcase filled with prizes that she had won on ship quiz nights. She had a wonderful memory for trivia, was excellent at chess and Scrabble, and was imaginative in fancy dress. She would fill me full of wonder for the world as we enjoyed viewing her photos as they screened on the wall on slide nights.

Her later journeys were by air and were quite tortuous. On one such occasion as a 70-year-old she had an angina attack in Saudi Arabia and was taken to hospital by ambulance, guarded by a soldier with a submachine gun. She was very frightened as a few months before, this had happened to another old lady who was never seen alive again. She was checked at the local hospital and discharged to resume her flight.

On her return the fights would start again and as a child I longed for my parents to divorce but they never did. Father believed in duty and his marriage vows meant marriage for life. Mother looked at him as a cash source so she could escape reality and Australia. Thus they grew old together. They lived in separate flats on the same property with me as the unwilling arbitrator.

Mother was a paradox for me when it came to my studies. On the one hand she would say that she would love me regardless of my level of success, because at primary school I was no scholar, and on the other would not acknowledge when I succeeded. When I attained my degree all I got was that her friend's son was a dentist with the title of doctor. I felt she longed to be titled again or at least be able to boast of her son the doctor. I constantly felt that I was a disappointment for her. Even in later life when I proved to be a very competent and successful businessman, I felt she would rather have me as a titled failure.

My mother was very broad-minded for a person of her generation, and advised me to live with a girl before I married her. When I met the love of my life, Cilla, and she moved in whilst Mum was overseas, Mum was not as pleased that I had taken her advice as she had been when she gave it. Her background of servants and nobility coloured her view of my wife-to-be, as Cilla came from working-class English parents, had no title and was not well educated. She would often refer to her as coming from the slums. She worked diligently to split us but it didn't work.

She begrudgingly put up with Cilla, even though my now wife cared for her and was a wonderful daughter-in-law. She was jealous of the love we shared as her life had been devoid of such affection. When our sons were born she enjoyed being a grandmother but love and hugs were always at a distance.

As she headed towards her 80th birthday her health began to fail in a major way. She had increasing attacks of angina, she had glaucoma and became frail. Cilla and I were visiting our Yankalilla farm when one of our staff members rang, concerned about Mum. I immediately rang home to be told that she had been suffering from unrelieved angina all day. When I got home I found Mum still in pain, ashen grey with cardiac arrhythmia. Reluctantly she allowed me to take her to the RAH. We visited her for the next two days in coronary care. The next evening we were phoned by the RAH to say she was dying and would we hurry in to say our last farewell. We found her in great distress with severe pulmonary oedema; I gave her a hug, caressed her brow and said our goodbyes.

We had just arrived home when the news came of her death. She died just after midnight on 8 April, Cilla's birthday. She was now at peace. We had said our goodbyes and I didn't shed a tear till I buried her ashes under her favourite tree on our Yankalilla property. We have placed a plaque on this tree in memory of her life. I feel good to have her so close to where we live. Strangely I feel closer to her in death than I did during her life.

I have often wondered about this intelligent, talented person who was my mother. I have pondered what she would have been like without the horrors of war. I think she would have been the medical doctor that she had aspired to be as a girl, a spirited individual full of life and of hope. Most likely I would not have come into existence as she would have remained in Austria and of course I would not be writing this account.

Gertrude's Austrian Rice Auflauf

Austrian Rice Cake (can be used as entree, main or dessert)

My mum used to cook it as a special treat because the ingredients were hard to get at the time. Some years ago I remembered how she made it and as a result the Rice Auflauf, as my mother had made it, was resurrected. I made one today in order to write down what I did by memory so I know the recipe works. Enjoy!

Ingredients

1½ cups white rice
6 eggs (700 grams or equivalent weight)
⅓ cup milk
½ cup sultanas (optional)
⅓ cup white sugar or stevia powder
½ teaspoon vanilla essence (optional)
Ground cinnamon

Equipment

2 mixing bowls (one microwaveable)
2 dinner plates
1 non-stick 25 cm baking dish (different width can be used – just changes cooking times)
Spatula
Whisk

Part 1

Fluffy rice can be cooked whichever way you like but below is my method.

Place 1½ cups of rice in microwavable mixing bowl, just cover rice with water and cook on high for 9 minutes. I place a dinner plate above and below the bowl to keep microwave clean and keep moisture in bowl.

Carefully remove hot dish from microwave. Using spatula or spoon, break up rice so grains separate. Cover rice with just enough water and again cook on high for 9 minutes. Again carefully remove hot bowl of rice.

Break up lumpy rice with spatula or spoon. You can add the milk to help free the cooked grains of rice so rice ends up fluffy.

Let rice cool to room temperature (can also refrigerate if you wish).

Part 2

When rice is cold place bowl with rice next to empty second bowl. Separate yolks from whites adding yolks to the rice and placing whites in the other bowl.

When this process is complete mix yolks thoroughly through the rice till rice turns golden in colour. Add optional sultanas at this point and stir them through mix. Add sugar or sweetener to egg whites with vanilla essence and whisk till frothy. Fold the whisked egg whites into the rice mix so that it looks frothy throughout the rice mix. Gently pour contents into baking dish. Dust top with ground cinnamon.

Place in oven and cook at 150°C for about 45 minutes. You will know it's ready when top turns golden brown and rebounds when pressed. Remove cooked Auflauf from oven.

Can be eaten hot or cold.

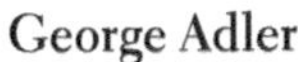

George Adler

Baby boomer George Adler was born on 13 August 1950 to Leo and Trudy Adler. He attended Linden Park Demonstration School and later Norwood High. Having completed his Bachelor of Business he worked for two years for the State Public Service Board as a Research Officer and later conducted all the State Government's induction courses. He left the Public Service to develop the family business and was successful in his career. As well as managing Glenelg Holiday Flats, a 130-guest establishment, George successfully bought and sold properties. He volunteered with the CFS for over 45 years and as an ambulance officer with St John for 18 years. He has been happily married to his soulmate, Cilla, since 1977 and has two boys. Having taken early retirement at the age of 55, he spends his time with Cilla boating, fishing and exploring the world.

Della JOYNER

née Greenwood

(1917–2011)

Steve Joyner

Mum was born in Sheffield, England in 1917. Her parents were Willie and Winifred Greenwood. Mum's father worked as a conductor for Sheffield Tramcar and her mother was a milliner. Mum had a younger sister and an older brother. At the young age of 15, Mum started work at Lipton Grocers, Sheffield.

In 1935, Mum was working at Weston's Toy Wholesalers in Sheffield when she met her future husband (Stan) who was there installing telephones. A long-distance courtship ensued, as they could only see each other at weekends on Sunday rail excursions as Stan was based in London.

Mum married Stan on Sunday 27 August 1939 at St Timothy's Church, Sheffield, just a few days prior to the outbreak of World War Two. After the wedding they caught the evening train to London and to their first house together in Harrow. No honeymoon and back to work the next day.

Mum left England, moving to New Zealand in 1946 with my

older brother Peter (born 1943) to follow Stan, coming out on the ship *Akaroa* via the Panama Canal, a long journey for a young mother on her own with a three-year-old. I, the second son, was born in Wellington, New Zealand, in 1950. The family moved to Melbourne in late 1950.

My recollections and memories of my mum pretty well start when I was about three or four. By this time Mum and Dad had purchased a new dark blue Vanguard car and a Bondwood caravan. Our caravan holidays to Lakes Entrance, Victoria, are still vivid, with my brother and I in our bunks and Mum and Dad squeezed into the converted dining table/bed at the front of the van.

In 1956 Mum was yet again on the trail of Dad as he had returned to England for a short period. This time Mum and her two boys ventured by ship from Melbourne to London and on return, also by ship, the family disembarked and settled in Adelaide.

In 1957 the family home at 45 Hay Road, Linden Park was built. As this was the first new home Mum and Dad built, it had all the 'new age' furniture with the bright-coloured Fler TV recliner chairs, the lightning-blue couch, the Vulcan Conray electric heater to supplement the open fire that burnt mallee roots, the red-painted feature wall in the lounge room, the red Laminex kitchen benches and table. Mum must have had a wonderful time selecting all the new furniture. This must have been an exciting time for her.

My recollections of Mum during the late 50s and early 60s are very much centred around home life, school, and trips to the city on the trolley-bus and lunch at the John Martin cafeteria, a real treat for a young boy. In those days Mum ordered from the back of the greengrocer's van – this was real home delivery. Mum always seemed to be there when we needed her. There was always something special in the fridge, like my most favourite dessert – lemon curd pie. The home-made lemon cordial was to die for.

Mum's idea of a school lunch was to take it from home not to buy it from the school tuckshop. Having said that, I didn't complain about the smoked salmon sandwiches she prepared with a Kit Kat to finish off. Mum was a good cook and a wonderful hostess to many a dinner party held at home for friends and Dad's overseas business colleagues. Mum was the ultimate entertainer.

This was also an era of great memories as Mum and Dad had a ski boat and a holiday shack on the River Murray. Mum's catering skills helped her whip up a dozen egg burgers with salad and of course Golden Circle pineapple rings to feed the hungry family and friends.

During the 60s Mum did much fundraising and charity work for the Adelaide Children's Hospital Auxiliary. She also did similar fundraising work as President of the Mothers' Rowing Committee for King's College culminating in raising sufficient funds in six months to enable the College to buy the new King's IV boat for the first eight rowing team. In recognition of her tireless work for the Rowing Club she had one of the new open four boats named in her honour. It is with pride that I can say I was in the King's IV as part of the winning crew that won the subsequent Head of the River in 1967.

In 1965, at the age of 48, Mum learned to drive and got her first driving licence. It is hard to imagine that up until then Mum had to rely on lifts from friends or catch the bus to get around. Mum's first car was a red Renault Dauphine (that my brother crashed); her next car was a new white Renault 10 (that I crashed). Mum's love affair with French cars must have been because of her numerous European trips that included Paris. Her favourite city was Vienna in Austria.

Mum was fortunate to travel back to England and Europe on many occasions. For a young woman leaving all her family behind in England back in 1946 it must have been of some comfort to all concerned to be able to meet up on each visit. I remember going on a couple of these trips, and being able to meet grandparents, uncles, aunts and various cousins was great. Mum and Dad were the only family to ever leave England and resettle abroad. The distance made contact somewhat difficult but Mum was a regular airmail letter writer. The regular phone link-ups and the annual Christmas parcels probably made it a little more bearable.

It wasn't long, however, before Dad's work had them moving again, to Canberra in 1973, home for the next five years. During this period Mum went to work as a saleswoman with a friend's real estate business. According to Mum she had a short, enjoyable and successful career.

Mum returned to Adelaide when Dad retired in 1979 and they decided to settle in Mannum, building a new house next to the golf course. Mum loved watching sport with golf and cricket her favourites. Of course Mum always struggled with deciding whether to barrack for the Poms or the Aussies. I reckon Mum switched sides as each Test unravelled. If challenged she would say she was following New Zealand. You didn't dare ask her opinion on the fateful Trevor Chappell bowling incident.

Mum loved playing bridge and had regular bridge nights, and always gave Dad a hard time as her card partner because she reckoned he always seemed to deal the wrong cards. She didn't like to lose at bridge.

Grandchildren had started to arrive, firstly with my brother's three boys and later my two girls. Mum was lucky enough to witness a further family generation of some 10 great-grandchildren. The great-grandkids seemed to keep Mum highly amused with all their energy and different personalities.

After Dad died in 2003, Mum stayed in her house in Mannum and continued an independent life until she was 92 when she moved to Adelaide. Mum died in Adelaide, South Australia, on 4 December 2011; she was 94. As they say in cricket, nearly a ton but let's call it 94 not out.

What I got from my mum and carry with me to this day is varied. There is undoubtedly a continued strong sense of family unity, support and participation. Also instilled is the need to take up opportunities, particularly in your working life, and not to be afraid to change direction and travel if needed for that opportunity. This has certainly featured in parts of my life. The support of a great partner (wife) is immeasurable in all aspects of your life and I count myself fortunate in this regard. I aim to have fun and involve my family, something I try hard to fulfil.

Steve Joyner

Steve was born in Wellington, New Zealand, in 1950. He came to Adelaide with his parents and brother in 1956. He lived at 45 Hay Road, Linden Park, and attended Linden Park Primary School, then went on to King's College (now Pembroke). At school he was a keen rower and was a team member of the King's first eight that won the Head of the River in 1967.

He commenced his professional career in the commercial real estate industry, working predominantly in the leasing field with such companies as Jones Lang LaSalle, Knight Frank, Colliers International and an independent property consultancy firm. He is currently working with the South Australian Government in Adelaide.

Steve has been married to Lea for some 35 years and lives at Norwood. He has two daughters, Sarah and Amy, plus four grandchildren, Sophia, Elsie, Oscar and Jake. He enjoys family and friends and always looks forward to that next holiday or caravan trip.

Meta SARAP
née Aksel

(1910–2000)

Helene Sarap Lockwood

My mother, Meta Sarap, was born Meta Aksel in April 1910. She was born in Estonia in the rural hamlet of Johvi, halfway between Tallinn, the national capital, and St Petersburg, Russia. Estonia was, at that time, a part of Imperial Tsarist Russia. It is interesting to note that at one point the family name was changed to Raidma by the authorities in an attempt to 'Estonianise' Germanic names.

Her father Wilhelm was a carpenter and her mother Helene busied herself at home raising eight children. From what I know, my mother's childhood was a happy one, growing up as she did in a large family. She recalled summer days herding cows to pasture on the family farm. Her grandfather was a respected choirmaster. This interest in things musical was passed on. My mother sang with her village choir often as soloist, and performed duets with one of her brothers.

The defeat of the German and Russian Empires in 1918 provided the opportunity for Estonia and indeed the entire Baltic region to take up arms and fight for their freedom. Incredibly the Baltic States managed to throw off the yoke of Russian rule. Estonians, Latvians and Lithuanians have lived on the shores of the Baltic Sea for over 5000 years. All three countries share a similar history. They have variously been ruled by Swedish and Danish kings, Teutonic knights, German barons and Russian tsars. Estonians also share a Viking heritage with their Scandinavian neighbours. The Estonian language is very similar to Finnish, as is the national anthem. This suggests a tribal separation at some point lost in the mists of time. The Gulf of Finland separates the two.

In the independent period between the two world wars, the Baltic countries made considerable progress in all aspects of economic, social and cultural life. In this breathing space, my mother finished her elementary schooling and went on to study home economics. This was quite a formal and demanding course undertaken in a trade school setting. Here was the foundation of her exceptional home-making skills in later years. As she got older, she worked as a nanny, a secretary in a bank and legal office, and as a sales assistant in a fabric store.

In 1934 she married a farmer. His name was Aarund Puu ('Tree' in English). In 1935 she had her first child, my sister Maret. Shortly afterward, she separated and divorced. With family support she carried on as a single mother. (Unheard of in those times!)

As a result of the Molotov–Ribbentrop pact of 1939, the Red Army invaded the Baltic States in 1940. Stalin and Hitler did not remain friends for long. The Germans pushed the Soviets out, but not before a program of arrests, executions and deportations had terrorised the populations into numb submission. World War Two was a time of genocide and torture during which many Baltic people perished in Siberian labour camps. The close of the war saw battles raging back and forth across the Estonian borderlands, the Germans in full retreat and Soviet forces once again massing to overrun the Baltics. Fear of the Red Army was widespread and many fled their homelands.

My mother was one of them. Her instinct was to leave her home, her family, everything she had ever known, and flee towards a less than certain future. As history now reveals, from the beginning of the first Soviet occupation in June 1940, until the end of the Stalinist era in 1954, the Baltic States combined population of six million lost 605,000 souls.

Fight or flight? Her instinct served her well!

Years later she told the story of how her sisters Tatiana and Alma together with their children had just escaped towards Sweden and of her plans to join them. Suddenly flight in that direction became impossible.

In Tallinn, alone with her child, the Russians only days away, she tells of opening a Bible at random. Exactly what she read there, she never said. She maintained from that point on, she was guided. Calmly and determinedly, and quite possibly with help from her brother-in-law, an officer in the Estonian Army high command (still at his post), she left. She gained a place as a laundress with the retreating German Army, under the protection of ranking officers. She was not concerned with politics. This was survival! A young mother and her daughter embarked on the most perilous of adventures. What followed is something most of us only ever experience in the cinema.

Fighter planes strafed the retreating columns. There were bombings and worse. Chaos reigned. Maret developed a high fever, which blocked her memory of the madness. There was no going back. Waiting to board a military transport in a Latvian port, mother and daughter had to hide in trucks being lifted from the quay onto ships. Civilian travel was forbidden. Nevertheless they got away.

Their ship made the Baltic crossing to Germany without incident, often lying motionless at sea, engines silent because of the ever present danger of being torpedoed. Many (including hospital ships) did not make it. In Germany, more bombing. Entire cities just piles of rubble. Refugees of all nations everywhere. Food supplies virtually non-existent. The war ended.

The Allies occupied Germany, and the various Allied zones came into being. The Western powers fell out with their Soviet allies, and the Cold War commenced. Everything was in short supply, but the Marshall Plan, an American initiative aimed at rebuilding a shattered Germany, helped ease the situation. This was more the case in the Western zones. Life was harsh but survivable. Mum found work as a domestic for a well-to-do family and Maret continued her schooling.

My mother met my father Aksel Sarap (born February 1906 in Rakvere, Estonia) in a displaced persons camp in the British zone. As a boy he was schooled mostly in Narva, a fortress city close to the Russian border. His family came from a town not far from Mum's village. His father Juri and mother Leontine were teachers and reasonably affluent. They had a large farm and also maintained a farm shop and townhouse in Narva. Mum had never met him, but knew of him. He and his brothers were party boys, and his sisters somewhat proud and aloof. Mum had seen his picture somewhere in the past.

Land-owning lesser descendants of Germanic 'Baltic Barons'– though not titled – were defined by their habit of speaking German amongst themselves and 'en famille' and speaking Estonian with 'the help'. Dad had already been married twice. The first marriage ended in an amicable divorce and the story goes that he and his wife Minna walked arm-in-arm into court. The marriage had produced two sons, Nicolai, who died in infancy, and Ants. Ants died in Siberia where he, his mother and new stepfather (the Mayor of Narva) were deported during one of Stalin's many purges of intellectuals, politicians and business leaders. The mayor also perished. Minna survived and eventually returned to Estonia.

Although this story is about my mother, events leading to her marriage to my father need to be explained. How did he find himself in the British zone as war in Europe ended? He had been fighting in the Estonian divisions of the German Army. As the tide turned in favour of another Soviet occupation of Estonia, Estonian Army diehards took to the forests. These 'forest brothers' fought a guerrilla campaign against the Red Army as well as the excesses of the Nazi regime. Even so, many Estonian fighting men found themselves captured and forced into German uniform, fighting the 'greater Soviet evil'. Take your pick – Dad's choice was to be shot by the Russians as Estonian bourgeoisie trash, or shot by the Germans for desertion of an army he was not keen to join in the first place. This is the kind of madness that only all-out war can unleash. Reading, writing or speaking fluent German was either a help or hindrance depending on which way the political winds blew. He survived being thrown out of officer's school in Poland – drunk on duty apparently. This is interesting because the father I knew was disciplined and correct in his bearing – he was a social drinker not a regular drunk. The historical record indicates that a group of Estonian trainee officers rebelled in Poland in the last years of the war. I am not sure if Dad was a part of that.

By that time most Estonians realised they were no longer fighting for an independent homeland. Like many in Europe they were simply swept up in a greater Soviet, Nazi, Allied catastrophe – betrayed and sidelined by all the competing powers of the day. Never was this more so than in the so-called 'Eastern Bloc'.

Dad found himself disciplined and transferred to the Western Front. Cannon fodder basically. After the Allied victory, he washed up in a British prisoner of war camp in Belgium, and was eventually repatriated to Germany. Thankfully to the British zone.

Mum and Dad met. A displaced persons camp is no picnic. Nevertheless, cultural life flourished. Art and craft, choirs, English classes. Mum fell seriously ill. A life-changing decision was made. Meta Aksel married Aksel Sarap. If Mum died, Maret would have a legal guardian, her new stepfather. Dad was free to marry as he understood from information received through official sources that his second wife Adele and their two children, son Juri and daughter Malle, had perished.

My mother had no such information about family still in Estonia. It took much longer to learn her parents were alive. Imagine the stress. In fact all but one of her siblings survived the war. Her favourite youngest brother (Olev) had been killed in defence of Narva early in the war. As conditions in the camp and in

Germany improved, Mum recovered her strength and purpose in going forward. Few were aware of the fate awaiting those forcibly repatriated to their now Soviet-occupied homelands by overzealous Western Allies. The horsetrading continued in part from a need to appease the Russian 'bear'. Refugees in the British zone fared better than those under French and American control. A cruel joke. The extent and severity of a new wave of Soviet aggression became less visible behind a new phenomenon – the Iron Curtain. More horror and loss. The hard-won peace in Europe now had a distinctly chilly edge. East v. West.

The International Red Cross helped track down Mum's sisters who had made it to Sweden. The much loved brother-in-law who was such a help in Tallinn did not survive. He had been executed by the Soviets. Another sister, Milda, had somehow surfaced in Berlin and was forcibly returned to Estonia – much of this took years to discover. For Mum, Dad and Maret emigration became a possibility. Sweden, Canada and America were discussed.

The new family decided to go as far away as possible. Australia. Before being approved, medical checks and political screening were undertaken. Most Estonians are of the Lutheran faith so armed with certificates attesting to being of good character they presented themselves to the British and Australian emigration authorities. Australia's White Australia Policy, never so much in evidence as after World War Two, facilitated their acceptance. Australia was very welcoming of tall, blond, and blue-eyed Balts. Many were educated professionals. Immigrants had only to agree to work for the government for two years on arrival. The Snowy Mountains Scheme, together with road, rail, mining, agricultural and industrial projects, absorbed a willing and grateful workforce from war-torn Europe. The lucky country fuelled its nation-building postwar economy.

On 14 April 1949, after a lengthy rail journey across Germany, through the Alps to Italy and more processing via a transit camp near Naples, the family boarded a former US troopship, the *General Sturgis*, and sailed to the 'new world'. On 21 May 1949 these latest 'new Australians' disembarked in Sydney Harbour. Dad had a few British pounds in his pocket; family possessions were a few battered leather cases. The first money spent in the new land was on a banana for Maret. Another train journey through an unfamiliar landscape to an immigration hostel in Bathurst, New South Wales. It was cold. It was winter. Odd, wasn't Australia supposed to be warm and sunny?

Mum worked in the staff canteen in the Bathurst hostel and Dad undertook various labouring jobs. Maret entered Bathurst High School. Mum had studied some English at school and was therefore able to communicate. In fact, Mum spoke four languages: Estonian and German fluently, English, with an accent, quite well and Russian (as little as possible!). Dad struggled. He never fully mastered English. It was passable but never brilliant. He spoke Estonian, German and Russian. Maret spoke Estonian and German. Although English was new to her she astounded everyone with good passes in English (French and Latin) at school and within a few years she was proficient with no accent.

By the time of my birth in the Queen Victoria Hospital on 3 January 1951 the family had settled in Adelaide. I was named Helene after my maternal grandmother but the family call me Lena. Mum worked briefly for Farmer's Union, Dad eventually went to work for General Motors. Maret continued school at Unley High (then situated on the current site of Mitcham Girls' High).

My mother now focused on 5 Cedar Avenue, Glenunga. She settled into raising a family and creating a home. Mum had insisted – on arrival in Adelaide – on buying a home at the earliest opportunity. She chose Cedar Avenue and Glenunga for its charm and affordability. She loved the tree-lined streets, the gardens and the peace and quiet. Glenunga had jacaranda and cedar trees, wide streets and gentlemen's bungalows. Mum was always careful with money. Dad earned it, she stretched it. He deferred to her in all matters financial. Within a few years of settling in Cedar Avenue the house was paid off. She had taken out a private mortgage with the vendors as the banks were not interested.

Mum took in boarders, other refugee Estonian families who were choosing Adelaide as their home. Like many displaced nationalities that arrive on distant and unfamiliar shores, a community establishes itself. Help is offered, everyone pitches in be it by building a new shed, laying concrete, seeding a lawn or growing food and cooking meals. As these Estonian friends found their feet and moved away, our home life became more ordered.

My brother Olev (Ollie) was born on 20 May 1953. My birth and Ollie's helped comfort our parents. New life brings new hope and nurturing children can be healing. The ache of loss, thoughts of home, family and old friends never left our transplanted family, but life now had new meaning. My mother led by loving example. The shocks and trauma of the war years were in the past. Australia made that possible. Ollie and I often feel a kind of survivor guilt, possibly from information picked up by osmosis in our formative years.

Maret finished school and commenced work in the front office of Adelaide University. In 1955 she married Robin Kneebone and started the Kneebone branch of our family. Andrew and Ian arrived in 1958 and 1960.

At the time this love match was frowned upon by Robin's Establishment parents. His father was a veterinary surgeon highly regarded by the South Australian Jockey Club. His mother, an arts graduate, opposed marrying her youngest son off to the daughter of European refugees. Robin's two elder brothers were studying medicine. Praise the Lord, Maret was a stunner! Robin was no slouch in the looks department either. He was great fun and Ollie and I absolutely adored him from day one. We have family jokes and sayings that are down to him.

Mum and Dad took all of this in their stride and determined to give Maret and Robin the best society wedding they could. Maret was 19, Robin four years older. I was four and Ollie not quite two.

Mum was a marvel on her Singer treadle sewing machine. She made most of her own clothes and those of Maret. I was well dressed as was Ollie. Complicated pleated drapes did not faze her. She could crochet lace and made her own Estonian national costume. She did not, however, knit. Mum made me a fabulous pale blue poplin party dress with tiny kittens printed on the fabric. I have only recently discarded this favourite dress of mine from the 50s. With so many moves I have finally had to let go!

This particular wedding however, could not be a home-made affair. The wedding dress, Dad's suit, Mum's outfit, and Ollie and my sailor suits (mine with pleated skirt) were all professionally tailored. I look back at the wedding photos and still go, 'Wow!' Maret a princess. Robin's beaming smile. Dad the proud stepfather giving his daughter away, handsome and dignified. Ollie and I scrubbed and immaculate. The mother of the bride wore dark-blue velvet, coordinated hat with fascinator, gloves, black velvet evening bag and elegant heels to match. Her traditional Estonian heavy rolled silver necklace the only jewellery. Perfect. The marriage was celebrated at Saint Stephen's Lutheran Church, Wakefield Street. The reception was at Burnside Town Hall. I was so young I can't recall if I rode inside the white Jaguar wedding car.

Mum was of the school of 'less is more' when it came to dressing. She didn't have lots of clothes, but what she did have was elegant in its simplicity. She had an eye for high quality fabric and construction. She wore little jewellery, usually only her wedding band and watch. She had a beautiful solid silver Viking ship brooch – one of the national symbols of Estonia. Strangely, she lost the brooch on a family holiday to Wallaroo while chatting with a group of Russian sailors – they were crew on a Russian grain carrier loading at the jetty.

Mum hated wearing hats and gloves and when catching the bus into the city would have a quiet giggle. Not for her the obvious discomfort of corseted and stockinged eastern suburbs matrons – in century heat! Her one great extravagance (or Dad's) was an 'autumn haze' mink. Ah! The feel of it against the face and the scent of Yardley perfume!

In 1958 Mum became critically ill with rheumatoid arthritis. The onset was rapid and the pain crippling. She couldn't stand the weight of a sheet. She tried every conceivable treatment including gold injections! Nothing worked. Ollie recalls Dad taking him to enrol in Linden Park School as Mum flew to Sydney that day for specialist consultations. Eventually, in desperation, she undertook to cure herself. A crackpot idea at the time. Mum took to her bed and fasted. Instinct? She read up on natural diets as a source of wellbeing. She cut down on sugar and processed foods. She recovered and never looked back. Along the way, and much to Ollie's and my horror, she discovered cod liver oil as a universal cure-all.

She was overjoyed to re-establish letter contact with family and friends. Letters with exotic stamps would arrive from different parts of the world. She read these letters out to us, extracting every ounce of information. Through her we began to understand our own place in this worldwide family. Communication with relatives locked firmly behind the Iron Curtain was not easy. The Soviet authorities censored every letter. Great care had to be taken not to compromise anyone. No politics! Care packages sent to Estonia were often looted or delayed without explanation.

Mum and Dad got quite a shock to learn that Dad's second wife, son and daughter were still alive. There had been a mistake. What to do? The law to the rescue. The second marriage was annulled. Mum revealed later in life, on meeting Dad's son in Adelaide in 1990, that she received a deeply personal, kind and understanding letter from Juri's mother many years ago. It put the matter to rest. (She had long since passed when Juri met our mother.) Mum reduced us all to tears when she quietly said to Juri, 'You are my son now.'

Juri said that his mother never spoke badly of our father, or of our mother. He also told us for the first time that our sister Malle never recovered from the shell shock suffered during massive wartime bombings. She was in and out of mental institutions for most of her life and died in her early 30s.

Back to Cedar Avenue and the 50s and 60s. Our life was a suburban idyll. Our dad's German cousin Heinz, wife Erica and daughter Ursula lived with us briefly until they moved to Rostrevor. Ollie and I spoke German, which we now struggle with. Estonian, no problem.

We had a large garden. We had chickens, fruit trees and vegetable plots. Every summer there were strawberries – the baker's horse providing manure. Mum was an exceptional gardener. Any weed was 'the enemy'. We had a large lawn out the back rolling gently down to a huge willow tree. We spent hot summer nights sleeping out on this back lawn. Bliss, except for mozzies! We played with the neighbourhood children who all attended Linden Park School. The Lehmanns next door, the Langsfords across the street. My best friend from school (still now) was Sandra Harrison from Allinga Avenue. Sandra recalls I wasn't allowed to play until I had done half an hour of piano practice. Our ancient piano teacher, Miss Ivy Munn, came to the house once a week.

We knew every kid for miles around. Mum didn't worry overly if we disappeared on a bike. We turned up eventually. There were other Estonian kids at Linden Park School. The Koldits boys from Sturdee Street and Peter Idol. He and Ollie were thick as thieves throughout primary school. His parents ran 'The Cottage' deli on Portrush Road and they delivered lunch orders to the school. The boys would have sleepovers, and we would all play 'spooky in the dark'.

We had big family lunches on Sundays. Mum was a terrific cook never consulting a recipe. She just understood ingredients. Her tortes and pastries were works of art. As children at Easter we helped dye hard-boiled eggs in the orthodox style – onion skins and coloured wool gave a marvellous marbled effect. She was amused by the smell of lamb drifting across the suburb at six o'clock. 'Don't Australians eat anything else?' Mind you, lamb appeared on our table too.

We had great birthday parties.

My parents sang in the Estonian men's and women's choir. Our parents went to parties, concerts, and balls at the Estonian House, Jeffcott Street, North Adelaide. Ollie and I attended Estonian school on Saturday mornings.

Every year the Baltic Communities held (and still do) a commemoration ceremony for victims of mass deportations. In earlier years these were standing-room only concerts held in the

Adelaide Town Hall. The massed Community choirs sang. Not a dry eye anywhere. Mum was proud of Maret's involvement with these events in later years. Maret shared a role as President of the Baltic Council of South Australia for a considerable number of years. There were always lots of visitors at Cedar Avenue. More often than not, our godparents.

Though Mum was interested in our schooling she didn't involve herself with school life. She didn't do Mothers' Club. She met other parents but simply put, she wasn't a lady who lunches. She was busy. She rode a bike to the shops. The only other mum in the neighbourhood to do so – that I knew of – was David and Margaret Rowland's mum from Queen Street. These days lots of mums ride bikes.

Mum and Dad encouraged our appreciation of music and art. Youthful obsessions with Elvis and The Beatles were taken lightly. Not so the Rolling Stones. Ollie had violin lessons as well as piano. Mum was a talented amateur painter. We still have some of her work. Dad played the trumpet – badly! Both parents read like fiends. Mum until her eyesight failed her, at which time she gave herself over to recalling poetry learnt in her youth and creating her own which she committed to memory.

She had simple tastes and indeed was an uncomplicated person. She had the strength of character to be herself. Children sometimes want their parents to be something else and Mum never succumbed to this notion.

In 1967 we moved to Burnside to a new house our parents built on Greenhill Road. Mum set about making this our new home. Years after she died we found her account book from that building project. Architect fees, foundations, Tasmanian oak floor. Everything accounted to the last cent.

Dad died suddenly in May 1968 on my brother Ollie's 15th birthday. Mum was devastated but stoic, she was only 58. In 1969 I married Gary Lockwood, a police cadet from a family of police. Ollie was still at school and quite a handful. His and Dad's relationship had never been easy. Dad could be emotionally distant and Ollie felt this more as a boy. Ever the rebellious type, he often got into scrapes just to get Dad's attention. We now think Dad's 'distance' was his armour. He had already lost three sons and did not want to lose another. Mum understood this and protected both. Her relationship with Dad was unique – we never saw them argue as mostly they were on the same page.

Both Ollie and I have given Mum a few anxious moments. I married at 18. She was accepting but not thrilled. I had my first child and suddenly all was well. Mum doted on baby Simon, then Scott and my twins Jason and Grant. Before I married, Ollie and I had to be confirmed. We were confirmed in St Stephen's in Wakefield Street and had a huge party at Estonian House with all our confirmation classmates, friends and family.

Ollie finished high school and went on to the South Australian School of Art and Western Teacher's College. With Dad gone he discovered 'The Age of Aquarius' – his excuse, it was the 70s – even the clothes were out there. He then spent three-and-a-half years teaching high school, and several years as a globetrotting party boy (shades of Dad). He studied languages and anthropology at Adelaide University for a year, working weekends at the original Toucan Club in King William Road, Hyde Park; absolutely *the* scene in Adelaide then. Mum's relief was palpable when he finally settled (at 35,000 feet) into a corporate travel management and airline-marketing career. (Air France, Finnair, TWA, Lan Chile …)

Family life can be a roller-coaster ride. Mum understood that. She loved us all deeply. Her children and grandchildren. She was much loved in return. All the grandchildren call her Meme (granny). My mother-in-law Jean Lockwood adored her.

In 1974 she moved to Stonyfell Road, Wattle Park, where she lived in virtual seclusion until her death in 2000 aged 90. She walked every day through Ferguson Park to the new house my husband and I built in the mid 80s in Stonyfell. If I was working Mum was always there when my boys came home from school and she had long talks with Simon about world history.

Apart from quick trips to Melbourne and Sydney she didn't venture much outside The City of Burnside. In 1981 she made an exception. Ollie travelled around the world with her to visit her sisters in Sweden and Canada, and my godmother Keete in the UK. Estonia – still under Soviet rule – was on the itinerary. At Stockholm airport she refused to board the plane. Her fear of 'Reds' still strong despite Maret, Robin and their boys having visited Estonia in the early 70s (admittedly travelling on diplomatic passports, as Robin had at that time been appointed to a position in the South Australian Agent-General's Office in London).

My mother was a deeply private person. She shared her thoughts with her children and grandchildren and with a few long-term friends. Her love of nature was a spiritual thing. She often said that life in Adelaide was blessed and we all lived here by the grace of God. She was a believer, not in a God held up to us by religion, but in a creator, and in creation itself.

I have known her to be angry, stubborn, disappointed and displeased. But I have never heard her speak ill of anyone. She used to say, 'I have never met a bad person.' Extraordinary, considering her life's journey.

I like to tell the story of 'the cat'. As cats do, it appeared one day and stayed for over 10 years. Mum had a curious relationship with pets. She liked them but they were animals and did not belong in the house. The cat would often try to slip past the door police and when discovered, was always repelled with a stamp of the foot and a clipped 'get out'. However, she was often in a hurry to get home to feed it. The cat would rarely leave her side in the garden. They spent hours together and were great companions.

My mother remained involved with her family to the last. At 90 she could be forgiven for slowing down. She passed away quietly just after midnight on 26 May 2000. In those last hours she shared her love in the most reassuring and motherly way.

Ollie recalls the day we attended to her funeral arrangements. Later in the day he went to the Central Market. While at a fruit stall a woman tugged his sleeve. At first he did not recognise her. She had been one of the nursing staff during a brief period in respite care. She said the staff had just been talking about Mum as the plant we had given them as a thank you, had flourished and just flowered. 'Your mother is such a lovely lady, we all liked her, how is she?' Ollie had to tell her Mum had just passed away and thanked her sincerely for stopping to talk. Mum's ashes are next to Dad's in the Centennial Park Rose Garden.

My mum was brave, beautiful, intelligent and profoundly human. I am happy to share her story here, amongst those of my classmates' mothers (and fathers).

She made it to mothers' club after all.

Beetroot Salad (Rosolje)

The recipe is for beetroot salad, which we called Rosolje. It varies among the north Europeans – it is made differently by the Swedes, Russians, Latvians and, of course, my family who are Estonian.

Serves 12

10 medium potatoes boiled in skin, allowed to cool, then peeled and diced

3–4 dill cucumbers, diced

450 grams roast beef diced (veal is okay, if you can get it) – optional

1–2 apples, cubed

2–3 cooked beets, diced

2 boiled eggs, diced

1 herring

Soak herring overnight in water or milk. Remove skin and bones and dice. Mix all the diced ingredients and pour the dressing over the salad – chill and decorate with parsley.

Dressing: 2 cups sour cream, 1 teaspoon vinegar, 1 teaspoon mustard, 1 teaspoon salt and ¼ teaspoon pepper; a little sugar can be sprinkled in.

Second dressing: 200 grams sour cream, 200 grams egg salad mayonnaise, 2 tablespoons horseradish (Newman's), 2 tablespoons mustard, salt and pepper.

Helene Sarap Lockwood

After completing primary school at Linden Park, Helene attended Adelaide Technical High School and Unley High School. She commenced a secretarial career in the State Public Service in 1968 with her first position as a shorthand typist for the South Australian Police Department, attached to the Police Commissioner's office. She went on to transfer to many departments as a secretary to high profile people, including the Deputy Premier's office, Premier's office, and Supreme Court. She was also invited to interview for a position with the Governor of South Australia. When her son Scott was diagnosed as an insulin-dependent diabetic at the age of 14 she retired from the Public Service and worked in a family business as this gave her the flexibility to educate the family on how to live with a diabetic in the family. When the family business closed Helene began working as a casual temp for various employment agencies. During this time her eldest son completed his medical degree at Adelaide University. He commenced general practice in Roxby Downs and Helene has spent several years assisting in his practice. In July 2014 she returned to live in North Adelaide. Two of her other sons also live in Roxby Downs with the youngest living in Kadina. She has been fortunate to have travelled the world extensively. Those trips away to different destinations were sometimes solo, with her brother Ollie, her in-laws, her own boys and her friend Sandy Harrison. In fact Sandy and Helene are still travelling on great adventures together.

Helene's sister Maret is now retired and living in Linden Park and brother Ollie is also retired currently and living in the former Stationmaster's Residence in Clare. Helene has nine grandchildren. Her greatest pleasures are spending time with them. She enjoys interior design, renovating, reading, travel, music and gardening.

Gudrun STROKOWSKY

née Birgden

(1922–2012)

Michael Strokowsky

It is the summer of 1937, and the sun glitters off the fast flowing water of the Rhine River as three girls cycle along the banks of one of the major waterways of Europe. They include a tall blonde girl who is to be my mama. They were on an epic cycling tour 400 kilometres up the Rhine, from their hometown to the junction with the Main River.

Mama was born in Remscheid, Germany, on 4 February 1922. On a clear day she could see the spires of the Cologne Cathedral 40 kilometres away from the attic window at home. She had an elder sister, and a brother who was born in 1927. Germany was in turmoil after World War One and things got much worse in 1929, after what the world later called the great stock market crash and the beginning of the Great Depression.

Mama's father lost his job, and with a young family to support and a home mortgage to manage, it was only due to the support of his mother, who had savings, that it survived together until my grandfather was able to return to work in 1933.By the late 1930s the Birgdens had survived and begun to prosper. In 1937 Mama and two school friends undertook that bicycle trip from Remscheid for 400 kilometres upstream on the Rhine River. In August 1939 the family was on holiday on the Baltic Sea when they saw troop movements heading east, and decided to cut their vacation short as they feared war would again break out, and they might not be able to obtain fuel to get home. On 1 September Germany invaded Poland.

Mama completed her matriculation in 1940, and was required to undertake a year of compulsory duty similar to the British Land Army, working in the fields planting and sowing crops. After her discharge, she went on to Technical College in Wiesbaden, where she studied as a chemical technologist. In 1943 she started work in a laboratory in Trosberg, southern Germany, not far from Munich.

In mid-1944 a young Russian born in Vilna (now Vilnius) was walking down a street in Trosberg with a friend. He saw Gudrun walking past him, and said to his friend, 'If she turns around I will marry her.' She did, and on 14 April 1947 John and Gudrun married in the Russian Orthodox Church in Marburg, West Germany, where John had started studying at the university. They were married a second time in a civil ceremony (to comply with German law) in Remscheid on 7 May 1947.

There was a final twist to my mother's experience during the war. She was conscripted into the military in December 1944, and was posted to Berchtesgarten in Bavaria as a switchboard operator at the airstrip used by Hitler. With the arrival of the American forces at Berchtesgarten, she stole the curtains from the office at the airport, and later made two dresses, one for herself and one for her elder sister, from the curtain materials.

By 1948 it looked very much as though another war could break out in Europe. My Mama had lost her German citizenship when she married John, who was classified as a stateless person. Accordingly they decided to get away from Europe, and Australia was the only country which would accept married couples as immigrants. They boarded the SS *Goya* in Genoa after spending three months in a transient camp, and arrived on the first migrant ship to travel directly to Adelaide on 7 May 1949 (coincidentally their civil wedding anniversary). They were greeted at Outer Harbour by the then Immigration Minister, Arthur Calwell, and then sent by train to the Woodside Army Camp, which was being set up as a migrant camp.

Mama was already pregnant with me. She had concealed her pregnancy from immigration officials for fear that it might jeopardise her departure. My dad, who had trained as a microbiologist in Germany, was given his first job in Australia – cutting firewood (with an axe) for the camp kitchen. I was born at Woodside hospital on Melbourne Cup Day, and it snowed in the Adelaide Hills on that day. By then my dad had been sent to Woodville to work on the Holden assembly plant, and Mama and I moved to a basement cellar in Parkside. There was a severe housing shortage in Australia, together with continued rationing of essential foodstuffs, and life in that cellar became even more difficult when my parents sponsored Mama's younger brother to migrate to Australia from Argentina. Papa had a part-time job on weekends to do photography for weddings and social events, and he borrowed the money from his boss to pay for my uncle's fare from Buenos Aires to Adelaide. He arrived in Adelaide on my first birthday.

By 1953 Mama and Papa had built a cement block home in Woodville Gardens (with my uncle's help) and the family had grown with the addition of the first daughter. Within 18 months my parents sold that home, used the proceeds to buy a block of land in Duncan Road, Beaumont, and moved into rental housing on Military Road, Semaphore. Mama collected threepenny and sixpenny pieces in a jar, and when it was full she had saved enough to arrange for a Klepper tent to be sent by her parents. This tent was the height of luxury for Australia in the 1950s; it had an in-built rubberised floor, mosquito-proof windows and a fully sealed door. No snakes or creepy crawlies in our tent!

I started my schooling at Largs Bay Primary. I spoke hardly any English, as the language at home was German. A second girl was born in 1956, and by 1958 we moved into the house that my parents had built in Beaumont. Like so many of my classmates, we found ourselves living in the area because of the quality of the schools available, not just Linden Park Primary School, but also Unley High School.

Mama's father had died in Germany in 1963, and later that year her mother came to visit. It was the first time they had seen each other since Christmas 1948. She spent about three months in Australia visiting both our family and that of Mama's brother, who had also settled in Adelaide. Grandmother never came to Australia again, but over the subsequent decades Mama's elder sister, who had never married, visited on many occasions, sometimes to commemorate noteworthy occasions such as birthdays and anniversaries, and Mama was able to visit family in Germany on several occasions.

I was enrolled at Linden Park Primary School, with my little sister, in September 1958. This was the start of 15 continuous years of Strokowskys at the school, as the last of my sisters was born in 1960. Mama started to volunteer at the school canteen in the 1960s. She took out Australian citizenship in 1961 (I can remember attending her citizenship ceremony at the Burnside Town Hall); Papa had taken out his citizenship as soon as he became eligible in 1952.

Life in Beaumont was good. Papa had a steady job as a salesman with a pharmaceutical company, travelling all over South Australia and western Victoria. The job included a new Holden car every three years, so we were able to go on camping holidays in our Klepper tent to the Flinders Ranges in spring, and travelled extensively throughout South Australia. Mama provided a stable home for her four children, and relished her stay-at-home status. In the late 1960s, while volunteering at the Linden Park Primary School canteen, she came across a school jumper with my name sewn into the back, which I had obviously lost at school about eight years previously. That jumper had been through several other hands before it finally came back to one of my siblings.

Social life revolved around friends coming to dinner parties at home, and the Strokowsky family visiting those friends at home. We did not go out to restaurants, firstly because they were too expensive, but also because the food and drink available did not suit my parents' palates. We ate Russian and German dishes such as raw herring, salami and sauerkraut, and drank vodka, coffee liqueur, eggnog and schnapps. Parties went well into the night with music a feature, including light classical and Russian folk. Papa was choirmaster at the Russian Orthodox Church, and so we often went to church either on Saturday night or Sunday morning. Mama always came, although she spoke no Russian and had grown up in the Lutheran Church.

When my sister and I finally left home in 1970, Papa took the leap and went into business for himself. Mama undertook some business training, and joined Papa in running an import/export business selling abalone shell to South Korea for manufacture into jewellery boxes and inlay on musical instruments. She and Papa then expanded into the manufacture of sheepskin products (seat covers, ugg boots etc.), and eventually Papa set up an interpreter and translating business. As a speaker of numerous European languages, including English, German, Russian and Polish amongst others, and using his extensive contacts in the migrant community of Adelaide, he was able to offer translation and interpretation services to the business, legal and medical professions. Mama did the office and coordination functions of a thriving business.

Mama was never a great cook. In the early years she did the best she could with the ingredients that were available. Shortages and rationing were a problem, and wild kangaroo, rabbit and hare (the product of many hunting trips north of Morgan) and mutton were common staples. Kangaroo-tail soup, rabbit stew and baked hare were considered delicacies at home. No meal was considered complete without potatoes, usually boiled. Mama was a great cook when it came to cakes. She had brought many recipes from home for tortes and cakes, and these have become legendary within the family as my sisters and my wife have taken these recipes over and continued a tradition for the family.

Eventually, in the mid 1990s, Mama and Papa decided to retire. The Beaumont house, or more particularly the huge block of land, became too much to manage, so they sold after almost 40 years in the home which had seen four children grow up in their own version of paradise. They moved to a townhouse only 50 metres from my middle sister in Magill, and spent another seven years there until Papa was diagnosed with Alzheimer's disease. At this point Mama and Papa moved into a retirement village in Paradise. They had a little two-bedroom self-contained independent-living unit, but within 12 months Papa was admitted to a nursing home. For the next three years Mama would travel daily to visit Papa, at first driving herself, but eventually as she became less confident in her ability to drive, she travelled by taxi. In 2005 Papa eventually passed away. They had been happily married for 58 years.

By 2009 Mama was no longer able to look after herself properly, and she moved out of her little unit into supported accommodation in the nursing home. In February 2012, the family gathered together to celebrate Mama's 90th birthday. Present were her four children, three of four grandchildren, and one great-grandchild. She had just become a great-great-grandmother, and did get to see photographs of Lilliana, who had been born only a few months earlier in Cooma.

Three weeks later, on leap year day, 29 February 2012, Mama passed away peacefully in her sleep. She is buried in the Russian Orthodox section of Dudley Park Cemetery, with Papa. Although she was baptised as a Lutheran, she had attended the Russian Orthodox Church from the time of her marriage, and her funeral service was conducted by the same Orthodox priest who had buried Papa seven years earlier. She had picked out the headstone and the inscription. It includes the words 'Ruhe in Frieden'; 'Rest in Peace'.

Michael Strokowsky

Michael Strokowsky was born on Melbourne Cup Day at Woodside, and in the Russian tradition was christened Mikhail Ivanovich Strokowsky, and known by the family as Mischa. He is the eldest of four children, with three younger sisters, Marina, Barbara and Tatiana, who all went to Linden Park Primary School and then Unley High. He spent his youth playing in the Adelaide foothills, hiking through Waterfall Gully and Mount Lofty. Shortly after enrolling at Linden Park he commenced studying the violin, initially under the tutelage of Mrs Roselaar, a teacher at Linden Park. He went on to spend a decade studying at the Elder Conservatorium of Music, where he also took up the viola.

In 1970 he moved to Alice Springs, where he joined the Commonwealth Public Service, and in 1975 married Helyn. They moved to Canberra in 1978, and in 1986 he was appointed as New South Wales State Director of Aboriginal Affairs for two years.

He was self-employed for a number of years in Canberra, and spent six years as a political advisor in the Australian Capital Territory Legislative Assembly. In 2007 Michael and Helyn retired, and moved back to Adelaide to be closer to his mother and siblings. Helyn got bored with retirement (mainly because Michael kept going away on fishing trips), so she went back to teaching.

He now spends his time between Adelaide and the Mid North of South Australia. Michael and Helyn enjoy music and travel, having travelled extensively through Africa, Europe, North America, Asia and the Pacific. Michael also goes fishing regularly, particularly the Snowy Mountains (for trout), the gulf country of the Gulf of Carpentaria (for barramundi) and the Coral Sea (for giant trevally). He has also fished in Alaska, Florida and Fiji.

Homemakers

Iris May COREY

née Sullivan

(1924–2007)

Di Corey Skull

My mother, Iris May Sullivan, was born on 16 September 1924 to parents Elsie Mira (née Marr) and Alfred Stanley Sullivan. She was the older of two children born of this marriage. The early years were spent in their home at Leane Avenue, Allenby Gardens. Then tragedy struck the family. Her father died 15 October 1933 aged 39 years when my mum was nine years old – he caught the pneumonic flu from his mother who had died of the same illness three weeks earlier on 25 September 1933. His father Tom recovered and lived until he was 91 years.

There being no safety net with government widow's pensions etc., her mother had to cope the best way that she could and to depend upon family. Her father's death also occurred during the years of the Great Depression, but fortunately he was employed as a carpenter at Lloyd's Timber Mills. So with the income gone, the family home at Allenby Gardens was rented out and the family of three moved to her other grandmother's home.

Her maternal grandmother's name was Elizabeth Constance Marr. Both her grandparents came to South Australia as pioneers in 1839 (Roberts and Smart). She was also a widow from a young age. Her husband owned and operated the general store at Modbury. He fell on iron spikes placed in his back shed to catch rats, and by the time he staggered to the front of his store he had lost a lot of blood and died half an hour later on 8 April 1908, aged 39 years. He left his wife with seven children and another was born after his death. The baby died aged six months. The eldest child Daisy was 14, and Elsie, the second child, was 12. Upon her husband's death the Marr family moved to Walkerville and the store was taken over by another family member.

Elsie, Iris and Harold later moved to live in Walkerville with her mother and Iris attended the Walkerville Primary School in Grades 5 to 7. Elsie ran a milk round for a while assisted by a younger brother, Cecil, still living at home, but he was taking the money and spending it on alcohol. So Elsie took Harold and moved to her elder sister's home (Daisy Smith at Maitland) and did housekeeping for her (they were farmers and were able to help), while Iris remained with her grandmother.

Iris attended Nailsworth Central School for first year high school and then attended Miss Mann's Business College for 12 months. While there she studied shorthand, typing and bookkeeping, and topped the state in the Intermediate typing exam that year. Her first job was at the Friendly Society Medical Association as an office worker aged 15 years; she received 15 shillings a week. She travelled into the city by tram.

War broke out and Iris joined the Liquid Fuel Control Board, a government department controlling petrol rationing. By this time Iris had moved to live with her Aunty Ruby in Broadview as her alcoholic uncle frightened her with his drunkenness. Aunty Ruby was married with one son Keith, and was happy for Iris to stay. Iris loved her Aunty Ruby who lived to over 100 years. Harold moved back from Maitland and lived there too for a time. Iris kept in touch with her mother while they were parted and in the same year that Iris married, her mother married a farmer, Jack Thomas, from Maitland and lived there for many years.

Mum's early life was difficult, having lost her father at a young age and her mother making do with her circumstances as best she could for her family. Her childhood friends and work friends became friends for life. Towards the end of the war Mum worked for the Shell Company, a private firm. Her brother, upon turning 18, enlisted in the RAAF and served some time in Manila.

It was while she worked for the Shell Company that a young man, William Thomas Corey, returned to Adelaide having served for five years with the Australian Army. They met at a dance at the Druid's Hall on North East Road, which still exists today, and I regularly drive past it as I travel into and out of the city. It is a time when I think of Mum.

Iris and Bill were both quiet people and Dad often tells their story. He was introduced to Iris at the dance by a friend who asked Bill if he would walk her home to Broadview. He did this, and then walked back to Gilberton where he lived. On the second occasion he saw her he thought he should ask her to the pictures. It was the Shell Company Annual Ball and she asked Dad to be her partner. On that occasion she wore her gold key brooch (given to her on the occasion of her 21st birthday by her mother) so that Dad could see that she was 'old enough' for him. Dad was 28 at that time, and Mum seven years younger. Mum wanted to be engaged for this Ball so they got engaged, and then Dad suggested that they might as well get married, which they did on 19 October 1946, at Walkerville Methodist Church. As simple as that – no romantic settings etc.

Dad found out some time later that Mum, on arriving home the first night, had declared to her Aunty Ruby, 'I've met the one.'

Things weren't easy after the war. Upon returning home from war service Dad was fortunate to be offered a job with his prewar employer, Powell's butcher shop at St Peters. Upon marriage Mum had to resign as it was the policy at the time. Housing and housing materials were in short supply and they spent the first three years of marriage living with Dad's parents at Gilberton. Their first child,

Don, was born 12 months after their wedding. He received much attention from his doting grandparents during this time.

Dad soon started his own butcher-shop business on Glen Osmond Road, Frewville, which he operated for 25 years. Mum and Dad built a house nearby in Conyngham Street, Frewville, with the help of a war-service loan, and moved there in December 1950 just prior to my birth in February 1951.

Mum, like most others at the time, was a stay-at-home mother, looking after all the family's needs. She loved sewing and knitting and spent many hours making clothes and knitting warm jumpers for my brother and me, and continued to do this for my children. And of course I had to learn sewing and knitting too. I enjoyed knitting, but not the sewing, and so Mum always did my sewing and mending. She made all the curtains in my house when I married.

Mum cooked wholesome meals for the family, which of course included a plentiful supply of good quality meat. It was mostly meat and three vegies, as was traditional fare for our time. It was always followed up with dessert – rice, sago or steam pudding, fruit etc. Never did we eat an evening meal without dessert, a tradition that I did not carry on. When Mum and Dad visited my home in Quorn, Mum would be responsible for dessert, as my abilities were limited. Little cakes, lamingtons, biscuits and log cakes were cooked regularly for lunches and snacks.

I can remember my first day at Linden Park Primary School. It was the day before I turned five and Mum took me to school. I remember lining up with Mum saying yes to bottled milk supplied daily by the government for all children attending school. I drank it in infant school, but refused from Grade 3 on, as the bottles were regularly left in the sun until recess time – obviously no refrigeration provided. Yet I developed a love of milk again in my teenage years.

My brother had started at Linden Park three years earlier, although our neighbour's children went to Glen Osmond Primary School, as that was the only school in the area when their children started school. Mum used to walk me to school in those infant school years, but after that I rode a bike with my friend Bronte who lived nearby, meeting friends along the way.

Our house looked out over Glenunga Oval and this was always used as our playing-field as children. There were buildings there for the local footy club and we were warned regularly by Mum not to use the downstairs toilets and to be ever watchful of strangers. It was instilled in us.

Monday was always washing day and I remember helping load the small Hoover washing machine and then wringing the clothes in the wringer attached before putting them into the cement wash trough for rinsing. Then they would go through another wringer and into the other side of the wash trough where Bluo was added (to whiten and brighten clothes) and wrung again before being put into the cane basket for hanging on the clothes line, originally a line or two strung between two posts before the Hills hoist was purchased. Dad's butcher work shirts were always boiled in the copper to ensure they were white.

On special occasions we attended the Hectorville Drive-In as a family, and the Norwood Swimming Pool when it was hot.

Mum became friends with some of the local ladies and they met regularly at each other's houses each month. Their children attended Linden Park too. We would delight in coming home and finding 'the girls' as Mum called them and leftover afternoon tea at whoever's house it was held. The families included the Cranwell, Laws and Pearson families (Don Cranwell and Margaret Laws were in the Class of 62), and a few others along the way. The Cranwell, Laws and Pearson families remained great friends throughout the years, and their daughters now meet annually for lunch.

My dad had a yacht moored at the Royal South Australian Yacht Squadron for about 25 years. We spent many Sundays there with the Cranwell and Norman families (Dad's crew members on Saturdays). My mother couldn't swim and sailing wasn't her pleasure. The only time she would go out on the boat was with a life-jacket on when the weather was perfectly fine, and she liked the motor going – she was not a fan of sailing.

We had a collie dog called Lassie and Mum cooked meat for her to eat as she thought raw meat wasn't good for her. She was a faithful family pet for many years. When Mum took me to the Parkside picture theatre to see the film *Lassie* she had to take me outside as I cried whenever she was hurt in her adventures; I obviously thought it was my Lassie. I can still remember that day.

Mum was protective of her two children, and I think that was particularly because of her upbringing. Her home was her domain and she spent many hours keeping it looking lovely. Many times I would come home from school and the furniture had been moved or changed in some way. Dad provided balance in that regard as he believed in doing things outside the home and encouraging us in our careers.

Mum would attend open days and sports days at the school, and I think was involved in the Welfare Club (mothers' support group). But Dad was always busy with his business so his involvement in school life was limited.

We regularly drove to Maitland to visit my grandma and Uncle Jack (my step-grandfather) and they stayed with us in Adelaide when they visited. A lot of our social life revolved around visiting Mum and Dad's brothers and sisters, and Sunday drives.

In winter we would all be together in the lounge room with the wood fire. In summer we would sometimes sleep outside on the front lawn during heatwaves. When it became available we installed air-conditioning for summer. A television was purchased a year or so after they began broadcasting in Adelaide. I can remember looking in shop windows and visiting friends before we had our own.

With the advent of supermarkets, business slowed a little and Mum began helping Dad in the butcher shop. She did home deliveries and helped at the counter. I can remember her working in an office for a short period, but although capable, she didn't enjoy it as she always felt her place was in the home tending to her family's needs.

When Dad retired from work he sold his boat and bought a

Melting moments

5 oz, S.R. flour
3 oz. custard pdr.
6 oz. butter
2 oz. icing sugar
vanilla.

cream B. & sugar, add sifted flour, custard pdr. roll in balls and place on greased tray. press with fork. cream tog.with icing sugar & butter

---

Chocolate hedgehog.

½ lb. sweet biscuits plain
4 oz. sugar
4 oz. butter, 1 egg
1 tab. cocoa, 1 cup chopped nuts and fruit.

Add rolled biscuits and cocoa and stir over low heat until blended. Press into well greased tin and leave until cold. Ice with choc. icing and cut into squares.

caravan and they travelled around the state with friends and also as part of a caravan club. They regularly travelled to Quorn to visit and Mum always enjoyed helping me with the children. They were regular visitors at shearing time, Dad helping in the shed and Mum with the food and children. After about five days living in the same house Mum and I were ready to part company, but always looked forward to the next visit in a month or so. She was always available to help my brother with his family.

Mum and Dad made the decision to sell their home in 1994 and spent 13 years together in the Leabrook Lodge Retirement Village. Mum enjoyed the village life and made many friends.

Mum's last five years were a battle with bladder cancer. She had regular cystoscopies after having a kidney removed. We thought it had been contained, but we discovered it had spread and she died within two weeks of receiving that information. She remained at home until that time when she was hospitalised.

Mum is remembered as a good and caring mother whose life revolved around her family.

Melting Moments

5 ounces (150 grams) self-raising flour
3 ounces (90 grams) custard powder
6 ounces (180 grams) butter
2 ounces (60 grams) icing sugar
Vanilla

Cream butter and sugar with a few drops of vanilla. Add sifted flour and custard powder. Roll in balls and place on greased tray. Press with fork and cook in moderate oven.

When cool, join together with icing (mixed icing sugar and extra butter).

Chocolate Hedgehog

½ pound (225 grams) sweet plain biscuits, crushed
4 ounces (120 grams) sugar
4 ounces (120 grams) butter
1 egg
1 tablespoon cocoa
1 cup chopped nuts and fruit

Combine sugar, butter, cocoa in a small saucepan and stir over low heat. Add crushed biscuits, nuts and dried fruit. Stir in the egg.

Press into a well greased tin and leave until cold. Ice with chocolate icing and cut into squares.

Di Corey Skull

Dianne (Di) Corey was born on 9 February 1951 to parents Iris and Bill Corey of Frewville. After attending Linden Park Primary School, Presbyterian Girls' College, and Metropolitan Business College Di graduated from Adelaide Teachers' College as a commercial teacher. She was posted to Quorn Area School (six years) and ended up spending the next 33 years living in the town of Quorn. She married Mark and subsequently had three children, Julia, Michael and Matthew. Although Mark was a train driver with the Commonwealth Railways driving trains in the outback of South Australia, he and Di bought a pastoral property north of Quorn for sheep and cattle grazing, and later a mixed farm closer to Quorn. As well as bringing up children, helping with farm work and being involved in community work, Di worked at Caritas College in Port Augusta for three years, then in administration and finance at the Quorn Hospital and Flinders Ranges Council for 11 years. After Mark's death Di sold the property and moved to Adelaide in 2004. After working at Calvary Central Districts Hospital for nearly 10 years Di retired in August 2014.

Margaret Jean COLLETT

née Andrew

(1921–2014)

Andrew Collett

Picture this. A 93-year-old woman sits, slightly listing to port, in her wheelchair struggling with her mobile phone. She eventually finds the appropriate speed-dial number and rings. The phone is answered by a 92-year-old woman.

'Are you there, dear?' they both say.

This is Peg Collett maintaining her 86-year friendship with Jean Abernathy Woodhouse Crompton, the first girl she befriended at PGC – in 1927. (Presbyterian Girls' College in Glen Osmond is now known as Seymour College.)

From 1927, Peg Andrew, as my mother was then known, and Jean went through PGC together as best friends, studied subjects at Adelaide University together, spent the war years together in Adelaide, were bridesmaids for each other, godparents to each other's children, went on holidays with their families at a shared beach house for decades, shared the trials and tribulations of their children and consoled each other after their husbands died following long and happy marriages.

They both came to PGC from Protestant middle-class suburban Adelaide families. Jean was not Presbyterian. The Crompton family were Unitarians from the middle of England who worshipped at the Unitarian Meeting House in Adelaide.

Peg Andrew was from a Scottish family. Her father's father had settled, after a time in Broken Hill, in Goodwood and was a pillar of the Goodwood Presbyterian Church. Her great-uncle, Adam Andrew, was a celebrated Presbyterian missionary in India. Peg's father, Burns Lyle Andrew, looked after his mother after his father died at 43 – thus exempting him from the horrors of World War One. He subsequently established a successful business as a manufacturer's representative and retailer of radios and became a skilled amateur photographer.

Peg's mother, Clarice Ruby Holmes, was of German stock. Her grandfather, Harry Haucke, had left Military College in Hamburg in the 1870s to migrate to Australia. He changed his name to Holmes and established Holmes' Garage in Plympton.

Peg was born on 10 November 1921 and was brought up in Trevorten Avenue, Glenunga – about 1.5 kilometres from PGC. She was an only child. Her mother was advised to have no further children on medical grounds. All of her schooling was at PGC where she was very happy. She did well academically and excelled at tennis, being selected in the First Tennis squad at the age of 14. In that year her coach wrote of her in the school magazine, the *Black Watch*: *Peggy Andrew; Has improved very much. Strong service and forehand drive, but there is still room for further improvement in her backhand.*

Peg was fortunate to have been able to stay at PGC during the Depression whilst a number of her school friends had to be removed on financial grounds. Peg formed strong friendships at PGC, which, like her friendship with Jean Crompton, continued until she died.

In 1936 when she was 15, Peg left PGC to study at the South Australian School of Art where she studied under the famous South Australian portrait and landscape artist Ivor Hele. She also studied dress design and made and exhibited a rather elegant but rakish dress in the Royal Adelaide Show. This period nurtured a lifelong interest in art and design and fostered her talent as a watercolour painter.

After the School of Art, Peg worked as a dental nurse and studied at Miss Mann's Typing School. Having qualified as a typiste, she obtained a job as a secretary at Goldsborough Mort and Co., one of South Australia's leading stock and station agents. Peg worked at Goldsborough's for the rest of the war and until she was married. During the war she managed her department whilst the male staff was at war.

In wartime she and a close group of ex-PGC friends performed voluntary work providing entertainment for troops who were visiting or home on leave. The group was not beyond travelling to Mildura and Mount Gambier to provide companionship to troops stationed there – or was it to check out the most eligible men?

Peg met George Collett in 1949. They married in October of that year and had their first child (me) in 1950. My sister Diana came along in 1955. They built a house in Craighill Road, St Georges, as soon as building materials and a builder were available in about 1953. When they started building, there were few houses in the street but rapidly the street filled with homes for young families whose children went to Linden Park. Our street alone accounted for Rob McConville, Rick Frolich and Michael Kryvoviaza.

Life was not easy for a young mother in St Georges in the early 1950s. Many families, including ours, did not have a car making shopping and getting young children to kindergarten and school difficult. Fortunately the baker and the milkman delivered door to door – in the 1950s in horse-drawn vans.

I can vividly remember our first car – a two-door green Morris Minor. Three years later Dad traded up – to a four-door green Morris Minor! I can also remember Mum getting her licence to drive a car (and a truck). It only involved her filling in a form at the local police station whilst we waited outside. This may have explained her less than confident driving for the next 25 years. Fortunately the truck part of the licence was never put to the test.

Mum and Dad stayed in the house in Craighill Road until the 1990s – long after my sister and I had left to go into student houses. Originally, the house had only two bedrooms but renovations in 1957, after my sister was born, and again in 1967 made it a comfortable three-bedroom home with an upstairs lounge and work area for Mum. The renovations were planned and superbly furnished by Mum where her interest in design and Danish furniture came to the fore.

The 50s and 60s were times of strong neighbourhood friendships. People generally did not move from St Georges and they helped each other to create gardens, tennis courts and amusements for the children.

Craighill Road, being quite steep, was excellent for soapbox carts made by Harold McConville and Dad. We would start a fast (and dangerous) race down Craighill Road and across two side streets from Rick Frolich's house and often end by crashing out of control into the McConvilles' front wall at the bend in the road. Mum and Pat McConville did more than their fair share of patching up cuts and grazes and tending to gravel rash.

It was a time when there were no concerns that children would be abused or abducted. Rob McConville and I were allowed to roam free in the foothills above Craighill Road where there was an old biplane in Professor Cleland's olive grove and old silver, lead and zinc mines dotting Mount Osmond. We relished the freedom our mothers allowed us. Mum and her fellow mothers, including Pat McConville, Greta Frolich and Rosemary Michell, formed a formidable support network for each other – marked, not infrequently, by brandies at five.

As we grew into our teens, a beach house was found. Mum's parents had a beach house right on the cliffs at Port Noarlunga (where I caught my first fish) but after an Easter at Port Willunga with the Jeffries (Jean Crompton's family) and the Rossiters, Mum's father sold Port Noarlunga and purchased a beach house for the family at Port Willunga.

Port Willunga then became the focus of joint holidays with the

Jeffries and Rossiters for the next 15 years at Easter, Christmas and the other school holidays. This beach house saw Mum at her happiest, with her best friend Jean and her family at a wonderful, relaxed and safe beach. Mum and Jean did not swim much, but they took great pleasure in their husbands fishing from a boat out in the bay, their children enjoying the surf, and in the landscape of Ivor Hele and the history of the Willunga region.

Mum was an assiduous parent. Like most mothers of that era, she did not work after she married Dad and so was always there for us. She would not have had it any other way. She was there to facilitate play and interaction with grandparents, support our sporting and extra-school activities and encourage and supervise homework. She set high standards for Diana and me and never wavered from them. It was made clear that we were expected to do well at school, to try our best at sport and to go to university. Mum would always come to support my sporting efforts – including long after I left Linden Park. When I was 15 and played cricket against the youngest of the famous Chappell brothers, Mum found a way to get Trevor Chappell's mother to impart her secrets as to how to get grass stains from cricket whites.

Diana and I took for granted the always washed, ironed and laid out school and sports clothes, the sewn-on badges, numbers and house colours, the dinners cooked and carefully kept in foil in the oven after late lectures and all the university essays lovingly typed.

Great care had been taken by Mum to get us to the best schools within my parents' finances. It had been decided early on that they would not be able to send me to St Peter's College, where my father had gone. So I was booked in to Pulteney Grammar School. However, when I was in Grade 7, Mum suggested that I sit the St Peter's entrance exam to gain some experience for the Pulteney exam later in the year. As it turned out, I was offered a Headmaster's bursary to St Peter's – despite my abject ignorance of all matters Anglican.

Mum was very keen that Diana go to PGC for the whole of her schooling as she had. The family finances could not run to this but Mum's father was asked to assist – and gladly did. The expenditure was considered well worth it with Diana in due course becoming a Prefect and Clan Chief of Clan Cameron – Mum's old clan.

At the same time, Mum was asked to play a key role for the school. Since leaving PGC she had been very active in the Old Collegians' Association (President 1959–1961 and representative on the PGC Council of Governors 1962–1967) and later the Parents' and Friends' Association (President 1971–1973).

In the late 1960s the Chairman of Council asked Mum to write the history of PGC for its 50-year anniversary in 1972. This was a very daunting task for her. She had never written a book before and her involvement in public life had been confined to PGC associations and a public speaking club known as 'Penguins'. However, she took to the task with determination and great enjoyment. After years of researching the archives and minutes of the school, of contacting and interviewing former principals, teachers and Council members she produced a meticulous history. As much as she enjoyed the research and the writing, she loved the historical analysis and the resultant friendships with the school principals and Council members. Later she compiled a further volume, *A Handbook of Historical Notes to Celebrate the School's 60th Anniversary 1982*.

Unlike those of many of her peers, Mum's culinary skills did not qualify her for gold, silver or, indeed, bronze medals. Luckily, Dad was a great cook – a legacy of knocking about with the Chinese cook on the merchant navy ship on which he spent the war. As a result, the combination of Dad's huge vegetable garden and his cooking had us eating fresh, healthy and sometimes exotic food as we grew up.

It was something of a relief when Mum completely retired from cooking in 1970. However, before she retired she had developed an expertise in one particular dessert. It was something of a necessity as Dad did not have a sweet tooth and had learnt nothing about the art of Australian dessert or cake making from the Chinese cook. So Mum had to master at least one dessert for special occasions. It was called 'Coffee Cream'. We always knew we were going to get it for dessert when we had guests and, miraculously, it was great. The recipe is attached.

Like all of her contemporaries, Mum had not travelled overseas until after Diana and I left home – unlike Dad who had seen much of the world as a merchant mariner during the war. From the early 1970s, Mum and Dad travelled a lot – often with their dear friend Kath Carter – to the British Isles, the Channel Islands, Europe, America, South Africa and New Zealand. Horizons were expanded, great art museums absorbed, many overseas friends were made and some wartime friendships renewed.

Towards the end of Dad's working career Mum helped as his bookkeeper. Before Dad retired they sold the beach house at Port Willunga to me and bought a vacant block on the esplanade. Mum said that after 26 years the novelty had worn off the outside toilet and promptly designed a two-storey beach house flush with inside toilets. In retirement Dad and Mum saw the new beach house built and spent increasing amounts of time out of the city down at Port Willunga – when not enjoying the company of Diana's two young children Yvan and Christie.

Mum and Dad were admitted to the Kirkholme Retirement Home in 2008 after Mum had suffered two falls during that year as a result of advancing degenerative deterioration of her spine. This came as a great blow to someone who had played tennis until well into her 70s. By the time she returned from hospital and rehabilitation from her falls, Dad's advancing Alzheimer's disease rendered him unable to care for her.

They adjusted well to life in Kirkholme, in the circumstances. Dad, by then, was 84 and Mum 87. They were the only married couple in the home until Dad died in 2013. By then, Mum was confined to a wheelchair.

As a parent, Mum sought to inculcate in us the values instilled in her. These included the importance of strong family ties, great loyalty to friends and family, intellectual rigour, conservatism and upward mobility. She succeeded with most.

Of these, loyalty to her friends was foremost for Mum.

Her story starts and must conclude with her oldest friend Jean. When Peg was about 10, she had one of her very rare arguments with Jean and was found by another girl on the PGC drive in tears. This girl asked her what had happened. Peg explained she had had an argument with Jean Crompton. The girl, trying to console Peg, said, 'Oh well I never liked her anyway.' Peg bristled and snapped back, 'How dare you criticise my dearest friend.' Eighty-six years on, the loyalty and friendship was undiminished.

Peg died at the Kirkholme Aged Care Home on 5 December 2014.

Coffee Cream

1 tin Bear brand evaporated milk (chilled in refrigerator overnight)
½ cup sugar
1 tablespoon gelatin
A dessertspoonful (or a little more) of instant coffee dissolved in very little water.

Beat milk and sprinkle in sugar. Add gelatin dissolved in warm water (not too much water). Mix again with beater, then add coffee powder.

Garnish with nuts, cherries and cream (not in that order).

Andrew Collett

Andrew Collett studied Arts/Law at Adelaide University during the Vietnam War. Consequently he looked for something that combined the practice of law with political activism and established a practice in Aboriginal legal rights, which still keeps him off the streets.

He has lived in the Adelaide square mile since 1975 and carried on his Linden Park sporting pursuits of lacrosse and cricket to university and beyond as well as running some slow marathons far from home. However, his sporting highlight was catching up with his old Linden Park pals Don Cranwell and Phil Higgins to play cricket for Kensington and football for Sturt.

In the 1990s he established a small Shiraz vineyard in McLaren Vale, which produces a palatable antidote to the rigours of the law.

In 2014 Andrew was awarded an AM for significant service to the law, as a supporter of Indigenous legal rights, and through contributions to professional organisations. He is married with two sons.

Peg MITCHELL
née Polkinghorne
(1926–1996)

Terry Mitchell Sleigh

My mother was born Peggy Patricia Polkinghorne, the youngest daughter of Anne and Frank Polkinghorne. Her mother was 40 years old when she was born. They lived in Croydon, South Australia.

She had a brother and two sisters and went to Croydon Primary School. Her father was a stonemason and her mother was very strict and head of the household. She was in awe of her mother, but could still be a rascal as she had an impish nature.

In her early years she went to singing, dancing and elocution lessons with her sister Beryl, and they often performed for various audiences and were quite popular. Her elder sister was a dress-maker and would have made their costumes. Mum was quite the performer, winning many medals. We found 21 of these in later years when emptying Dad's house for sale.

The family used to go for annual holidays to Victor Harbor. Her father liked going to the trots and would give his daughters a halfpenny as a treat, which was a lovely bonus in those days as they were not a wealthy family.

Peg's nickname at school was 'three peas in a pod' due to her initials PPP. I do not know where she went to high school. She worked as a sales assistant in Harris Scarfe, a department store in the city of Adelaide, and I have a lovely portrait of her, a prize for being 'Miss Harris Scarfe' when she was about 17 years of age. She loved to go dancing and even rubbed shoulders with the singer, Bobby Limb.

In the latter part of the war she was an ammunition inspector at Salisbury, checking .303 bullets. She earned 9/6 a week – that's nine shillings and sixpence. She had to give her mother 7/6 for 'board and keep' and the weekly fare for transport was three shillings, leaving her sixpence a week for herself. It was fortunate her elder sister was able to make her clothes!

She met our father, Donald Mitchell of Woodville, at a dance, having been invited by Dad's mother who knew the family. They made a handsome couple. They courted and were married in February 1949. Mum became a chair-side assistant to a dentist Fred Trotter, later to become a close family friend. Dad was studying to be a civil engineer. They lived with Dad's family in Woodville for a while, then Mum's parents' place while they were slowly building their house in Hazelwood Park. They'd bought a corner block for £250; it was covered in olive trees, which of course had to be uprooted. They made the sandstone bricks for the house themselves and each one had to be sun dried. Dad worked for the Harbours Board and studied at night.

Dad had a wartime Harley Davidson motorbike with a sidecar for Mum. On the day I was born, he took her to the Hindmarsh hospital in it with her sitting on a cement bag to avoid the bumps. I was the firstborn child on 24 April 1950. Dad designed the house with a large separate outside laundry complete with an old copper. They moved into it before it was completed as they felt it was time to be independent, and not under the ever watchful eye of Peg's mother. My brothers were born in 1952 and 1954.

I can remember a happy childhood. Dad was definitely the 'boss', strongly supported by Mum. Her weeks seemed to have a strict routine of washing and housework on Mondays, playing tennis on Tuesdays and shopping for groceries on Fridays. She always greeted Dad with a kiss at the door when he arrived home from work and had the meal ready to serve. We ate together in the kitchen. If you had bad manners you had to sit next to Dad.

She wasn't keen on cooking but there was always variety and a tasty homemade slice in our school lunches. Mum loved it if Dad was away for a meal as then we could relax and have tinned spaghetti on toast. It was a treat if we were allowed to have tea on our trays in front of the TV – which we didn't get until I was about 12 years old! It was also a treat for us kids if Dad suggested a barbeque in the backyard when he would cook! He always cooked breakfast on Christmas morning. Every summer we had to help with the odious task of making plum jam from our own plum trees. The cupboards were full of jam and other preserved fruit, from trees in our back garden.

Dad used to play tennis on Saturdays in Toorak Gardens and Mum always had his clothes laid out for him and his shoes cleaned. They were quite social and often got invited to 'well to do' balls, so my wardrobe had a selection of Mum's ball gowns in it. She had beautiful long hair which was always smartly done up in a bun. Mum was a very stylish dresser and I loved to know what she was wearing and with which shoes. I can remember some very snappy, maroon velvet slingbacks with peep-toes.

We did go on lots of outings to the beach or the hills. Dad liked to go off-road and we'd discover all sorts of tracks. We collected all the rocks for the rock wall at the front of our house. We had camping and caravan holidays too that always seemed to have some sort of disaster. We once lost the roof off our hired caravan on the way to Tumby Bay.

Mum packed our school lunches each day except Mondays as no fresh bread was delivered, so our treat was to order from the tuckshop on Portrush Road. We either walked or rode our bikes to school at Linden Park or she might drive us if it rained. She loved it if we offered to make her a cup of tea and if you made her toast it had to be buttered and spread right to the corners.

Mum was mostly a housewife but did have a stint working at Demasius department store as George Demasius was a good friend of Dad's. That is now the site of Burnside Village. She also taught ballet at home for a while but had to give up on her daughter as she just didn't have it!

Dad used to like to entertain at home and would invite friends to dinners with wild duck he had shot himself. Mum would have the dining-room table set days in advance and be well organised. She was quite a planner. You didn't argue with Mum as she was never wrong! Mum had a wonderful laugh and lovely singing voice and it was always good to hear singing about the house.

It is good to reminisce about those early years, though rather hard to remember much detail as now that my father has passed away and Mum's siblings have gone there is no one to ask. I am proud of both my parents and I was brought up to appreciate good manners and thoughtfulness. I think my mother was the most thoughtful person I have known and I thank her for that and try to emulate her.

Christmas Fruit Pudding

2 large cups fresh breadcrumbs (2 slices)
2 large cups mixed dried fruit
1 cup nuts
2 large ripe bananas
1 small cup milk
1 level teaspoon carb soda

Mash bananas with the fruit and bread and mix in the mixed dried fruit. Dissolve carb soda in the milk and mix in well; include nuts. Can add a bit of brandy.

Steam for three hours.

Date Slice

Melt 125 grams butter or margarine. Add 1 cup brown sugar, 1 beaten egg, 1 cup chopped walnuts or pecans, 1 cup chopped dates, 1 cup self-raising flour.

Mix together well and pour into a lined slice tin. Bake for approximately 20 minutes at 160°C.

Nut Loaf

½ cup walnuts
1 cup raisins or sultanas
1 teaspoon carb soda
1 beaten egg
2 tablespoons butter
1 cup sugar
2 cups self-raising flour
1 cup boiling water

Put raisins in bowl with the carb soda, pour in boiling water. Add butter, stir well, then add rest of ingredients.

Bake in 2 lined loaf tins – 200°C for half an hour.

Bola of Beef – Dad's favourite

1.5 kg meat (approx.)

Line a baking dish with foil, then brush with French or Italian dressing.

Sprinkle meat with a packet of French onion soup and 3 tablespoons of red wine. (This recipe might have been later in Mum's life as no packets of soup way back then, pre 1962.)

Fold over foil and bake for approximately 3 hours. You can open up foil to brown for the last half hour.

Great served with baked potatoes, mushroom sauce and green salad.

Terry Mitchell Sleigh

Teresa Anne Mitchell, known as Terry, born 24 April 1950, is the firstborn child to Peg and Don Mitchell. She has two younger brothers, Stephen and Grant, who also attended Linden Park Primary School through Grades 1–7.

She attended St Peter's Collegiate Girls' College and Hales Business College and commenced her nursing training at Royal Adelaide Hospital in 1968, one of the last groups to study in their own time.

In 1971 she left Adelaide to do a theatre course at Royal Perth Hospital. She met her future husband Hamilton in Perth and married in February 1973. Her parents moved to Darwin in 1975 as her father had applied for an engineer's position with Darwin Reconstruction Commission to rebuild Darwin after Cyclone Tracy. As her mother had had a mild stroke, she and Hamilton decided to go to Darwin to be supportive, and 'make their fortune'. She planned to just go for a year or so but has remained ever since …

Terry and Hamilton have two handsome sons, Mitchell and Jason, and new daughter-in-law Katie, all living in Darwin.

Terry worked as a theatre nurse both at Royal Darwin Hospital and Darwin Private Hospital, and retired in February 2014 after 24 years at DPH. She bought her parents' huge house in 1994 and is still finishing it off. Thank goodness Hamilton is a builder.

Terry enjoys the lifestyle of Darwin but tires of the heat and humidity in the 'wet' season so needs plenty of holidays.

Ruth RINDER

née Iverson

(1918–2012)

Greg Rinder

On 27 June 1918, Ruth Iverson was born to parents Henry William and Edith Joyce at St Kilda in Melbourne, Victoria, the second of four children. Her father was a prosperous Collins Street real estate agent and the family, which by 1924 comprised Joyce, Ruth, Marjorie and John, grew up in a range of lovely old homes in and around the seaside suburb of Brighton.

On a number of occasions Ruth fondly recalled travelling up to the Picnic Races at Hanging Rock as a little girl. With her sisters and brother close at hand, the children wandered around the racecourse collecting threepences and sixpences dropped by the punters. The volcanic monoliths of the Hanging Rock did not have the sinister overtones that the movie engendered in those days but by coincidence in later years, Ruth grew to love the haunting pan flute music used throughout the film. Music was to play a major role in Ruth's life.

With the children in their early teens, father Harry decided to lease a stately bayside mansion near St Kilda known as Kooringie, and it was here that Ruth developed another passion, her love for the sea. She was given a small sailing dinghy that she painted red and called the 'blood vessel'. In this tiny boat she sailed around the treacherous Port Phillip Bay with her little dog Rusty, braving the conditions and often arriving home after dark, soaked to the skin. Her parents were often to be seen pacing the windswept shores of the bay, looking out to sea and wondering if they would ever see their daughter again. She always returned safely and those early adventurous days in the salty seaside environment would always hold special memories for Ruth and draw her back to a similar lifestyle later in life.

By the time the children had reached their mid-teens, Harry decided to purchase Moana, a grand old two-storeyed property on Port Philip Bay. Many happy years were spent here in what could best be described as a privileged life, as by now the Iverson name had become one of the most respected real estate firms in Melbourne. Ruth, together with her two sisters, attended the Oberwell Private School for young ladies and though she did not excel academically, she proved to have a natural talent at the piano. She won many awards and reached concert pianist status by her early 20s. Her ability was recognised by a Melbourne-based symphony orchestra and Ruth was invited to join the company for a world tour. She declined as she felt she could not leave her parents for any length of time, a mind-set that was to change in the not-too-distant future.

Ruth spent many happy hours on her Steinway piano and composed some lovely pieces of music, one of which is a hauntingly beautiful piece entitled *Evening*. It was presented to an ABC producer and selected for the main title theme in a mini-series. Her talents were later recognised by a number of eastern suburbs schools for whom she composed the music and lyrics for school songs.

In 1940 brother John joined the Australian Imperial Forces and shipped out to the Middle East where he fought at El Alamein. During the terrible years of World War Two, when the family were constantly concerned for John and about the encroaching Japanese Army, Ruth did a great deal of voluntary work in many fields. One of the roles she enjoyed immensely was with Sister Kenny whose radical cure for polio was daily immersion in the healing salty waters of Port Phillip Bay. Ruth helped to carry the little polio-affected children down into the water and comforted them as the tides washed over their legs and brought relief from the cruel disease.

As brother John battled Rommel's Afrika Korps in Libya, a young man from Maitland, South Australia, was flying missions over Germany with the Royal Australian Air Force. Following the declaration of peace and his discharge from the RAAF, Flight Sergeant Gordon Samuel Rinder decided to take a cruise along the eastern coast of Australia from Sydney to Cairns. It was on this voyage that he met Ruth Iverson and a shipboard romance developed.

Ruth and Gordon were married at St Andrew's Church in Brighton, Victoria, on 11 December 1948, and returned to Adelaide where they lived with Gordon's parents in a large Tudor-style house on Greenhill Road, Toorak Gardens. Their only son Gregory Edward was born on 19 April 1950, and grew up with both parents and grandparents, which was probably more fun for him than it was for Ruth. With Greg at preschool age, Ruth transported him up to Linden Park Junior School each day on the back of her pushbike. It was a quite a climb up the Greenhill and Fullarton roads to the school but she had always loved riding in her younger years and now the exercise paid off.

After working with his father for a number of years, Gordon decided to purchase John Farmer Pty Ltd, a manufacturing business that produced saws for companies such as Black & Decker. With ongoing contracts and now a good income, Gordon and Ruth purchased their first home in 1955, a little stone cottage at Burnell Street, Linden Park. By now Greg was attending Linden Park Primary School and could walk up an adjacent lane rather than being 'donkeyed' by Ruth, which must have been a great relief. It was around this time that Ruth composed the Linden Park School song that was sung on a regular basis at assembly each morning.

This quaint old custom has long since died out though many former Linden Park students will still remember it, I'm sure. The words are reproduced below as they appear on the original manuscript.

> *A Tempo* (Majestically)
>
> To Our School we pledge our Word,
> To bring Honour, Truth and Loyalty –
> We are proud to stand before,
> Our Flag of British Royalty –
> Our Standards high shall far excel,
> All others ever set,
> At work or play we will do well,
> This pledge we shan't forget –
> We'll be ready for the Test,
> Through the years that lay before us,
> To Linden Park, our School that is best,
> We hail in hearty Chorus.

Footnote: they don't write songs like that anymore, something that was recognised by a former student of Linden Park School who requested that the old school song be sung at the 50th anniversary celebrations. His mother had loved the song and he had it played at her funeral service. Ruth was contacted by the headmaster at the time and invited to attend. She told family that she was very proud to be asked but had sadly declined as it had been but a short time since her granddaughter Emily had died tragically.

Ruth and Gordon shared a mutual love of golf, a game they played at Mount Osmond and Royal Adelaide Golf Clubs. Ruth was a member of the Mount Osmond Molla Cup Team of four ladies and was proud to win the Cup on a number of occasions. She and Gordon loved their golfing holidays, especially to the Victoria Golf Club in Melbourne and country courses such as Horsham. By the 1960s Gordon purchased a larger home at Glenunga where his elderly parents came to live after selling their home on Greenhill Road. The Rinders were all together again and stayed that way until

Gordon's parents passed away and son Greg married. By now the house was too large and Ruth and Gordon moved to a smaller property on a Glen Osmond hillside overlooking Adelaide.

Once Gordon sold his business and retired from his working life, he and Ruth decided to move from the city to a beachside property south of Adelaide at Silver Sands on the Fleurieu Peninsula. Once again Ruth was living near the ocean and she and Gordon often walked together for miles along the deserted beaches, played golf at the Willunga Golf Club and explored the local area together. Greg's daughter Emily was a regular visitor and often stayed with her grandparents at their lovely home near the beach. Like her father, Emily attended Linden Park Primary School but would be the last of the Maitland Rinders to do so.

Ruth and Gordon's 'sea change' lifestyle at Silver Sands was brief but extremely happy and fulfilling. Ruth was able to continue her correspondence with Melbourne family members though her parents; eldest sister Joy and brother John had by now passed away. Letters and cards to nieces and nephews were important to her and she never missed a birthday or Christmas. Her habit of sending a $2 note to each of her family's children on birthdays and at Christmas, right up until the note was replaced by a coin, was a quaint custom that all appreciated though by the 1990s not for its monetary value. Ruth did eventually upgrade to a $5 note though by this time most of the children had grown up and the old custom was eventually discontinued!

Within two years of moving to Silver Sands, Gordon developed cancer and passed away after a short time in hospital. Ruth was naturally grief stricken, as they had been married for over 35 years, and could not bring herself to leave their relatively new home as Gordon's ashes had been scattered on a hilltop overlooking Silver Sands. She stayed on for a number of years looking after herself and taking long walks along the lonely beaches with her faithful Labrador Sam. Most things in her life stopped after Gordon's death though she still kept in touch with old friends and loved her fortnightly visits from Greg and granddaughter Emy.

In 1987 Ruth decided that it was time to move back to Adelaide and settled into a townhouse at Fullarton, which proved to be an ideal retirement home. Still active at 79 years of age, she and Sam continued their long walks around Victoria Park and the local area whilst enjoying regular visits from family and friends. The old Steinway piano that she learned to play as a young girl in Melbourne so many years ago was kept in excellent tune and even into her 80s, Ruth still played beautifully. Recitals to friends and family were always fondly remembered though they were by now becoming rare. Ruth's passion for classical music never left her and she continued to play her old piano, often alone, up until she was 90 years of age.

Apart from a trip up the Western Australian coast by ship to Singapore with Gordon and Greg in 1969, Ruth stayed in Australia all her life. She had always loved the Australian bush and made a number of 4WD trips into the outback following her move to the city. At 76 she was sleeping in a swag under the stars with Greg and Emy in the Flinders Ranges, canoeing down the flooded Cooper Creek to Burke and Wills Dig Tree a few years later, and playing Chopin on an ancient piano for a dear friend and a group of shearers in the front bar of the historic old goldfields hotel at Milparinka in outback New South Wales.

In her early 80s Ruth was still fit enough to accompany son Greg, his wife Rosalie, family members and old friends on a number of houseboat trips along the River Murray. These were exciting times that she enjoyed immensely though by now health issues were impacting heavily on her life.

The loss of her faithful dog Sam and most of her friends and family hit her very hard and the tragedy of Emy's death in 1999 had a huge impact on her life, affecting her health and wellbeing in many ways. By her 90th birthday Ruth was taking a substantial amount of medication but was still in good spirits and ready to celebrate the occasion with all of the special people left in her life. It was a truly memorable day and one that Ruth talked about constantly afterwards. Sadly it was also the start of a slow decline in both her mental and physical health that changed her life so much in the next two years.

Just after her 92nd birthday, Ruth was admitted to the Royal Adelaide Hospital for tests and diagnosed with bowel cancer. After a three-hour operation to remove the tumour, followed by another month in hospital, she slowly recovered at the Fullarton Lutheran Home and finally decided to stay at that location. Ruth settled into her new home, a lovely unit overlooking gardens with a wonderful group of carers that she now required on a constant basis.

Ruth's old Steinway piano was relocated to Greg and Rosalie's home and is now being played again after Rosalie decided to take piano lessons. In this way Ruth's tradition has continued but one final link in her long life was about to be fulfilled at Christmas 2011. Eighty-eight years before, Ruth had met a little girl at kindergarten in Melbourne and they had stayed close and dear friends ever since, phoning each other on a weekly basis and exchanging letters and cards for nearly nine decades. Lornie Anthill, now very frail, blind and almost unable to communicate, spoke briefly to Ruth from her son's home in Sydney, New South Wales. The old friends were once again reunited which proved to be a moving experience for them both. It was to be the last time they would speak to each other.

Ruth's health declined further in 2011. She enjoyed simple pleasures now such as sitting in her comfortable recliner that faced out over the garden and, with help, still managed to get down to the dining room for lunch each day. Greg and Rosalie, together with the her few remaining old friends and family visited as often as they could and sometimes shared a little glass of sherry from a decanter hidden away in a cupboard under the sink as alcohol was 'prohibited' on the premises. The spirit was still willing though in her 94th year Ruth was rapidly losing ground.

In November 2012, Ruth contracted a chest infection that spread rapidly. She was transferred to the Royal Adelaide Hospital where X-rays showed that pneumonia had attacked her lungs and she was now battling for life with few prospects for any long-term recovery. Ruth's last days were difficult for her but she fought on bravely for every breath with Greg by her side. Her old heart finally stopped beating at 11.25 am on Thursday 29 November 2012.

All in all, Ruth had led a very happy and eventful life amongst wonderful family and cherished friends. One of her favourite sayings was always directed at Greg and Rosalie on their birthdays, starting at age 50 and going on from there. 'Fifty, why 50 is the old age of youth and the youth of old age!'

Ruth, forever a staunch monarchist, had always informed everyone that she intended to reach her 100th birthday so that she could receive a telegram from the Queen. She fell a little short of her target. Ruth was a proud Australian from the old school with somewhat Victorian values and expectations. In her 94 years she had watched 22 Australian prime ministers come and go and witnessed many world conflicts and changes, a number of which she did not approve of. She loved nature and specifically requested a basic casket in the hope that perhaps one more tree might be saved. Ruth will always be remembered for her strong will, her strength of character, her independence, her sense of humour, her piano recitals, her hot roast dinners, her devotion to Gordon and her family, her long and enduring friendships and last but not least, for being a wonderful loving mother.

Postscript: On the evening of Monday 10 December 2012, Ruth's ashes were scattered by the water's edge within sight of her old home at Silver Sands. As the sun slowly set on a calm and serene south coast landscape that she had often strolled along, the salty waters slowly washed over her mortal remains and returned Ruth to an environment she had been at one with all her life.

Greg Rinder

Gregory Edward Rinder was born on 19 April 1950, the only child of Ruth and Gordon Rinder. He attended Linden Park Primary School and later Prince Alfred College. Greg studied surveying and geological mapping whilst employed by a Canadian mineral exploration company in the late 60s. His work took him to the outback and he has continued to explore the remote vastness of Australia for both work and pleasure ever since. He joined the CSIRO in 1972 and throughout his 40-year career with that organisation, has worked as a cartographer, photographer and graphic artist in the field of communications. During this time Greg was also involved in the hospitality industry as a part-time working partner in two Adelaide-based businesses. Greg's only child Emily, from his first marriage, died tragically in 1999. Fortunately he had met a special lady, following his marriage breakdown, who helped him through an extremely difficult decade. Greg and Rosalie were married in 2000. After accepting early retirement at the age of 55, Greg was given an honorary fellowship with CSIRO and continues to work with that organisation on a contractual basis. He and Rosalie spend much of their free time on their River Murray houseboat with friends and family, touring outback Australia and exploring exotic locations around the world. In their 17 years together they have managed sheep stations in the Flinders Ranges, a country hotel at Mount Mary and a houseboat company on the river. They are making the most of every moment.

Barbara Langdon TOMS

née Parsons

(1921–)

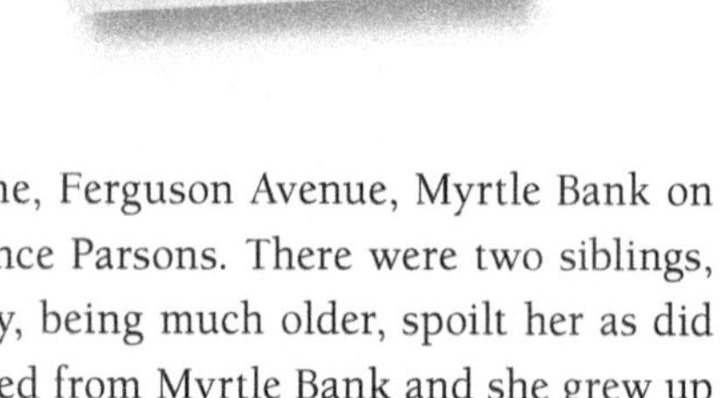

Andrew Toms

My mother was born at home, Ferguson Avenue, Myrtle Bank on 16 July 1921 to Rita and Lance Parsons. There were two siblings, Langdon and Margaret. They, being much older, spoilt her as did her parents. The family moved from Myrtle Bank and she grew up in Leabrook.

My mother married my father, Seymour Toms, on 27 January, 1945 at St Peter's College Chapel. They met on a blind date in 1939 just before war broke out. They corresponded whilst he served overseas with the 2/27th Battalion. When the war ended, it seems that there was a great sense of freedom. Freedom prevailed. People threw caution to the wind. Life became simpler.

I was born on 22 November 1949 and had two siblings, Christopher (now deceased), born July 1947, and Elizabeth, born September 1948. So, I was the third baby boomer born to my parents and a boom and boon I was. We lived with my grandparents at Leabrook until the red-brick postwar home at Linden Avenue,

Hazelwood Park, was completed early in 1950. In that year Linden Park Primary School was built and my mother turned 29.

In those days bread was still delivered by a baker via horse and cart. The 'fish man' delivered via a bicycle with a side-cart containing fish on ice. My father was working at the wool stores at Port Adelaide and left for work early returning around 7 pm. Mum read to us in the evening, and each morning was up and dressed to say goodbye to him before she made our school lunches. Did anyone else have their sandwiches wrapped in vine leaves in the summer to keep them supposedly cool?

My mother initially walked us to Linden Park School, but when the three of us were attending we walked without her. Later we were allowed to ride our bikes. We felt so lucky to have bikes. I have memories of my mother in a floral dress.

In 1952, my mother's parents moved into our house for a year while they were building a house six doors from us on Linden Avenue. My mother did all the cooking 'because she loved them' she said. I was three years old so I probably only remember my mother's story and not the actual facts. At this time, to help out, my grandmother paid for a Mrs King to help my mother clean and iron. This continued into the early 70s.

On 1 March 1954 there was an earthquake that rocked our house. We awoke and were scared. Our mother told us that it was a 'truck going up the street'. One believes, as a kid, what one's mother tells one. And around about this time a circus came to town – on Linden Avenue. We did not go as there was a polio epidemic and my mother would not take us anywhere where there were crowds due to fear of a polio outbreak. My mother says that 'polio was a constant fear' around this time.

My mother, along with my father and thousands of others, helped at Mannum during the floods. This was 1956. My father helped with sandbagging and my mother cooked cakes for the volunteers. We grew a lot of our own fruit and vegetables. My mother preserved a lot of fruit and made pickled onions and jam. My mother was a lover of cheese and pickled onions and, at 93, still is. There was always a large ceramic container of pickled onions for us all to delve into.

My mother accompanied my father to many cocktail parties at the Officers' Club at Keswick Barracks. He was in the Citizen Military Forces (CMF). Apparently the army cooks did their best to outdo each other. They ate *lobster.* There were dances at times. I remember her wearing long evening gowns. Anzac Day was very important. My mother always took us to the Anzac Day march.

Though not a committee person, my mother was involved in the Linden Park School Mothers' Club. She tells a story that she and a friend sat at the back of the room and darned socks! No cups of coffee in those days at meetings; only tea which she did not drink. She made many cakes for school fundraising events and also for the Linden Park Cubs and Scouts. My mother was very proud that my father helped build the Scout Club building.

We went camping to the south coast areas of South Australia and to the South East via Portland. I remember my mother's amazement when she first saw the enormous dump/mining trucks as the port was being built. There were wonderful botanic gardens at Portland which she took us to. It was hot. My mother and father bought us ice-creams and milkshakes – an expense they could not really afford.

My mother's very favourite time was the time spent at Port Willunga. My dad built a house there in the mid 50s. We'd had a lot of camping holidays at the camping ground, so a house called 'The Shack' was the next course of action. My mother coped initially with no electricity or indoor loo, no fridge till the gas one. She made do. Summers were for her and us, sun, sand, salmon and lettuce sandwiches, ham sandwiches from the Christmas ham, fresh fish caught by Bill Howe and whoever was around to help with the catch. She had afternoon siestas. My father would come down on the weekends. My mother felt the holidays had begun when we drove by the vineyards and almond trees.

She loved the winter holidays also and collected wood and pine cones for the wood heater which she also cooked on. She loved playing Chinese checkers and making card houses with us on those cold, rainy days. Then holidays would finish. Back to Linden Avenue and for us, back to school.

Life was not always on an even keel. I told my mother one day that I had been 'making beer in the shed'. She asked what was in it and I said something like 'kerosene and water and … and …' so off to the hospital my mother took me. Oh! Another time I swallowed a key. My mother tipped me upside down and hit me on the back and out came the key, but still a trip to hospital. I have always felt grateful that my mother saved my life.

My mother's life revolved around many things apart from us kids. I do not think that I thought about her hobbies (is that word still used?) or whether she had any, until now. I would say her hobbies were cooking and reading.

So to cooking. I remember my mother's roasts with the cheese cauliflower. Roast lamb with home-made mint sauce and sometimes roast hogget. She cooked curries. She made ice-cream but it never tasted as good as Golden North or Amscol ice-cream. She made pizzas and 'Chinese' food – usually sweet and sour pork. She was a great cake maker and always made our birthday cakes that ranged from Dolly Varden cakes to ocean liners. She made Bombe Alaska, the ice-cream covered in meringue and baked in the oven, sitting on a bed of coffee biscuits. And I remember my mother making Mount Everests. More later.

My parents entertained a lot. The meals were fairly simple but tasty. There would always be the obligatory French onion dip. She made lots of little toasted things in the oven which they ate whilst drinking sherry and hock, which came in a flagon.

My mother received a magazine from the USA, as a gift from her mother, *The Ladies Home Journal* (*LHJ*). She would try these new, and then, innovative, recipes from the magazine. My mother used the *LHJ* recipe for meat loaf. She covered the meat loaf in Heinz tomato soup and flavoured the mince with garlic (fresh). Garlic then would have been considered a bit foreign. The recipe called for sour cream to serve with the tasty meat loaf. One could not buy sour cream so my mother soured the cream with a little lemon juice.

The Mount Everest Dessert is so named because Edmund Hillary had just climbed Everest in 1953.

The Mount Everest Dessert

Take a pear and core it. Place the cored pear in a dish on a bed of whipped cream. Fill the centre of the pear with grated, dark chocolate. Cover the pear with stiffly whipped cream. Sprinkle with grated dark chocolate. (I guess now we would quickly poach the pear in spices and vanilla.)

In 1958 we moved from our red-brick Linden Avenue house to one in Rose Park. There was a cellar filled with the usual preserves etc. We continued to attend Linden Park Primary School. I rode my bike as did Christopher. Elizabeth caught the double-decker bus.

In 1958 the Queen Mother visited Adelaide and my mother was in awe of her.

My mother's mother died in 1958 and she cried a lot. Her father died six months later. This was a very sad time in her life. She was very, very close to her parents. They had always spoilt her being the youngest sibling.

We purchased a television in 1959.

The 60s arrived. My mother went along to see Billy Graham to get some sort of help or enlightenment due to the death of her parents. We had one television set. We had a radiogram. My mother still cooked inventively. She was still an avid reader. We still had idyllic holidays at Port Willunga. My parents still continued to entertain and as kids we had Saturday night low-key get-togethers at our house and my mother would make American doughnuts for us and popcorn! My mother took us to our various sporting activities and as they say today, our car was 'Mum's taxi'.

Life was good. We kids went on to the next level of education. My father was working at Legacy. I realised at this time that although we were wealth-poor we were rich in life until my mother's life changed forever in October 1966 when my brother Christopher was killed in a motor vehicle accident at Middleton along with four of his friends. And then in May the following year my father died.

My mother was inconsolable.

I then joined the army. This made my mother happy and sad at the same time … happy for me but sad for her. I remember her being proud at my Passing-Out Parade at Kapooka.

My mother met a wonderful man a few years later, Harry Wheaton. They were loving companions and friends up until his death in 2005.

Though I married and Elizabeth married and grandchildren came along, there has always been a great sadness and emptiness for her along with a kind of 'Why did God do this?', 'It's just not fair' – and angry feelings came to the fore.

At 93, none of those feelings or words have dissipated … and sadly she has become sadder and lonelier. We still love her. I guess it is not for us to stand on the sidelines and make all sorts of pronouncements about how she could have handled the sad situations. Perhaps we have forgotten an essential truth: there is no appropriate way to react to the worst that life can throw at you. These are sad and happy memories of my mother, the woman with the always red-painted nails and matching lipstick.

(This story of our mother, Barbara Toms, was kindly written by my sister, Elizabeth, who also attended Linden Park Primary School.)

Andrew Toms

Andrew is the youngest of three children, all of whom attended Linden Park Primary School. He was always destined to go to the bush. It is all he ever wanted.

After a short stint at Pulteney Grammar he went to Urrbrae High School. He had his eyes set on being on the land. He left school at 14 and went to work on Lambina Station near Oodnadatta. In 1967 he joined the regular army. He was in the army for eight years. He went to Vietnam on the 27 January 1970 and returned home on 19 August 1971.

With plant equipment experience in Vietnam and discharged from the army at his own request, he was employed by McMahon Construction Company. He worked on road constructions between Nullarbor Roadhouse and Yalata. He then transferred to the Northern Territory and continued on road constructions. In 1977 Andrew went back to the land in the Northern Territory to work on a property. His wife Wendy and two young children went with him. He and Wendy both love the vastness and remoteness of the Australian outback. They eventually moved to Western Australia in 1986 to help run a property.

Andrew is the father of Vanessa, Warren (deceased) and Kate from a previous marriage. He has five grandchildren and one great-grandchild. He is now retired and he and Wendy live 100 kilometres from Esperance on one of the properties owned by his daughter Vanessa and son-in-law Brad.

Andrew just takes life as it is served up to him.

Beatrice (Betty) DYSON

née Webb

(1924–2000)

Susan Dyson Burt

It was only 8.6 miles (14 kilometres) from Croydon to Beaumont. However, as she packed the family's belongings and climbed into the family Holden with her husband and four children, I wonder to what extent she felt she was travelling to a new country, a new world. Most of the furniture would remain behind. Only the 'babies' room' (as she referred to the four- and five-year-olds) would have some recycled pieces.

She had lived all her 34 years in the one suburb: a house, a street, or a few streets from parents, grandparents, great-grand-parent, cousins, aunts, and parents-in-law. She had been a regular attendee of the same church as her parents, her grandparents, and her great-grandmother before them. Even marriage did not change this. Her children attended the very same school and Sunday school as she had done. Four generations of family, social life, and work all entwined; social, status, and gender boundaries clearly defined.

Everyone has a story, something that has shaped them, changed them, or set their path; big, small, captivating, ordinary. While there might be common threads in our stories, 'Every family', says Biff Ward in her book *My Mother's Hands*, 'develops those intimate ways of being, those patterns of connection that no one else really knows about'.

This is part of Betty Dyson's story. Or rather, it is my story of my mother, as I remember it.

Born in the family home in which her mother had lived since she was 14, Betty's arrival made four generations living together, along with an uncle and any other relative in need of a bed. A photograph of the attending midwife handing a beautifully dressed newborn to her maternal grandfather, and another photograph of the midwife with the baby and both grandparents could suggest the patriarchal, matriarchal world into which Betty was born. I wonder…

The story of her name-giving is, perhaps, an illustration of what would be much of her life: living to cultural expectations and as an extension of another.

Born to Beatrice Ivy and Richard James Webb, my mother was never known by her given name. My grandfather wanted desperately to name her after his beloved wife, but Grandma would not have a bar of it. Having chosen to be known by her middle name, Ivy, rather than her first name, Grandma argued that Beatrice was not an appropriate name for their firstborn. Thinking her beloved would not do anything to 'hurt' her, Grandma suggested that Grandpa register the baby and surprise her with the name. Surprised she was! Grandpa registered the name Beatrice. Grandma let him know, in no uncertain terms, that the baby would *never* use the name. Betty, she would be. Her second given name? Betty's grandfather moaned and complained how none had named a child after him. A vowel was added to the end of his name, and Beatrice/ Betty was registered as Beatrice Alfreda.

Newly-weds Ivy and Richard lived with Ivy's parents. They had purchased a block of land but had not yet built their dream home. Betty was born within the first year of their marriage. The Great Depression was closing in, and employment became increasingly difficult for my grandfather. His days were filled seeking work, and as a volunteer firefighter and ambulance officer. It was during the Great Depression my great-grandmother died in 1932. My great-grandfather was a fit and able man, but this was the 1930s and there were clearly defined boundaries for men and women; it fell to my grandmother to maintain hearth and home. My grandparents sold their block of land, and the dream of their home was not realised. The home in which Grandma had lived since she was 14 years of age, 16 Day Terrace, would be their one and only residence.

Mum would say she lived in an adult world with great expectations of perfect behaviour, and knowing her place. Although the house was filled with visitors and family, school friends were not encouraged. Mum told how Grandma often reminded her that it was not their house; they were living there as guests, and should behave accordingly. Grandma and Grandpa eventually inherited the house, as Great-grandfather recognised all they had given up to care for him, but that was after Mum had married.

Talented Betty was studying piano, tap dancing, elocution, and singing by around age five. Talent, she was taught, was a gift to share and not for financial gain. From a very early age, she performed with her father's charity concert troupe. He was a talented baritone. Dancing and singing her way through such songs as 'On the Good Ship Lollipop' and 'Won't You Buy My Pretty Flowers', she was the 'talk of the town'.

There are moments in someone's story when a window opens, and you see a little more than maybe they intended. While Mum would sometimes 'replay' her 'On the Good Ship' routine and tell about her singing and dancing performances, a window was opened during a fundraising concert in the Beaumont Methodist Church hall. We, cheekily, chose to vote with our pennies by throwing them onto the stage – as if they were flowers being thrown to the principal dancer. Mum recoiled and was a little shaken. She told how all those years ago, when singing 'Won't You Buy My Pretty Flowers', people threw pennies at her feet. It was frightening for such a young child.

It seemed that something had to give. Betty shared her bedroom with her great-grandmother, an idiosyncratic Cornish woman who went to bed each night with a candle perched on her chest, and reading either from the Bible or the sermons of John Wesley. The flickering light frightened Betty, but she said nothing. One evening, she knocked over a candle that was burning on the bedside table, and cried out in fear. Her mother rushed into the room and raised her voice; Betty began to shake and twitch. It was the beginning of a nervous breakdown. Betty was only seven- or eight-years-old. Were there lingering effects? Did this episode contribute in any way to her occasional moods?

Tap dancing, piano and singing lessons stopped, but elocution lessons remained. Mum was an exceptionally talented elocutionist. From age six and into her teenage years, she received numerous awards from many Eisteddfod competitions, sometimes two or three awards within one competition. She was in great demand as a guest performer at church concerts, socials, 21sts and weddings. Performing continued late into her life. But true to her upbringing, she did not pursue acting or reciting for financial gain.

Betty was 17 when a handsome 19-year-old moved next door. They would sometimes meet as they walked to their respective churches: Don, to Croydon Methodist; Betty, to the Church of Christ. Betty rather fancied him, so she invited him to partner her at a party. That was it! Mum was 22 when she married the boy next door. As housing was unavailable after the war, she moved next door and lived with Dad's parents for the first two-and-a-half years of marriage. During this time, their first child was born. Dad had set up a manufacturing, engineering business in the backyard garage, worked long hours, and 'came in' for lunch every day! I am sure Mum was available for morning and afternoon tea breaks as well. In order not to give her mother-in-law cause to criticise, she would not venture far from home. A side-gate connected her to her parents, grandfather, and siblings. Did she feel hemmed in, supported, or not supported? I wonder.

Together, Don and Betty purchased land on Torrens Road,

Croydon, just one mile (1.7 kilometres) away, and built, not a home, but a factory! Rooms at the front became the family home, and later the business offices and storerooms. The family laundry and bathroom was shared by the employees, and located to the side of the factory floor. Mum rose at 5 am to complete the clothes washing before the workers arrived. Two more children were born during this time.

I have fond memories of life in and at the factory. Being rocked to sleep by the sound of the automatic lathes that hummed when the swinging door between the kitchen/dining room and the factory flapped open then closed, open then closed. The smell of oil, clean, clean floors where we could ride our bikes when the machines were not running, staff parties, Guy Fawkes, and so on.

With the arrival of their second child, Mum and Dad purchased their first car, a brand new Morris Minor ute. Until then trams, trains, bikes and foot were the modes of transport, with Gaynor being carried in a basket on the back of Dad's bike. Mum, licensed in the days when only a written test was needed, didn't drive, except on the very odd occasions when we were driving on country roads. Mum was, however, the licensed (albeit a non-experienced) driver who accompanied us when we were learner drivers! Without a ride, we often found our own way to netball, tennis, school, and friends' homes.

Ah, the ute. It was a squeeze for two adults, a toddler and a baby, but car safety was loose in those days. Later, we would pile into the back, wrapping blankets around us on colder days. Mum would keep a firm eye on us, and a tap on the window would have us toeing the line again. Such was her ability to control and discipline.

A few weeks before baby number four was born, the family moved to Bedford Street. With only the Croydon High School oval between the house and the factory, Dad could still be home for lunch each day and pop in when need be. It was 1954; 12 years before the infamous 'Beaumont children case'; 'stranger danger' was not part of the vocabulary. When just four, I would run errands to the corner store, which was not on the corner but around the corner, for any last-minute items. On one of my first trips, I turned the wrong way as I left the store and became quite lost. Mum, frantic (and very pregnant), combed the streets before heading to Dad at the factory. Dad was out, but there was I, quietly riding my bike about. I had found my way to Torrens Road, recognised the area, crossed the busy road, and settled into familiar surrounds. By age six, we could find our way to school and Grandma's.

Mum left paid employment when she married, but as a milliner and dressmaker by trade she continued to sew for the family. As youngsters, the two older girls were dressed identically, each outfit complete with a petticoat and frilly apron. The two infants – a boy and a girl – were dressed *almost* identically: a male and female version of the outfit. The pressure of perfection was at play again. She told of the time she had dressed all four but had neglected to drain the bathwater. One fell in the bath, and the saturated clothes had to be changed. Dad was in the car and ready to go; Mum was reduced to tears because there was no time to change two children into matching outfits! Mum continued to make our clothes, up until and including, wedding dresses for her three daughters and their bridesmaids, and a wedding dress for one daughter-in-law. There was a new dress for every Sunday school picnic and every Sunday school anniversary, and hemlines had to be perfectly straight! With my sway back, I had to stand still for what seemed like forever!

Mum was a snappy dresser, as early photos indicate. Dad's company manufactured small parts for Holden cars, and Mum and Dad received an invitation to the prestigious launch of the first Holden car on 3 December 1948 at Centennial Hall. Mum, window-shopping in Rundle Street, spotted a designer dress she quite liked, sketched and replicated it. Approaching the receiving line at Centennial Hall, panic and embarrassment swept over her; the wife of one of the officials was wearing the original of Mum's copy!

Business in the 50s began to boom. During the recovery from the days of the war, household goods were almost unavailable. New cars, washing machines, refrigerators, and building materials were in great demand. Dad won significant contracts with companies such as Simpson Pope and Holden. More labour was needed. Skilled migrants were coming to South Australia, and Dad offered employment to several. With Dad, Mum befriended these 'new Australians'; most were struggling with the English language in a land that was also struggling with such radical change. Lifelong friendships were built.

Mum reflected on those boom times, writing:

For quite a time things were good, even to the extent of working two shifts to get all the work out. But the unions began to flex their muscles and some serious strikes became too frequent. The strikes led to gas and electricity being rationed and only obtainable a few hours a day, or running at night. This prompted a night shift, but that was not the answer to the problems. The next few years were to be a string of ups and downs and recessions. With the push for higher and higher wages, Australia began importing goods produced overseas by cheaper labour. Australian companies could not compete, which meant disaster for many engineering firms. But D.G. Dyson and Co managed to stay in, fighting.

Industry was not the only thing to boom in the 50s. With four children, the two-bedroom bungalow at Bedford Street was stretching at the seams. In January 1959, we moved to a brand-new, three double-bedrooms, triple-fronted, double cream-brick home, on a quarter-acre block on Dashwood Road, Beaumont. Three of us were enrolled at Linden Park Primary School.

Mum's world was changing. From a short commute to the factory for Dad, to a thirty- or forty-minute drive – depending on traffic. From regular contact with each other, to Dad leaving at 6 or 6.30 am and not returning until 6.30 pm. From morning tea, lunch, and afternoon tea conversations, to a short telegram delivered from the post office on Greenhill Road, Burnside. (Before the phone was installed, Dad would send at least one message via telegram a day.) From flat ground to steep inclines, and a quarter-acre bare block in need of landscaping. So much soil to cart! From a network of family and support just streets away, and a cultural and social life developed over four generations, to a need to build a new network of friends. From corner shops, familiar surrounds and contained space, to open space, vistas, no fences or footpaths. From four children to five.

Mum was houseproud and clutter was not tolerated. The kitchen floor was polished every day to a high sheen. She was chuffed with her new house. She would usher family and friends into the back lobby and close all four doors that opened into it, to give the impact of the different pastel colour on each of the doors – coral pink, turquoise, mint green, and lemon. Did she intend them to match her brand new kitchen canisters, proudly displayed on the laminate benchtop? She delighted in the large kitchen window that flooded the kitchen with light and looked out to Mount Osmond, with very little between our property and the foot of the hill. The double sink was a luxury. She gushed about the large picture windows in the dining and lounge rooms, and the French doors in the lounge room that opened to the 'top' patio and a view to the city. 'On a clear day,' she would boast, 'you can see the sea.' Three double-bedrooms, a large block, and no fencing meant space for the children to play, roam, and mingle with neighbourhood children.

Mum adapted to the surroundings easily and well. Church would play a big part in her life: Sunday school teaching, Women's Fellowship, Overseas Aid, community and service work. Linden Park School Mothers' Club was also a place of social interaction. She quickly made friends with neighbours, including the 'tennis girls' who enjoyed what she called a 'hit and giggle' on a neighbour's court. Bread and milk were delivered daily. On Thursday, Bradshaw Grocers collected Mum's written order and delivered it on Friday. I think we thought the delivery boy's name was 'grocer', as that is what he would call at the back door as he opened it and walked in! Mr Vella, the butcher, phoned on Thursday and delivered on Friday. The bus took a direct route to the Port Road, so it was a relatively easy trip to visit her parents, and it was a pleasant and scenic route to the city. Trips to the city were a highlight, a chance to dress up (a hat and gloves were always worn) and enjoy a quiet sandwich and pot of tea at Balfour's Tea Rooms.

Mum was a good cook, but we were mostly a 'meat and three veg family'. Mum cooked for Dad's tastes. A side of lamb each week, some mince, and, occasionally, chicken. There were no snacks between school and the evening meal. So we ate heartily at mealtime. While I loved Mum's roast dinner, I hoped there were no leftovers. Leftovers meant cold lamb sandwiches for school lunches the following day. I still shudder as I remember those lamb sandwiches sitting in a school bag on a warm day! There is a drain on Hay Road that I am sure I blocked with the lamb sandwich lunches I ditched on my way home from school. I developed a pretty good swing; hardly anyone noticed as I disposed of the said sandwiches.

The credit squeeze that led to a slight recession in the early 60s had an impact on D.G. Dyson Pty Ltd (as it was now named), but Dad refused to lay off any of his workers, especially those who had come seeking a new life in South Australia. With diminishing orders and contracts, Dad set about stocking his storeroom with bolts, washers, screws, fasteners – things he expected would be in demand again once the economy improved. Unfortunately, he could not foresee that Australia would soon move to metric measurements, and the stock would be reduced to scrap metal.

This, in turn, affected the household budget, which Mum maintained. It must have been a stressful time. Her housekeeping allowance that needed to meet all household utilities and food, as well as insurance, which she would not neglect, was reduced. Mum managed the budget well and was very creative in stretching the weekly food supplies. Rice pudding and mock fish were a favourite, so we didn't complain if that was on the menu on Thursday night – pay night. Mum maintained our extracurricular activities, elocution, music, singing, art, sport, and money was set aside for education, 21sts and weddings. She planned well. In terms of education: it was to be Methodist Ladies College for the three girls, although our younger sister elected for co-ed and Adelaide Technical School (Glenunga International High School), and Adelaide Technical School for the boys. Their reasoning: the boys were likely to go to university, so their education money would be invested there. These were pre-Whitlam days and university meant fees. I don't think Mum and Dad questioned the girls' ability for further study, rather they assumed we would marry, be stay-at-home wives and mothers, and not continue with a career.

Mum was a strict disciplinarian, making sure we children behaved and performed in ways so as not to embarrass or shame, and showcased family life. There was always the threat of the strap. There were many times when we sensed her anxiety and frustration, and were often at the receiving end of swift and harsh punishment (not unusual for many children raised in the 50s). But there was also laughter, anticipation, times of deep satisfaction – good times. I remember such things as the vision of the laundry cupboard groaning under the weight of summer preserves and apricot jam; sitting or lying on the front lawn on hot summer nights, being cooled by the gully winds and watching/counting stars as a relaxed Mum engaged in conversation; pineapple pie, cream puffs, lemon pie, the best sponge cakes, stew, and vegetable soup made in the trusty old pressure cooker; being trusted with the best dinner set and silverware for special meals; warming ourselves by the gas fire in the best room when we arrived home wet and cold after a winter's walk up the hill; the fragrance of folded and ironed washing airing by the same fire. The rhythm and ritual of the weekly housekeeping would not be compromised. Rain or shine, the washing was always done on Mondays and Thursdays. We swung on the Hills Hoist until the cogs gave way under the weight; we still continued to swing but it was a bumpy ride. There were fun holidays at Pine Point, a relaxed Mum with relaxed rules, evening swims at Black Point and huge bowls of homemade chips made late into the night to fill hungry holidaymakers, and card games while the chips cooked. There was backyard cricket and no reprimand at the sound of breaking glass when the ball hit the louvered toilet windows. Instead, as we prepared to blame the other, we were met with an understanding that these things happen. We jumped through the sprinkler on hot summer days. There were holiday walks from home to the top of Mount Osmond, where we scratched our names on one of the trees there, and waved energetically to Mum who was standing at the back door waving a tea towel in celebration of our achievement. Although, I suspect the encouragement for the adventure could well have been to achieve an hour or two of quiet for herself. We enjoyed the special treat of midday movies while eating lunch during the holidays; holiday picnics with Mum, Grandma, aunt and cousins in the Botanical Gardens. There was freedom to go-cart down Dashwood Road in go-carts without brakes. We rode our bikes unsupervised to Hazelwood Park, and could roam and explore freely, as long as we were home by 5 pm. I remember Mum's sense of humour and her ability to, as Dad would say, not spoil a good story by getting the facts right. She had quite a capacity to exaggerate! She also loved parties to celebrate her important milestones – 40th, 50th, 60th, 70th birthdays, and significant wedding anniversaries.

Mum had health challenges. Thyroid, kidneys, heart, carpal tunnel. She was finally diagnosed with a benign tumour on the pituitary gland. It was found almost by accident and had been there for over 30 years. The doctor suggested this could have been the source of many of her health issues. Never reticent in coming forward, when she discovered Hazel Hawke also had an operation for this little known or diagnosed condition, she wrote an empathetic letter about her own experience. I can't know the content of Mum's letter but, from Ms Hawke's handwritten reply, I wonder what 'help' Mum was offering. Ms Hawke wrote: 'Your kindness in now wanting to help others is something I appreciate very much. You are generous, and typical of the fine community work I am privileged to see around Australia.'

After about 30 years at Beaumont and with the family having married and moved on, it was time for Mum and Dad to move, too. Dad was not as ready as Mum was. 'One day,' Mum would argue, 'you will need to either stop as you drive up Dashwood Road or drive around me. I will have collapsed on the road. I can't walk this hill any longer.' They moved to Clarence Gardens. Mum died in 2000, a year before the birth of her first great-grandchild. A loving grandmother, she was looking forward to being a great-grandmother. 'I am a great-grandmother going to waste,' she would say. She was also hoping, waiting, and planning for the day Dad would retire, and the day when she would not have to deal with machine oil on and in his clothes, but that was not to be. Dad closed his relocated, smaller factory seven years after Mum's death. He was 83 years of age. Now aged 92, he continues to 'turn up' some small jobs for selected customers, having installed a lathe in his shed. Machine oil, it would seem is in his blood.

Mum straddled an era of cultural and social expectations of being diligent in homemaking and housekeeping and the women's liberation movement. Feminist authors and activists challenged so much of what our mothers had devoted their lives to. To what extent did my mother feel her self-identity, self-worth diminished or challenged? Mum defended her role as homemaker and defended herself against what she felt were attacks from the feminist movement, but toward the end of her life she made a comment that I wish I had asked her to explain. 'I feel like I have been held back for most of my life,' she said. I wonder what she would have done differently, and what she wished was different. What window into her life would this discussion have opened? We can only wonder.

Susan Dyson Burt

Susan Burt is the second child and second daughter of Betty and Don Dyson. The family moved from Croydon to Beaumont in January 1959. Susan, and her sisters Gaynor and Judith, were enrolled at Linden Park Primary School. Younger brothers Donald and Raymond also attended. During her childhood and teenage years, Susan was active within the Beaumont Methodist Church, which included various clubs and groups, netball, tennis, and basketball clubs.

Susan went on to study at Methodist Ladies College (now Annesley) and Hales Business College. She worked as a personal assistant until the birth of her first child, Emily. Simon, Anthony and Victoria followed. Susan married Kenneth in 1973. In 1992, Susan was a student again, this time at Flinders University, where she completed a degree in theology. For the past 20 years, Susan has worked as the coordinating editor of an international, ecumenical, lectionary-based Christian education and worship resource, and works for a publishing company in British Columbia, Canada. The work has provided opportunity for much overseas travel.

Susan adores spending time with her growing number of grandchildren.

Dawn CHARLTON

née Edwards

(1923–)

Bryan Charlton

Dawn Charlton was born on 11 April 1923, the second daughter of Muriel and Francis Edwards in the then-thriving mining town of Broken Hill in New South Wales. This followed a family mining tradition going back two generations when her grandparents migrated to Australia from Cornwall, settling in the copper mining town of Moonta on Yorke Peninsula. It was here her mother, Muriel, was born. Her father, Frank, ran a successful grocery store in Broken Hill.

'As a five-year-old I used to visit my father's shop. He would sit me on a stool at the counter next to the Iced VoVo biscuits and I was allowed to indulge in a couple. My father spoiled me as a child,' Dawn recalls.

In the late 1920s, times became hard in Broken Hill. Prolonged strikes by the miners, with their union demanding free groceries from their shop, along with the start of the Great Depression of the early 1930s forced Frank to close his business and the family moved to Adelaide.

They rented a house in Keswick where Dawn and her older sister Avis went to Richmond Public School. Like so many others during the Depression, Frank could not find steady work, finally taking a job as a penciller with a Naracoorte bookmaker in the south-east of the state. Jobs came and went and moving house was a regular occurrence for Dawn and her parents. As the economy improved so did the stability of the Edwards family. They returned to settle for many years in a house on Anzac Highway from where Dawn attended Adelaide High School in Grote Street and forged life-long friendships with girls her age at school and the local church. Her parents were strict Methodists.

'My mother packed my lunch in my leather schoolbag, jam sandwiches were my favourite. I used to keep sweet with a teacher, Mr Roesler, by carrying his bag from the Keswick Railway Station to the Richmond School. I enjoyed playing netball for Keswick Methodist Church, travelling by bicycle to play at churches at Brighton and Croydon,' Dawn says.

Dawn left school after attaining her Intermediate Certificate and worked for Rundle Street grocery wholesaler Gordon Sym Choon shortly before the start of World War Two. During this time, at age 18, she met Leon Charlton, a young police cadet, while out with her girlfriends on a Sunday evening. A romance developed and Dawn reflects on the times Leon, now a mounted police officer, would ride past the Sym Choon shop adjacent to the East End Market on his police grey, Chagomar.

'I would time the cleaning of the shop windows as Leon would come by on his horse on market duty to catch a glimpse of him. During our courtship we would attend the Unley Star picture theatre on Unley Road, regularly sitting in seats D34 and D35. I was very shy and Leon would buy me a box of chocolates and I was afraid to eat them in his company, taking them home and hiding them in my bedroom.'

During the last three years of the war Dawn worked for Tusmore grocer Vernon Ellery at his Greenhill Road shop opposite Devereaux Road. Dawn replaced a man who had gone to war and she received a full male wage, often running the store single-handedly. At this time parents Frank and Muriel bought a home in L'Estrange Street, Glenunga.

'My father obtained a bookmaker's licence at the Tattersalls Club and raised the deposit to buy our first home, a three-bedroom Tudor-style home that remained in the family for 44 years. My first memory of living there was hearing the squealing of pigs being slaughtered in the abattoir across the road. Animal blood flowed down the gutter across from our home. We were glad to see the closure of the abattoir. Of course things got better when the Glenunga Oval and a school were developed on the site.'

After a four-year courtship Dawn married Leon at the Pirie Street Methodist Church on Guy Fawkes Day 1946 followed by a reception at the Arcadia Café, downstairs in King William Street. Returning from their honeymoon in Mount Gambier they settled in a rented maisonette in Fullarton, between Leon's parents' shop and residence on Unley Road and Dawn's parents at Glenunga. Two years later Leon took up a posting as the station officer at the Port Lincoln Police Station. Their home was attached to the station and Port Lincoln Courthouse. Leon conducted police duties in the town and often escorted wage deliveries to rail settlements and government agencies across the dirt roads of Eyre Peninsula. Dawn received a small payment for preparing and serving meals for the prisoners in the adjacent police cells.

'Leon was one of five officers in Port Lincoln and would take me around town in the sidecar of the police motorcycle outfit. Most of the prisoners were locals detained for drunkenness and I would feed them and in return they would clean the windows of the station and courthouse.'

I was born in October 1950 and spent the first two years of my life in Port Lincoln living at the Police Station. Mum's father died late in 1952 and we returned from Port Lincoln and moved into my grandmother's home in Glenunga. I grew up in this house, attending Parkside kindergarten with my father dropping me off by car on his way to work in the city and Mum picking me up on her bicycle with a cane child's seat on the back. On the way home we would often stop at the Frewville shops on Glen Osmond Road to buy the evening meal – vegetables from Mr Bradshaw's shop and a cut of meat from Mr Corey's butcher shop. I would eat the slice of fritz offered by Mr Corey on the ride home as Mum's pleated frock would blow around her legs in the breeze. Mum was on the kindergarten committee, always baking goods for the trading table and organising social fundraisers for the parents. Both my parents gave to the community, with my father establishing the Glenunga Cubs and Scouts with Keith Tuckwell in 1958.

At age five, I started infant school at Linden Park in 1956, with Mum walking me to the top of Queen Street and gripping my hand as we crossed the busy Portrush Road. During this time we had developed friendships with families in the area through the Glenunga Methodist Church and the school. Mum went to the Mothers' Club meetings at the school and held office at our church and taught Religious Instruction to Grade 3 students at nearby Glen Osmond School. One of her pupils was Gordon Whitrow who transferred to Linden Park School in Grade 4 and became a good friend of mine along with Don Cranwell, David Brecht, Kim Fuss, Garrie Hisco, Laurie Cousin and Mark Rosenthal.

Dawn recalls: 'Gordon was cheeky and often I would send him outside the classroom. A year or two later his mother became the local Rawleigh distributor calling at our house to sell household products. The baker and the milkman delivered their goods daily in a horse and cart.'

Mum played tennis regularly at the church and at friends' private courts. She made most of her own clothes, often dragging me along to Myer or John Martins in Rundle Street while she chose patterns and material. We took a tram or trolley bus from Glen Osmond Road to the city. Mum used to place items on lay-by at the city stores, which reflected her tight housekeeping budget. I could never understand how that worked and why we would take another trip to the city to pay monthly store accounts. Demasius Store, now part of the site of the Burnside Village Shopping Centre, was another source of fashion and homewares. My father left the police force in 1954 and began a successful career in shipping, taking up a management role at Port Adelaide in the 1960s until he retired in 1983.

Our Glenunga home was full of love and laughter, with my father being stricter than Mum. I fondly remember Mum's chocolate cake with coconut over the icing and sausage rolls as holiday and after-school snacks. Summer treats were home-made ice-cream, with juicy peaches and nectarines from our garden. Mum used to care for the garden, mowing the lawns with a push hand mower. When the motorised Victa mower came on the market, Mum saved her housekeeping money and bought one in the late 1950s. I remember our excitement when the salesman delivered it to our home and demonstrated how it worked to Mum.

'I scrimped and saved for that mower to make the task easier on my ailing back but as soon as I bought it Leon took over the lawn cutting duties.'

Summer holidays were always taken at Port Vincent, where we spent the last two weeks of January in a rented flat near the beach with 32-volt lighting, a kerosene refrigerator and wire-based bunk beds. Mum would roll Dad's cigarettes during the three-hour journey, mostly on unsealed roads, stopping for a while when the fully laden car had boiled. Dad took on the cooking duties there. Most evening meals were the fish we had caught off the local grain wharf. Mum was good at fishing and I remember one evening we ran out of cockles and Mum caught a bucketful of whiting by substituting cotton wool as bait. We would leave the beach around 4 pm each day so Dad could have a shower and return to the Ventnor Hotel in time for the 'six o'clock swill'. Dad would park the Wolseley 6/80 outside the hotel at 5 pm and bring out a shandy for Mum and a lemonade and raspberry for me. In later years a beer garden was set up where we would sit on the brightly coloured metal chairs. I fondly remember those holidays and regularly visit the hotel, where two large sporting photos of mine now decorate the front bar.

'Port Vincent was a wonderful holiday destination, it created a break from living with my mother. Bryan learnt to swim and fish there and to be back in the country reminded us of our time in Port Lincoln.'

The Adelaide Technical High School was built in 1962 opposite our house and I went there, along with a number of my Linden Park School classmates. Mum was on the school council and worked in the tuckshop. After leaving school I became a cadet photographer at the *Advertiser.* I lived at home until I was 20, when my parents bought a seafront block of land at Ardrossan and built a substantial holiday home. Mum and Dad lived in tents at first and made do with a 'long drop' toilet during the building of what became their retirement home in 1984. Mum learnt to drive at 50, buying a low-mileage green 1956 Austin A90 that was previously owned by Miss Garrett, principal of Linden Park Infant School when I went there in the mid 1950s. Mum and Dad forged new friendships at Ardrossan and always described this time, along with the few years living in Port Lincoln, as the best years of their lives.

I travelled and worked overseas for two years in the early 1970s, exchanging weekly aerogram letters with Mum; her news from home and mine from wherever I was at the time. I would call home on birthdays and Christmas from a phone box. With the arrival of two grandchildren (Daniel in 1986 and Lauren in 1988) Mum and Dad moved back to Adelaide in 1989 to a home on Cross Road, Myrtle Bank, and regularly picked them up from Linden Park School for after-school care. During this time both parents helped out with the renovation of my family home in Toorak Gardens. My father's health rapidly deteriorated in 1994 and he died in September the following year.

Mum moved to a home unit close to us in Toorak Gardens and at 91 years of age, and with most of her friends passed on, is still living independently with support from family, neighbours, friends and outside care. I enjoy her sharp mind and often share opinions on the news and sporting events of the day.

Mum loves the Crows while I am a keen Port Adelaide fan, which makes for some interesting discussions. She is fond of a meal at Paul's Fish Café on the Norwood Parade, and the occasional glass of wine. Most of all, she adores her family, especially grandchildren Daniel and Lauren and is dearly loved by all of us.

Brandy Cream

Ingredients

1 cup cream

2 eggs

1 teaspoon vanilla essence

1 tablespoon brandy

½ cup sugar

Beat egg whites. Add sugar and beat. Add egg yolks and beat. Beat cream with brandy and vanilla essence. Stir beaten egg whites, sugar and egg yolks into beaten cream, brandy and vanilla.

Delicious with Christmas pudding. Can be made well ahead and frozen.

Bryan Charlton

Bryan Charlton was born on 8 October 1950 at Rose Park, the only child of Dawn and Leon Charlton.

He attended Linden Park Primary and Adelaide Technical High (now Glenunga High) schools. On leaving school he began a 40-year career as a press photographer, firstly with the Advertiser *and later with the* Age *as the Adelaide bureau photographer with Fairfax Publications. Bryan also spent time in the early 1970s as a sports photographer in London covering major sporting events in the UK and Europe. He has won many awards, including Rothmans Press Photographer of the Year in 1980, Australian Sports Photographer of the Year in 1981, and, in 2004, SA Press*

Photographer of the Year. He currently works as a freelance photographer with clients in the mining and construction industries, government departments and the corporate world.

Bryan has enjoyed building and renovation of his homes, fishing and travelling extensively in Australia and overseas. He is happily married to Denise and the proud father of Daniel, a film-maker and audio-visual specialist, and Lauren, a physiotherapist. He regularly visits and cares for his mother Dawn and looks forward to enjoying the rest of his life with family and friends.

Juggling Work and Home

Greta Ellman FROLICH

née Dempster

(1924–1999)

Richard Frolich

It's a cold winter day. I am in front of the fire, at the beach, looking through the Adelaide Symphony Orchestra's program to book concert tickets for the rest of the 2014 season. Handel's *Messiah* is being performed on Thursday 27 November. Will we or won't we go?

Every year a serious choral performance is programmed by the ASO, I confront the same issue, season after season. Growing up as a child and then as a teenager, our house was almost a studio of my mother's music. The family radio would be constantly playing classical music. I could cope with the symphonies, piano, cello and violin concertos, but I had inordinate difficulty aligning with my mother's love for choral work ... Bach's *Masses*; Brahms' *Requiem*; Handel's *Messiah*; the *Carmina Burana*; Mendelssohn's *Elijah*, to name a few.

As a child I think it was just too difficult for me to understand what my mother loved so much about choral music. She would immerse herself in every note. Her eyes would close as certain passages clearly moved her so emotionally. Sometimes there was almost a feeling of embarrassment in me, as she would 'conduct' the work using a wooden spoon as she cooked. But it was clearly that part of her life that stimulated and motivated her so much, and gave her hour upon hour of endless enjoyment.

She had kept every program of every concert performance her parents ever performed, her father as conductor or as the organist, and her mother as a soloist soprano singer. Programs collected since 1929, when she was only five! It must have been the most amazing sight, and clearly a dominant force in her life to have her family home so enriched by music, and then to see both parents perform at the Town Hall and the Elder Hall month after month, year after year.

Greta was involved in the very fabric of the Adelaide music world after the passing of her parents, from 1938 onwards. Among the hundreds of recital programs, I found original letters from the University of Adelaide Elder Conservatorium of Music professors acknowledging her cooperation in bringing her school choirs to performances at the Elder Hall. Thankyou letters acknowledging her passion and drive to bring music into the lives of the youth of Adelaide in the 1950s and 1960s. Letters from Bernard Heinze and Henry Krips, all acknowledging her drive and commitment.

So for me, a rebel teenager, trying to connect with her choral music was impossible. Nothing could compare with my heroes, the Beatles, the Rolling Stones and Bob Dylan. But there it was, all the time, omnipresent, year after year, permeating my senses, so that without ever seeing her choral music performed live, I knew every bar. Every note. I have to give it to her though. Even when my brother and I each had our respective rock-and-roll school bands, she would come and watch us rehearse; that's how much she loved music and how diverse her music interests were.

So why am I still procrastinating, after 40 years, about purchasing tickets to something that was such a part of my life growing up?

Well to understand, I have to share with you the story of an amazing woman. A truly amazing woman of all seasons, and of all things artistic. Mum was born in 1924, into a very musical family. By the age of 18, both her parents had passed away, and she almost immediately assumed her father's role at Walford College, taking singing classes for their students. Her father, John Dempster, was a prodigious musician: a singing teacher, the organist at St Peter's Cathedral Adelaide for 30 years, the city's organist, and the conductor of the Adelaide Philharmonic Choir for 15 years. Her mother was the perfect partner for her husband. A soprano singer and accomplished pianist.

For Mum at age 17 to suddenly lose her father, when he was only 52 and in the prime of his life, must have been an immeasurable shock. To lose her mother the following year, also as suddenly, a life-changing tragedy. It was this sequence of events in her teenage years that I believe shaped her survival instincts, her determination, her agenda, her skill sets and her personality.

Greta Ellman Frolich née Dempster was a woman ahead of her time. By the time she married in 1947, she had been teaching for six years, from the age of 17 to 23. She had also performed solo at age 16 as a singer in Town Hall and Elder Conservatorium recitals.

She married a handsome Hungarian sportsman and gave birth to her two children, Rick in 1950 and John in 1952. She and her dashing husband Frank had a whirlwind social life in the 50s and 60s, Greta's centred around her musical interests, Frank's around his rowing, horse-riding and bridge-playing worlds. Yet they would cross over into each other's arenas, with some awkwardness, and do what was expected of their times – perform their moral duty to support each other in their respective interests.

And yet they would always find the time to entertain friends, in a most generous and warm style, with their two young boys eagerly hovering around, avoiding going to bed, just to see everyone connect and talk and laugh. As a couple they were formidable hosts.

Mum was an amazing and gifted person in the kitchen and a most gracious hostess. Her dinner parties were legendary. Our family dinners were memorable. She adapted to a European-centric cuisine within months of marrying Dad, using and adapting her mother-in-law's traditional Hungarian recipes. Despite her teaching obligations, my brother and I would arrive home from school every day to a fresh-baked cake or biscuits. Every night would see a beautiful meal prepared for her family by her.

On weekends, Mum would show her prowess in the kitchen by making yeast buns and pasties in winter, and in summer, preparing salads before they were fashionable, to accompany barbecues, fish and the occasional crayfish dinners. She would prepare innovative stuffings for her astonishing roast chicken. She would scour the Central Market every Friday morning for the freshest vegetables, breads, cheeses, fish and poultry, and the most interesting cuts of meat. And there would always be a treat for us from the confectionary shop, crude chocolate assorted crèmes in a brown paper bag from the lolly shop or Charlesworth's.

By the 1960s Mum had taken on additional teaching responsibilities at Presbyterian Girls' College and St Peter's Girls' School. I look back on this commitment she had for at least 20 years, and continue to be astounded at how she accomplished this. Thousands of students had the experience of being taught singing by Greta (nick-named Demi-semi-quaver by her students). Greta was respected by her peers and in particular, the headmistresses of the schools at which she taught. The headmistresses subsequently became her lifelong friends, entertaining each other, swapping books, and going to the movies.

By the time my brother and I were teenagers, Mum had many students call around to the house for coaching or mentoring. They were the daughters she never had. For my brother and me, they were the opportunity to meet and connect with dozens of girls. I don't think Mum ever knew what an amazing source of introductions she was for us both. They loved her. We loved her.

All the while, Mum would be there to support my brother John and me. Our clothes always washed and carefully put away in our bedroom wardrobes. Our football clothes, filthy from mud, restored to as new condition after her magic touch. Our beds always made. Our rooms always clean. The garden always tidy. In return we would wash her car, dry the dishes at night, sweep the bedroom floors if we made an extra mess with our friends, ride down to the shops to fetch something that the family had run out of, and vacuum the pool.

Aah. The pool. Mum and Dad built the family a swimming pool in 1962, and Mum swam in that pool every single day of her life. She worked to pay for it … she was going to get the full dividend from it. And until her death in 1999, she lapped that pool, keeping fit, rarely catching a cold, and loving every single minute of it – summer, autumn, winter, spring.

Perhaps her most significant achievement was the raising of her two boys…..the instilling of manners, social etiquette, courtesy, moral code, and a work ethic. The way she persisted with us to say our please and thankyous. Her insistence on making eye contact with people upon meeting and talking to them. The wiping of our feet on the doormat of our home and every home we entered. The importance of a firm and deliberate handshake when meeting people. The opening of car doors for women. Teaching us to speak correctly, and pronounce our words clearly. The completion of chores around the house to warrant our weekly pocket money. The encouragement to go out and clean neighbours' cars for extra spending money.

I am in no doubt that the reason I had £300 in the bank by the time I was 16 was due to the work ethic she instilled in me, and also the frugal savings ethic she taught us. We were a comfortable family, but both Mum and Dad worked hard to get us suitably educated and prepared for adult life.

By the 1970s, with her two boys now grown-up men, Mum had been teaching for over 30 years. She started to cut back on her commitments to the schools, and started to seek out fresh interests. One of those changes was her first grandchild, Jonothon – my son.

Jonothon became the next generation to be a beneficiary of the Frolich/Dempster value system. And continue it did: from a little boy through to his teens, Jonothon's life was shaped and moulded by this amazing family matriarch. It's quite spooky really, because today at 40, some of life's little anecdotal snippets have their foundations laid in Greta's philosophy. I swear I even see mannerisms rear their heads from time to time, in Jonathon's pointed and potentially dogmatic views on some issues.

She taught Jonothon everything. Like her two boys before, she went to the extreme to ensure that Jonothon would be prepared for life. A great story is about the day she fully set the dining-room table, at 3 pm in the afternoon after school, not for a dinner party, but to share with her grandson, in fine detail, how to sit, eat and talk at a dinner. She showed him how to use a serviette; how to use the cutlery from the outside to the inside; when to speak with an empty mouth; how to maintain eye contact; how to hold a knife and fork; how to tip the soup bowl away from you to get the last two spoonfuls of soup; how to write a thankyou note after being entertained by someone. Déjà vu.

Every conceivable detail of social etiquette was bestowed on that fine lad. Including, as Jono now describes it, adult conversation with his grandmother. She didn't believe in kiddie speak. She'd cut to the chase. Adult conversations about politics, friends, music and art. Life, and what to expect. No shade of grey for this matriarch; just plain black-and-white speak. I am so glad my son was able, through circumstance, to share in the same guidance and principles in life as my brother and I. And so, Mum had another opportunity to guide a young soul and family member with the same life skills as her first two boys.

I am absolutely certain that my son's commercial success is in some part due to the confidence she instilled in him socially, and he was always a very impressive young man in adult company. This has certainly aided and abetted his successful career.

When my father passed away in 1985, his death unleashed an even more independent woman. With her two boys long absent from home, Mum immersed herself even more deeply into art and music, advising the ABC on music broadcasting selections, reading profusely and enjoying her grandson on an almost daily basis, as his school was just around the corner. The wonderful Linden Park Primary School. Yes, two generations of boys, both coming home to Craighill Road after school for that fresh cake, lime cordial, and many dinners and stay-overs.

But back to the art. The loss of her husband gave Greta the room to express herself again as an individual. She took art lessons from Ruth Tuck, a professional painter and art teacher in the 70s. Greta loved painting watercolours, and Ruth was the perfect mentor. Greta would practice for hours and hours a day. She would spread her white Arches paper all over the house, and her paintbrushes and paints. She would have multiple paintings on the go.

Her 'clown series' gave her the most joy, smiling faces of clowns performing tricks; frowning unhappy clowns when a trick failed. She would drive to the beaches of South Australia and paint seasides. She even took Jonothon to Granite Island one day and painted a portrait of her grandson with the ocean backdrop, beating at the south side of the island.

Real imagination.

My mum passed away in 1999. An unfortunate operation led to her passing at age 74. I would have loved her to grow older with us, like so many of my friends have experienced. To see our lives evolve. To see the product of her guidance. To share in the successes. To be there in times of tragedy and failures.

This opportunity to write about Mum has been a very cathartic experience for me. For it took me until only a few years ago at age 59–60 to realise what an amazing person had brought me into the world, provided me with love, support, guidance and a life living at home to age 20 that was an absolute privilege.

My mother was an independent, intelligent, free-thinking, musical academic, sure of her principles, and firm in her opinions. She was informed, sophisticated, and outgoing. She was loved by many and respected by all. She was an emancipated woman before Germaine Greer even thought of the idea. She was her own person; she was not restricted by custom or tradition, yet valued both and used them as tools in her life with us.

Mum was forthright yet a listener; she was combative, yet empathetic; single-minded, yet could also be broad in her views.

She was Greta Ellman Frolich (Dempster).

PS: *Nearly forgot. The tickets to Handel's* Messiah *for November? Couldn't go. Staff Christmas party planned for that night. Next season!*

Richard Frolich

Richard (Rick) Frolich was born on 2 July 1950. He lived at St Georges with his family for 20 years, attending Linden Park Primary School until 1961, then Prince Alfred College from 1962–1967. Rick was a very involved student at PAC, finishing with representation in the school athletics team, the Cadet Corps as an officer, the lifesaving team and winning a school literature prize. After matriculating, he studied accounting and marketing at the South Australian Institute of Technology, and joined Myer as a trainee in 1969. He enjoyed a retail career with Myer, then Harris Scarfe until 1977.

Rick started a retail consultancy in 1978, which evolved into a specialist strategic marketing business over the next 15 years. Married in 1983 to Jan, Rick has two children, Jonothon who works in New York and Danielle who is a director of the family company in Adelaide.

In 1992, Rick joined with Jan his wife in Tynte Street Flowers as a partner. Together they have grown the business into Adelaide's largest fresh flower retailer and digital market.

Rick has been heavily involved in the visual arts community for many years, being retired treasurer and a director of the Melbourne Art Foundation, a retired Venice Biennale Council member, a board member of the Sydney Biennale, and the founding chair of the Contemporary Collectors benefactor group at the Art Gallery of South Australia.

Bertine Janet Cameron CRAMOND

née Mackintosh

(1924–)

Anne Cramond Sutcliffe

When I was a child I thought my mother grew up on Embo Farm, but later I discovered that she actually spent a large part of her childhood living in the neighbouring village, Dornoch, where she was born on 1 September 1924. Dornoch is the county town of Sutherland in the north of Scotland. Her grandfather owned the farm, large by the standards of northern Scotland, and it was on his death that she began to live there. In fact, the families swapped houses, and her grandmother and unmarried aunts moved to Mum's family house.

Mum was an intelligent child, a mixture of obedience and mischievousness, which led to my being told some wonderful stories of escapades quite at odds with the sensible mother I knew. How I would have liked to have had the nerve to do things like that! She did very well at school, winning many prizes. I was surprised to discover recently that golf was one of her subjects, presumably because golf has been played at Dornoch since at least 1616.

I never knew John Mackintosh, my grandfather, as he died when Mum was 19 and at university in Aberdeen. After her husband's death, my grandmother, Anne, was left to run the farm on her own, as her son John was too young to come in to his inheritance. This was not the first time that she had had to cope with disaster, as her mother died when she was 17, and she spent many years helping her father to bring up her sisters. Mum loved spending time with Grandfather Mackenzie (her maternal grandfather), following him around as he worked, but her Mackintosh grandparents seem to have been somewhat remote.

Mum told me that life wasn't too hard for them during the war, although the fact that the men had gone to fight made working the farm more difficult. I was surprised to discover that they had a German prisoner-of-war to help them. Food rationing did not affect them much as they had their own produce, but clothes were a different matter. In 1949, Mum's wedding dress was second-hand and was bought with clothing coupons; it was later worn by my aunt when she married Mum's brother.

Mum went on to study medicine at the University of Aberdeen, which is where she met my father, Bill Cramond. They married in 1949.

Mum's interest after she graduated was in obstetrics and gynaecology, but she did not practise this long as I arrived in 1950. Dad was studying for his MD and Diploma in Psychological Medicine in their early years together, as well as working at a psychiatric hospital outside Aberdeen. Mum did not work at this stage, but looked after me, and later my brother Stephen when he was born in 1952. About six months after I was born, she and I went to Embo where she looked after her mother who had had a stroke and required care that my uncle was unable to give on his own. Dad would visit us when he was able, and spent some of his time there studying.

Later on in 1955, we moved to Woodilee Hospital near Glasgow, where Dad was the superintendent. The house that we lived in came with the job; it was immense, particularly compared to the places we'd lived in before and to the small flat where Dad grew up. But

Mum was unfazed because it was very like the house where she had lived on the farm, the earliest part of which dated from the late 1600s. I didn't realise until I was older, probably in my 20s, that farm houses didn't usually have wings or three storeys, but that one did. So Mum relished the thought of living in a large house again, and did not mind the effort involved in looking after the house and family. (She did have someone to help with the cleaning.) I remember her saying that once she'd finished cleaning it, she had to start all over again.

It was in Woodilee that I first became more aware of her as a person as I began to realise that she could do all sorts of things. For example, she stuck stars made of silver paper on our bedroom ceiling which she had painted blue; she made me a doll's house that was open all the way around so that I could easily move the furniture and people in it, and a dressing table from a kit; and made us all sheepskin slippers. But she didn't seem to like the more traditional knitting or sewing very much, perhaps because my father's mother excelled in this area.

Christmas is a special time, and Mum made it very personal by making us Christmas stockings from felt, with our names painted on in gold, and filling them with gifts. They weren't limited to toys, as oranges (which were rare) were often included. After we came to Adelaide, the huge pine tree with beautiful decorations gave way to her version of an Australian Christmas tree. She would get a suitable small branch, place the end on a piece of cardboard, and put plaster of Paris around the base. When this was dry, she would paint the whole thing white with splashes of gold, particularly on the ends of the twigs, and then put on the tinsel and ornaments. We loved this unusual and individual approach to tradition.

She also played the piano. This she had learnt when growing up, and she took it up again at Woodilee; I also learnt from her teacher (I wanted to play the piano rather than dance because that's what Mum did).

I remember her being very firm with us, but she also allowed us a great deal of freedom, something which has gone these days, and was made easier when I was young by the amount of space we had to roam in. We also had this freedom when we stayed with her family on the farm: it was quite a contrast with the more restricted life in the city of Aberdeen when we were with Dad's parents.

Her reassurance is also something I recall, such as the time when my first tooth became loose. She had spent some time putting me to bed, a time I always enjoyed even if I may not have wanted to go to bed originally: I called her back because I got such a fright when I felt my tooth wiggling. What a relief to find that nothing was the matter and that the fairies would leave money under my pillow when the tooth finally came out. After that I remember poking it with my tongue to hasten the process. Mum was a good listener and good at explaining, for example, the facts of life – I remember asking all sorts of questions about this that she answered without making me feel embarrassed or foolish. I often enjoyed spending time with her, especially sitting at the kitchen table on a Saturday, chatting while she prepared dinner, perhaps for some friends; or walking to the shops to get the greengroceries, returning with each of us holding one handle of a heavy bag. (Mum has reminded me that often I would be peeling mushrooms while sitting talking to her.)

She would also try to spend time with us when we were sick: on one occasion I had measles or something, and Mum took the ironing-board and ironing upstairs so that she could do it in my bedroom. Now I realise what an effort that must have been. If we had a cold, she would make us a lovely warm drink from orange juice flavoured with honey, cinnamon and nutmeg; when we were older, a splash of whisky went in too. Perhaps that's where my taste for it developed!

Cooking is a large part of mothers' work, and I remember enjoying the food she made – all sorts of things, from scraping out the bowl when she'd made a cake to eating a roast or the crusts cut from sandwiches for an elegant afternoon tea, perhaps with bits of tomato or cucumber still attached. One thing in particular stays with me – because we didn't have a fridge (just a larder), we rarely had ice-cream. But Mum made a mean Bombe Alaska, so every now and then, Dad would dash off to the shops, and race home with the ice-cream which was put in a thermos until Mum needed it. Yum!

Life changed in many ways when we came to Adelaide in 1961, but because our way of life was so similar to the new one, many of the inevitable teething problems probably weren't very evident to others. Some of them involved food, were embarrassing at the time, and in retrospect, hilarious. One was the time when we had a barbeque with a family who had very kindly met us when we landed for the simple reason that their surname was the same as ours. Mum had bought the requisite supplies, and had frozen the sausages in her very first fridge. Unfortunately, she hadn't realised how long it took to defrost meat, so that our meal was still frozen when it came time to cook it. Another was a similar event where we were expected to bring our contribution to a mass barbeque; my parents didn't understand the technicalities, so Mum brought sandwiches. We had to eat those while all around were the smells and sounds of chops and sausages being cooked and demolished. We found it very difficult to understand why we couldn't accept the offers of sausages wrapped in bread and dripping with sauce. And there was the time when Mum was asked to bring a plate to a function, so she did – with nothing on it. She had thought that the request was extremely odd!

Going into town presented Mum with a special challenge. This was a woman who was used to visiting Glasgow, a large city near where we lived in Scotland, and, other than being presentable, one did not have to dress in a particular way. So she was shocked to find that she was expected to wear a hat and gloves when she went in to Adelaide. To this, she did not conform.

School was different for us too, as we landed in the middle of a school year and had to catch up quickly. I was in Mrs Roselaar's class where French was being taught and this required a lot of work on my part. Fortunately, Mum had learnt French at school and was able to coach me in vocabulary, grammar and pronunciation. Decimals were another challenge, overcome with the help of Mum.

Something else that changed was Mum's return to work. I don't know all the reasons behind this decision, but one was that being a housewife in Adelaide was not onerous. This gave her time that she wanted to fill by working. But she didn't resume her career where she left it – she began a new one by training as a child psychiatrist. In 1962 she began working part time at the Child Guidance Clinic in Wakefield Street and, under the tutelage of Dr Keith Le Page, developed an interest in psychoanalysis and family therapy. With her first pay she proudly bought us all a present: I imagine it must have been quite a thrill to once more be able to dispose of her own earnings. After a couple of years, she started full-time work, and as my parents felt it was important that we did not return from school to an empty house, they employed someone to help with cleaning and a bit of cooking. As I got older, I would sometimes start a meal and Mum would finish it off when she got home.

It was still unusual to have a mother who worked. We didn't much like having a stranger in the house when we got home, although we certainly understood the necessity, but it was much nicer to go to a friend's house instead (her mother didn't work). There she and I engulfed large quantities of cake and gem scones – what a long-suffering woman my friend's mother must have been. We benefited in other ways though, as Mum was happier working even though it was hard for her to do everything she needed to. And as she began to realise that there were different ways of bringing up and understanding children, she changed the ways in which she dealt with us for the better. In doing so, she also gave us valuable ways of understanding and dealing with the world.

I haven't said much about being taught to cook, clean and suchlike. My tuition was a bit patchy as Mum thought that it was better for us to concentrate on homework rather than chores. I certainly didn't help when we lived in Scotland, but in Adelaide I gradually learnt how to do chores. One was ironing, where I started off with sheets and pillowslips, then graduated to more complicated objects, such as shirts. Imagine ironing sheets! Mum was lucky here, as I actually liked ironing, and still do. Mum is a good and inventive cook, and we made pastry, pancakes, scones and cakes together. Somehow I learnt to cook meat, although I don't remember how. Making ginger beer was my particular pleasure. I obtained the plant from a friend, collected lots of Woodies' lemonade bottles, and was allowed space in the cupboard to store the finished product. We all enjoyed the results, and I don't think there were any explosions.

As I mentioned earlier, Mum wasn't interested in sewing, much preferring painting walls, which was sometimes a disadvantage. In Grade 7, the girls had to perform a club-swinging act at the end-of-year function, for which we had to wear a blue top and shorts, naturally made by one's mother. Not in my case – we had to find a dressmaker to make mine. This, coupled with the fact that a friend's mother made all her clothes, got me thinking about learning to sew. We learnt to sew by hand at school, but my family didn't own a sewing machine. I can't recall the details, but somehow Mum agreed to buy a sewing machine, I had a few lessons that I think came with the purchase, and started sewing my clothes. Part of the bargain with Mum was that I do any sewing that she required. The first was chopping up a tablecloth to make napkins. Later on, Mum trusted me enough to make dresses for her – it still amazes me that they were good enough for her to wear.

One of the defining skills of an Australian adult is the ability to drive, and this is something that my mother never did here. She had obtained a licence in Scotland in the days when very little in the way of skill was asked of one, but had never driven much. In fact, she told me that there were only two women in her circle who drove. When we came here, passing a test about the rules of the road was all that was necessary to obtain a licence, but she never used her licence. So all her life she has walked, been driven by someone, usually my father, or used public transport and taxis. But on the other hand, she has never had to adjust to the loss of driving, and walks to the shops every day, just as she always has.

In my late teens, I was sufficiently accomplished in the housewifely arts for Mum to pay me to do the housework and some cooking before I started university, as we were between home helps at the time. Watching Mum had taught me a lot but I didn't realise how much I knew until after I left home at the age of 20.

This coincided with my family returning to Scotland in 1971 while I stayed in Adelaide. The years in Britain were very productive for Mum and may well have been some of her best: she worked in Edinburgh, Glasgow and Leicester in child, adolescent and family psychiatry, as well as psychoanalysis and family therapy. Mum also had another job when they lived in Stirling where Dad was Principal of Stirling University, a position which also involved entertaining people as varied as students and visiting dignitaries as well as attending formal functions. Mum fulfilled her role splendidly although she found it difficult at first.

They returned to Australia in 1980 and, after spending three years in Sydney, came back to Adelaide in 1983, when she resumed work with what had now become the Child, Adolescent and Family Health Services. All this time, as well as clinical work, she had undertaken training and supervision and had read widely in her field, but had not pursued any formal qualifications, which meant that finding jobs commensurate with her skills and experience was difficult. Her worth was recognised in 1987 when she was made a Fellow of the Royal Australian and New Zealand College of Psychiatrists. Mum plays this down as she sees herself more as a psychotherapist than a psychiatrist, but I am very proud that her ability was marked in this way. She stopped working full time in 1989, and finally retired in 1994.

After 12 years of communicating mainly by letter, international phone calls being prohibitively expensive, my family was again in the same city, and, as with my father, Mum and I now discovered that some of the difficulties we had while I was an adolescent had not disappeared. Turning a parent–child relationship into an adult version is not easy, as I'm sure that all of us writing these essays about our parents would agree. Mum and I have worked hard on this over the years, particularly since my father's death 10 years ago, and I think we are very lucky to have reached a point where we have a relationship of deep understanding.

About the time that she reduced her working hours, my brother Stephen married and had two children. Mum and Dad willingly looked after their grandchildren, doing all sorts of things with them, such as taking them to the monthly children's event at the Art Gallery, as well as the more usual weekly meal with the new family. She is now amazed and very pleased that she has seen her grandchildren grow up, something she never expected.

Mum was 90 on 1 September 2014. Although frail, she is an impressive woman – she appears to be quiet and self-effacing, but she can stand up and be counted when necessary; she successfully combined a career with a family at a time when this was unusual and harder to do than it is now; and best of all, she continues to walk to the shops each day, read, listen to music, see her friends and engage with the world, as well as grow personally. She is an excellent example of how to grow old.

Chocolate Mousse

6 ounces dark dessert chocolate

½ gill strong black coffee (4 gills = 1 pint)

2 tablespoons caster sugar

½ ounce butter

1 tablespoon brandy

3 eggs

Whipped cream

Coarsely chopped almonds or crushed praline

Melt chocolate with sugar and coffee in a heavy pan until like thick cream, being careful not to let it curdle (omit sugar if chocolate is sweet). Remove from heat and cool a little, then stir in butter, brandy and egg yolks. When cold, lightly stir in stiffly beaten egg whites. Pour into a bowl or individual glasses and decorate.

Anne Cramond Sutcliffe

Anne was born in Aberdeen, Scotland, and emigrated with her family to Adelaide in 1961. After attending Linden Park Primary School and Presbyterian Girls' College, she obtained a BSc and BPharm. Most of her work was in hospital pharmacies and she is now an editor in a small publishing company involved in providing information about drugs to health care professionals. This satisfactorily brings together her love of science and of English. She has been divorced and has since remarried.

Renna May GILLIES

née Brinkworth

(1920–)

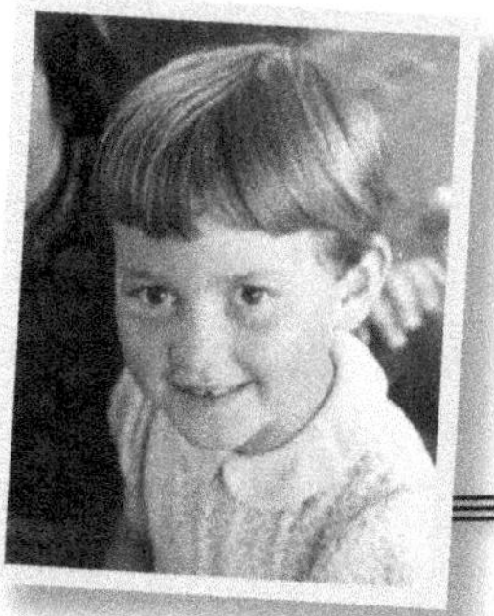

Julie Gillies Kernick

Renna May Brinkworth was born at Kadina on 19 October 1920 to Frederick George Brinkworth (born 7 August 1875) and Mabel May (née Rodda, born 13 May 1881), their seventh child.

Mum spent the first two years of her life at the family property Chinkford, just south of Kadina, before her father retired and the family moved to Alexandra Avenue in Rose Park. Her father was an innovative and successful farmer and her mother reputedly the 'district beauty' with a notable head of hair and a very slender waist, having been heavily corseted from an early age. May, as Mum's Mum was known, dreamed all her life of independence and a career but ended up moving from farm chores and caring for younger siblings at home to becoming a farmer's wife and raising a large family of her own.

Mum grew up as the youngest daughter in a large family of seven children with four older sisters and two older brothers, and a cousin, Pearl Skipworth, who lived with them after her mother died. This was an era where a widowed father was fortunate to have available relatives to care for his children as part of their family household.

Mum's older siblings were able to join in the lifestyle of the 1920s, the 'flapper years', and enjoyed parties and lots of socialising, especially the girls who, once they finished school at Methodist Ladies College (MLC, renamed Annesley College), were not allowed to undertake paid work outside the home as 'ladies do not work'. The two boys completed their schooling at Prince Alfred College (PAC).

Mum recalls that as she grew into her early teens the 1930s recession hit and relatives came to live at the house, such as Aunt Delsie while her husband 'headed off seeking work in the West'. While large family meals were common with often 12 or 19 at the table, the frugality of the recession era meant her social life was different to that of her older sisters.

She recalls the sleeping arrangements being tight for the children in a burgeoning household, and when the sleep-out on part of the back porch was full, sleeping on the back porch with canvas between them and the elements, sleeping at Aunty Laura's next door across Thomas Place, or in Mum's case, as the youngest child, sharing her parent's bedroom for a time.

In the 1930s, Fred became a State Bank Inspector and was known as very conscientious and fair in his dealings with farmers in financial troubles at this difficult time. His own investment in a property at Geranium in the Mallee, led to its ownership. Mum's two brothers worked the land once they left school, there being 'no jobs' then, and Mum lived there at times. There were lots of funny stories about life there, even the one very shallow bath a week for everyone to dip in, and becoming expert at cleaning teeth with water in a cup. The soil was so sandy Mum's brothers ended up putting fences one on another as the drifting sand buried them.

Mum attended Rose Park Primary School and then followed her sisters to MLC where she was able to be a day student in the 1930s so did not first attend a one-teacher country school and then become a boarder as her older sisters had. For several years when the family was not 'in town' the two older sisters lived with an aunt and then in a boarding house, and brought up their teenage youngest sister, Mum. She always thought that her sisters were stricter than their mother who let Mum get away with things that they were never allowed to do.

Mum completed her Intermediate Certificate (Year 10) after two years of high school in an accelerated program and was allowed to go to Business School to learn typing, shorthand and bookkeeping. While by far the youngest, Mum was the first of the sisters allowed to take paid employment and she worked in the then State Bank on King William Street. In those days it was a prestigious institution where one was invited to open an account. This broke the ice with their father for the other sisters who were able to broaden their employment pursuits and gain qualifications in subsequent years.

Mum developed a closeness to her two older sisters that never left them. In later years Joyce and Beryl needed to move into supported accommodation and in their final days, full nursing care, on Beulah Road, Norwood. Mum visited regularly and provided practical support, helping them with their clothes shopping, health issues and other matters. They always felt well cared for with someone to watch out for their interests at an especially vulnerable time in their lives although both enjoyed good intellect right to the end.

Mum found the start for a long-standing desire (shared with her mother and older sisters) for a career and some independence but in time felt stifled by her position at the bank. Roles for males and females were highly differentiated and duties on switchboard, as personal assistant to the Bank Manager, and general reception duties not all that exciting. She prepared weekly financial reports with 10 copies typed through carbon sheets rolled into the carriage of her typewriter – accuracy really mattered as any changes meant 10 corrections. However, there was no opportunity for her to win the positions and consequent pay enjoyed by her male colleagues. In her daily interactions, she became acutely aware that some of those males were a lot less bright than she was.

At this time Mum met Dad, Hugh Gillies, through mutual friends. Mum was a lifelong friend of Coralie, who knew the Soward family, and Dad had met Neville Soward prior to both entering the army. Mum's family home was near the Victoria Park Race Course where Dad had established a chiropody (podiatry) clinic as part of the army encampment there. Neville's mother was very taken with Coralie and determined one of her four sons would marry her. Coralie and Neville also married and became two of my godparents as did Mum and Dad for their younger daughter Robyn.

Mum and Dad married in July 1943 during the war and after Dad had been very ill. Married life commenced with renting a flat in Toorak Gardens where they had two daughters, my sister, Heather, and me. In 1950 they started building the family home in Beaumont. As Dad's father Archibald had just been widowed and was a frequent visitor, Mum and Dad moved to his house in Opey Avenue, Hyde Park, while building was in progress. My earliest memories are of life at Grandpa's.

I remember riding in a cane seat with footrests on the back of Mum's bicycle to kindergarten and on occasion to her felt-hat-making class. We also caught the tram on King William Road, Hyde Park, to the city. The family car then, and for some years, was a black Vanguard, with heavy manual steering and column shift gears; overall it was a very solid vehicle.

Because my father's work involved a large number of surgery towels and starched white coats, and nowhere could be found to wash them to a satisfactory standard, this task was undertaken by 'Page' as I knew her. She was an elderly woman who asked to have the job if she could wash and iron for the practice and the family in her own time and not be rushed by fixed hours. Page was much loved and a regular part of weekday life.

I remember the laundry on the back porch and the washing machine with the wringer top that swung around so that the washing could go through two troughs of rinsing water, the second of which might have had Bluo added for whites, and then finally through the wringer and into the laundry basket and out to the clothesline. That washing machine stayed in use for some years until I was old enough to be using it.

When the new house was completed in 1954, the whole family moved to Beaumont, including Grandpa. Page retired and Mrs Mickovitz came to clean, wash and iron for the practice and the family. She was a single mother postwar from Latvia. I remember how stressed she was and we gathered it was to do with her war experiences in Europe. She was a gem, but at that time no one really spoke about war experiences, and being from an English–Scottish heritage we did not understand the difficulty of learning English later in life, even for an educated multilingual woman.

Mum got going learning to drive as an adult on the deserted beaches near fishing spots when we were on family holidays. I remember being driven to school and picked up for the first six months of infant school by Mum driving that car. After that I walked to and from school each day.

With two young children, opportunity to work outside the home was not an option. Fortunately Mum's efforts to establish an interesting life which included more than home duties and caring for children were not limited to felt-hat making and learning to drive.

Mum's early introduction to bookkeeping would stand her in good stead in future years. It was not just her skill but her use of her knowledge and application to her own circumstances that enabled her to manage her finances to good effect throughout her life. She kept the accounts for Dad's chiropody practice and, at 93, is still preparing her statements to go to the accountant for her tax returns.

Mum sewed clothes, especially for my sister and me. Due to pricing at the time it was more economical to buy fabric and make clothes and they were generally of better quality. As Mum wanted to be a fashion designer rather than a bookkeeper/shorthand typiste/secretary, my sister and I had attractive well-made clothes to wear. Our clothes gave her some outlet and I remember she pleated tartan wool skirts for my sister and me for winter; they had a white cotton placket on top with several layers of tucks to let the hems down as we grew. I also remember two sundresses I wore to school in summer in Grade 5 when white spots were at the height of fashion.

While my sister and I were at school, Mum caught up with her old school friends weekly for tennis in summer and cards in winter. Her driving licence came in handy to get to Somerton from Beaumont! Following her retirement, Mum was able to catch up regularly again with these friends for some years. Mum was also able to drop and collect Dad from work some days and visit her mum in the family home in Rose Park.

Linden Park Primary School had a Parents' and Friends' Committee (P&F) which Mum joined. She thoroughly enjoyed being part of the Committee that planned for a swimming pool to be built, and she still comments today what an impressive group came together to fundraise and plan the pool. It was built and operating while I was still in primary school. Mum also organised netball posts and rings to be soldered onto metal wheel-shaped bases so the girls could play in the schoolyard on the asphalt by the original buildings. On Arbour Day one year in the late 1950s, the whole primary school was on the school oval to see trees planted along the Hay Road edge, bought with money from the P&F. Mum realised at Christmas time that no-one was watering the newly planted trees and organised for several students living close by to water them until Term 1 started in February the following year.

Mum has commented from time to time ever since how rewarding and interesting her time on the Committee was.

Mum thought about how my sister and I were going at school, especially by mid-primary when my dad was having significant health issues. As was often the case, I was shielded from all this and was told it was not unusual for a dad to rest in hospital for six weeks over Christmas, or that we went away for a week every term break. The associated pressure this could only have made for my mum and dad was not something I was particularly aware of because I had no idea at all how ill my father was. Other families I visited as a child all had their own household issues they were dealing with and I just assumed everyone was different in various ways.

When Dad died a year later, Mum became a widow at age 40. Fortunately, friends and family were supportive and arrangements were made to sell my dad's practice with Mum continuing to handle the accounts and also start work as the practice receptionist. I was in Grade 6 when Mum returned to work.

Mum's friend Coralie came to the house when it was time to bottle all the fruit from our peach and apricot trees and bottled a year's worth for us so we had dessert for that first year. At this time her own mum was waiting for a supported care place at Resthaven, Leabrook. Nanna moved in with us and shared a bedroom with me. My older sister had moved into Grandpa's room as he had moved house when he remarried a few years before.

The following year, when I was in Grade 7, Mum commenced podiatry study while still working during the week and made sure she passed every subject. Following her graduation, Mum bought her own practice in North Terrace, and so established her own career.

Mum was now working, running the household as a single parent, attending lectures in the evenings and studying evenings, early mornings and weekends. There was a weeknight meals roster to get the dinner on for a quick meal.

Mum worried about her mum's safety, being frail and alone in the house all day, and asked for help for a placement. Nanna then came for tea on Wednesday nights and we dropped her back to her room at Resthaven until she was bedridden in her final years in my late teens.

Shopping while working was quite a challenge as shop opening hours were limited. Shops closed at 5 pm weekdays and were open 9–11.30 am on Saturdays. That meant that if we needed to fit something else in at that time my sister and I were dispatched with a shopping list to the greengrocer, the butcher or the grocer, so we did one each. If that failed, Mum rang each shop from work and ordered for collection on Friday a little after 5 pm; all our shopping was left with whichever shopkeeper would still be there waiting for Mum. These were rather unique arrangements at the time and based on trust. With the opening of the first supermarkets in the early 1960s, all changed.

At home it was very fashionable to have a niche in the front hall with a decorative feature. In our case, we had a wrought-iron fitting with driftwood and plant arrangements. The kitchen floor had black-and-white square vinyl tiles that needed to be waxed and polished every week, and there was a floral carpet through the lounge-dining room, hallways and main bedroom. The kitchen doors were a high gloss red and there were padded red vinyl bench seats either side of the kitchen table. While Mum was at lectures in the evening, I remember cleaning the cooking splash marks off the red door surface that opened against the upright oven and taking off the gloss in the process. The electric floor polisher found a new use as I lifted it up and down the door to buff the shine back.

Our family pet dog Ritchie was our watchdog and he was allowed inside while Mum was out at lectures. He was a good watchdog, and Grandpa made him a very smart kennel fitted out to match the house including white eaves on the front.

Our meals at that time were predominantly the traditional fare. For dinners we ate a side of lamb each week with the usual boiled vegetables except for the roast for Sunday lunch and fish and chips or steak on Friday nights. In earlier years we ate freshly caught fish when Dad had had a successful day out. Mum used traditional cookbooks like the *365 Pudding Recipes* for every day of the year. Meals were practical and fitted into a busy schedule. In later years the breadth of the recipes changed as those of us of English–Scots heritage learnt to eat a much wider range of foods, to our great benefit. Mum did not like cake or soft drink herself and these were kept for special occasions. Icing and decorative items such as silver balls, chocolate sticks and hundreds and thousands and occasionally cream were used.

Apart from fresh or preserved fruit, we had lemon pudding or something similar on Sundays, jam and cream on bread or a slice of ice-cream from a cardboard-covered block of about 400 grams. Ice-cream cones were a great treat for birthdays as were jellies and fairy cakes.

By the time I completed Grade 7, Mum had been widowed for two years, had sold my father's chiropody practice, held a job and completed her first part-time year of study of her podiatry course.

Mum joined the Podiatry Association and, as an established podiatrist, held a term as President. Her specialty was, as for my father, foot supports. Mum's knowledge and physical skills enabled her to develop a number of techniques and approaches that helped patients with a range of problems. Dad's 'penguin parade' of nuns found Mum and came to her, especially for foot supports as many had been issued with the wrong-sized shoes in earlier times and had fairly mangled feet as a result.

While Mum's eventual career path was a practical solution to raising a family as a widow, it had elements of intellectual stimulation, both with the practice itself and the Podiatry Association involvement; a creative side with design of the business itself and with making foot supports; and the opportunity to run a successful practice and handle all the finances.

Mum moved house once my sister and I had left home, and later remarried and was subsequently widowed for a second time. Mum has pursued interests in bridge, which she still plays on occasion, theatre, travel, Probus Club, and her friendships with family and friends.

She wears well-fitted shoes and fashionable attire with cut, colour and fabric always just right and still has an eye for combining style with practicality and comfort. Just as her own mother took great interest in, and cared for others, so does Mum take great interest in her grandchildren and, now, great-grandchildren.

Julie Gillies Kernick

Julie grew up in Adelaide, first in Hyde Park and then in a red-brick house across the road from the Beaumont Common, Beaumont – until she graduated with an Arts degree from Adelaide University. She grew up with the neighbourhood friends and family, and was part of the community at Beaumont Methodist Church throughout her childhood and teenage years.

Julie attended Linden Park Primary School and then Presbyterian Girls' College (now Seymour College). She then taught in Adelaide high schools, completing a graduate Diploma of Education at Flinders University before studying at Stockholm University International Graduate School. Julie then won a scholarship to the Australian National University where she completed a Research Master's degree in Sociology using International Education data and a thesis proposal developed while in Sweden.

Julie has worked in education, training and research ever since with the Commonwealth, the National Centre for Vocational Education Research and the Independent Education Union. She has been a member of various education boards and committees. She has held the position of Manager, Research and Skills Development at the Construction Industry Training Board for the last three years.

Julie enjoyed learning music, sport and dancing and has been active in various community groups over many years. She still enjoys being active in community groups and has recently learned Scottish Country Dancing. Julie is very happily married to Phil and between them they have six children, five with partners, and nine grandchildren and a large extended family.

Merle HIGGINS

née Smith

(1920–2003)

Phil Higgins

From my very earliest memories, I can recall that my mother was someone who always had to be doing something. Whether it was sewing, knitting, cooking, gardening or entertaining, she never really stopped – ever! It was quite incredible.

Born in Melbourne on 5 April 1920, Merle Smith was the second of three children born to Leslie (Les) Frederick and Florence Ada (née Randall) Smith. They lived at Hutton Street, Thornbury, and later at Henry Street, Northcote. Les managed grocery stores and Florence was a wool winder prior to their marriage in 1918. Les was also an accomplished cyclist and won a number of trophies in amateur road racing throughout Victoria.

The marriage was to last only four years after Florence left him on 5 November 1922, taking with her only their youngest child, one-year-old son Leo. Les would later file for divorce on the grounds of adultery. With Les now the sole parent of two young girls, neither of whom had yet started school, he sought assistance from his mother and father, moving himself and the girls back into their home, not far from the Northcote State School where Mum and her sister, also named Florence (but known as Floss), commenced their education. From the day Florence walked out, Mum never knowingly had any further contact with her mother. However, as a young child, she and her sister were often dressed up in nice clothes and told to wait outside at the front gate where 'a friendly lady' would pass by at a certain time on Sunday afternoons and talk with them. It is also quite likely that Les never again saw Leo although I have been unable to confirm this. It wasn't until many decades had passed that Mum was able to reunite with Leo, but more about that later.

In 1929, Les remarried and in the following years his family grew with the addition of another son and daughter. It was at this stage that his employer required him to relocate his family several times. He managed grocery stores at Clifton Hill, where they lived upstairs above the shop, and at Burwood where they also lived on site, before buying his own business at Camberwell. This meant that Mum was always moving from one school to another. In those days, primary schooling went to Year 8 and with the country in the middle of a terrible depression, many children were forced to leave school on completion of Year 8 and 'go out and get a job' in order to supplement the family income. Mum was one of these children and after initially assisting in the shop, she obtained employment at the iconic Melbourne department store, Georges. It was while working at Georges that she completed her apprenticeship in dressmaking, a qualification she would continue to use throughout her life. During the war Mum was employed at the Government Clothing Factory making uniforms for the armed forces and she continued working as a dressmaker after she had moved to Adelaide at the end of the war.

Mum met my father in Melbourne when he was on leave from the army and they were married in 1947. It was not just her mother who did not attend the wedding but also her father who had passed away four months earlier. For five years Mum and Dad lived alongside the Unley Oval, sharing the home with an elderly widower, and both became actively involved in the local church as Sunday school teachers. I was born in 1950 and my sister Roslyn followed in 1952. Shortly after her birth we moved into our new home at Hazelwood Park. Ours was one of the last houses to be built in the street and was located directly opposite a reserve which is today known as Wood Park. There was even a Mothers' and Babies' health centre in the park to cater for the large number of young families which had moved into the area.

In 1955 I commenced my eight years at Linden Park Primary School and still have memories of Mum walking with me each morning and being there again at the gate in the afternoon. It wasn't until I was in either Grade 3 or 4 that they allowed me to ride my bike to school, Devereux Road being the issue. As most people know, married women of the day spent a lot of their time at home and Mum was never one to waste the day away. Using her earlier acquired qualifications, she would make her own skirts and dresses as well as clothes for my sister. She was also a prolific knitter and even made me a grey V-neck school pullover complete with the maroon bands. It was something that at the time I didn't really appreciate, as I thought it made me 'stand out like a sore thumb' compared to the others who wore the regular type.

With a young family, much of her time was taken up with routine tasks, the washing always being done on Mondays. Without modern appliances this usually took a lot longer than it does now, and in the case of the clothes wringer, which was mounted above the tub, it was potentially dangerous. She had heard of instances where hair had been caught and was generally very wary but on one occasion got her arm too close while it was moving, trapping it between the rollers, and she suffered a severely dislocated elbow. I can recall the sling and her arm being all shades of black and blue for several weeks.

It was also around this time in the late 50s that she decided to paint the entire inside of the house. At that stage the house was white throughout and Mum decided she needed to introduce some colour. She chose the colour scheme, my room being a combination of bright yellow, blue and orange, and progressively over the following weeks, completed every room!

Mum was also well known for her culinary expertise. Like most families in the 50s and 60s, all our meals were eaten at home and together at the table. Fast food outlets were virtually non-existent and takeaway was something you bought at the local fish and chip shop. This never mattered and although I may be biased, Mum certainly excelled in the kitchen with cakes and desserts her speciality. In those days doing the weekly shopping never seemed to be much of a chore and it was not necessary to have a car. You could phone the local grocer who would home deliver, there was a fruit and vegetable truck which went down the street once a week and a butcher on Devereux Road. Briefly diverting, I also have memories of the travelling salesmen who frequented our area. One was a chap who sold a product called Rawleigh's Salve Ointment, which Mum called 'bike chain ointment', and another sold Faulding's Castor Oil. The ointment she kept for my skinned knees, often as a result of the red rover games played during lunchtime at school, and the latter was something that Mum threatened to rinse my mouth out with if I continued to swear … But let's get back on track!

Almost all the food Mum prepared came from these three local sources. In earlier years, Dad had planted citrus and stone fruit trees across the upper half of the backyard. We had orange, mandarin, grapefruit and lemon trees as well as a passionfruit vine which grew over the back shed. However, it was the apricot and peach trees which offered an abundance and every year Mum would get out the Fowler's Vacola preserving kit and go into production. I can remember arriving home from school to find the entire kitchen occupied with the various stages of the process. Relatives and neighbours were usually the recipients of any surplus and as long as they returned the empty jars with their special lids and sealing clips, she was happy.

Mum continued to be heavily involved with church activities and even more so after Dad had bought their first car in 1961. On

Sundays she was one of a few who took on the responsibility of extending hospitality which included inviting people home to lunch. This was something that the church encouraged especially towards visitors from interstate or elsewhere, as well as singles and elderly widows who might otherwise have had nowhere to go. Lunch would usually be a roast with vegetables followed by something like baked apple or apricot pie or maybe even pavlova. Mouths would then drop open when she brought out the double-layered sponge cake topped with strawberries and cream! 'Where am I going to put this?' or 'Oh Merle, you didn't need to go to so much trouble' were common responses. But it never was any ' trouble', it was simply something she loved to do.

Throughout her life Mum never had any desire to learn to drive and Dad didn't do or say anything to encourage her to think differently, especially after an incident which occurred at a Sunday school picnic in the early 60s. We were at Paracombe in the Adelaide Hills and someone had managed to acquire a couple of two-stroke-motor go-karts for the day. Although reluctant at first and after a fair bit of encouragement, Mum finally relented and agreed to have a turn. Everyone was laughing, thinking it hilarious as the kart careered wildly all around the oval. In reality she was petrified, as somehow the accelerator had become jammed and the kart was out of control, eventually coming to a stop when she crashed into a partially collapsed section of wire fence which surrounded a tennis court. Badly shaken, she was fortunately otherwise unharmed. It was to be the last time she got behind a steering wheel!

Mum was always a stickler for cleanliness, with the home being spotless from one end to the other and she had the same expectations of accommodation when travelling. On one occasion in the late 60s, she and Dad had scheduled a trip to Melbourne to visit her family. Dad had booked ahead, planning to stay overnight in a motel at Nhill in western Victoria. Her usual habit upon entering such places was to inspect the sheets and the grouting in the shower recess. In this instance they must have been clearly off the mark as over the next few hours she proceeded to let Dad know, in no uncertain terms, that this 'joint' was not a good choice. In the months and years that followed, Dad, who was a serial stirrer, would relate this incident to quite a number of friends and one of them offered to make a small sign. The sign just had the letters MHPH (Merle Higgins performed here) and looked rather professional after he had attached it to a shortened tomato stake. On a subsequent trip to Melbourne this friend planted the sign in a garden bed alongside the driveway leading to the reception office and even brought back photos to show Mum and Dad. The sign remained for several years until finally succumbing to the weather, but not before many friends and family, including Mum herself, had passed through the town and checked it out.

In 1965, with my sister and I both now in high school, Mum approached George Demasius, owner of the fondly remembered Demasius department store on Greenhill Road. She had come to know George well as she regularly frequented his store and he offered her employment. As she did not have a driver's licence, Mum relied upon Dad to get her to and from work, which always meant for a rather long day. She worked in the Ladies Knitwear Department and became well known amongst the local 'blue rinse set' (her words not mine) and others who shopped regularly in the store. At that time, Australia still had a large clothing manufacturing industry, centred around the inner suburbs of Melbourne, and eventually she would become the knitwear manager, whose responsibility it was to purchase the stock. This required her to make trips to Melbourne where she would meet with manufacturers and agents, selecting a range and placing orders for the following season. I have memories of our kitchen table being turned into an office and being covered with stock control books and range catalogues and her working on them late into the night. Such was the devotion to her job that she would 'talk shop' during her sleep. Dad would often call me to their room to have a listen. He would play the role of the customer and would say something like, 'That's a lovely blue twin-set on that mannequin. Do you have one in my size?' Mum would usually answer back with a positive response but would always be in complete denial the following morning. 'That's just ridiculous, of course I don't talk in my sleep,' she would say.

It was during her time at Demasius that she was also making wedding and bridesmaids' gowns in her 'spare time' of an evening and at weekends. The word had got around among some of the young women at the church that Merle Higgins could be persuaded to make their bridal dresses. All that was required was for them to provide the materials, patterns and a bouquet of flowers upon completion. At least two of them, as well as another marrying for a second time, thought that was a pretty good deal! In the 70s she also made the gowns, including those of the bridesmaids, for both her niece's and my sister's weddings.

The 17 years Mum spent at Demasius was certainly mind-broadening for her and she developed a new circle of friends, which up until then had been restricted to neighbours and church members, all of whom had mostly conventional views. These people were of various age groups and ethnic backgrounds. In an era when many still harboured anti-Japanese sentiment and derogatory slang names identified a person's nationality, Australia's gradual shift to a multicultural population was something that a large number of people, including Mum, found difficult. However, over time she became much more tolerant of different worldly attitudes, opinions, and religious customs, and in the instance of one particular person, even their sexuality. She retired in 1982 when it would have been impractical for her to commute from Glenelg, where she and Dad had relocated.

Not long after Mum and Dad had shifted to Glenelg, she was reunited with her brother Leo after more than 60 years. This came about after Leo, who had been adopted by another family only a few months after the marriage fell apart, took it upon himself to trace his family. Having another brother was something that Mum had never mentioned to me until then. They met together several times over the following years and kept regularly in contact, but with Leo now living in Perth, distance was always a problem.

Dad died in 1995 and the following year Mum moved to a small

Anns Carrot Cake

1 Cup White Sugar
1 Cup Vegetable Oil
3 Eggs
1 1/3 Teaspoons Baking Powder
1 1/3 Teaspoons Carb Soda
1 1/3 Cups Grated Carrots
1 1/3 Cups Plain Flour
1 Cup Brazil Nuts (optional) or walnuts or almonds
1 1/2 Teaspoons Cinnamon
1 1/2 Teaspoon Nutmeg.

Method. Put all ingredients into a bowl together, and mix well.
Line bottom of round or square tin with lightly greased, greaseproof paper. and bake in oven for 1 hour at 300°. 150 C.

Icing One 4 oz pkt philly cream cheese
1 Cup Icing Sugar
1 oz Butter
1 Teaspoon vanilla essence.

unit in Netherby where she felt less isolated from her family and friends, most of whom still lived in the south-eastern suburbs. Until 2002 she had always been reasonably healthy, however in May of that year she was diagnosed with terminal cancer. In the months that followed, Mum spent much time in and out of hospital. It was her wish to spend her final days at home and this was made possible through the efforts of my sister and a couple of palliative care nurses. She passed away on 28 January 2003 with the family at her bedside. At her funeral, a friend entitled the eulogy 'Family, Friends, Food and Frocks'. It had been a life full of devotion to her family and valued friendship to many.

Ann's Carrot Cake

1 cup white sugar
1 cup vegetable oil
3 eggs
1⅓ teaspoons baking powder
1⅓ teaspoons carb soda
1⅓ cups grated carrot
1⅓ cups plain flour
1 cup Brazil nuts, walnuts or almonds (optional)
1½ teaspoons cinnamon
1½ teaspoons nutmeg

Place all ingredients in a bowl and mix well. Line base of a round or square tin with lightly greased greaseproof paper and bake in oven for 1 hour at 300°F (150°C).

Icing

One 4 ounce packet Philly cream cheese
1 cup icing sugar
1 ounce butter
1 teaspoon vanilla essence

Phil Higgins

At the end of 1964 his class teacher wrote, 'Philip has had a disappointing year. He has not found the work easy but with a bit more effort he could have done much better'. After breezing through primary school around the top end of the class, Phil found high school a whole different challenge where his best efforts were always reserved for the sporting fields rather than the classroom. After leaving school in 1966, he commenced a 26-year career with the Coles organisation, which included store management and regional management positions in two states. Since 1994 he has worked as manager of an automotive parts and accessories store in Brisbane where he has lived since 1989. Until her passing in 2014, he was married for 30 years to Nerida, a schoolteacher, and they had two children, Catherine who is also a schoolteacher and Ben, a Fine Arts student. His current interests include camping and four-wheel-driving activities, which he plans to devote more time to in coming years.

Edna Jean MACPHERSON

née Speirs

(1918–2012)

Judy Macpherson Kent

'Mrs Ross Hector Macpherson, 13 Playford Street, Glen Osmond, SA.' I clearly remember the letters addressed to my mother in my father's name. I wondered at the time if she resented this. Didn't she deserve to be addressed in her own name? Who was the woman behind the man? What were her aspirations? Was she happy and fulfilled? Did she have an identity apart from her husband and family?

I need to go back to her family of origin to answer some of these questions. She was born to William Goldsmith Speirs and Margaret Tweeddale – the third child and middle daughter of the family.

The story has it that her father Bill, who was born in Launceston, Tasmania to a Scottish immigrant ship-building family, was on his way to work for relatives in Perth with his twin brother Arthur, when Arthur died of tuberculosis in Adelaide. Bill, who had met Margaret (actually Maggie-May on her birth certificate) also of Scottish ancestry, decided to settle there and raise a family. He went into business as a picture-framer and managed to survive the recession while raising four children.

Mum, who was 'affectionately' called Poodie by her family (she was not overweight by the way), seemed to have inherited a dose of Scottish pessimism. Whenever she talked of her upbringing it was tinged with some regret. Regret that she was the only one in the family with blue eyes. Regret that she wasn't allowed to get her long plaits cut. Regret that she had to leave school at 16 to go to work as a comptometriste while her older brother, Bill, and sister, Margaret, continued on with their studies during the recession. Regret that she had been named 'Edna'. (She always wondered if it had been after Charlie Chaplin's wife!) Regret that she couldn't sign up to go to war because she worked for an essential service. Regret that she had to leave that essential service, Shell, when she married.

And when I compare her childhood with my carefree existence, I realise that she had a lot to be regretful about. But on the other hand, the grainy pictures I have of her show her beaming as a tow-haired child playing cricket in the garden of the family home at Black Forest; proudly straddling her bicycle with her plaits wound around her head; lying on the beach in bathers, giggling with her younger sister, Ailsa. The family home was in the middle block of three with an almond and fruit orchard on one side and a tennis court on the other. Her sister remembers that Edna used to sit in the fig tree singing. She remembers it as being a very happy childhood but then says that Edna 'didn't get much attention' despite the fact that she won the junior athletic cup for Adelaide High School and excelled at hockey and tennis.

Mum married Dad, whom she had met through the church when he came back from the war in 1943. Dad had been wounded in the hand in Palestine and was not considered fit for more active service, so he resumed his job at the Savings Bank of South Australia. Mum, who had had to leave the job that she loved at Shell, was pregnant in a couple of months and had my sister, Rosslyn, in 1944. She confided that she had no idea of sex or sexuality before she married. Periods were an embarrassment better not discussed – in those days they had to wash out rags and get them dried ready for the next day's service. You can imagine what it must have been like with three girls and their mother in the house! And all of it undiscussible!

Two more daughters followed at three-yearly intervals, Janet in 1947 and me, the youngest, in 1950.

On my fourth birthday we moved from Glandore to Glen Osmond and my first memories of Mum are of being sung to sleep with her gently caressing my eyelids. The songs were Scottish lullabies, which I remember to this day and have passed onto my children – 'A Nut Brown Maiden', 'The Skye Boat Song', 'The Bonnie Banks o' Loch Lomond', 'I Had a Little Nut tree' and 'Wee Chookie Birdie'. All of which I have been singing to my new grandson. Just the other week while on a flight from Melbourne to Adelaide, I was sitting next to a young woman who was trying to get her fractious baby off to sleep after a long international flight. I found myself showing her how to gently rub his eyelids until he subsided into a deep and long-awaited sleep.

Other memories are of cuddling kittens with Mum on the deck of our new house, surrounded by lots of concrete and newly planted lawn. I remember her in the kitchen, turning out rather grey offerings. Irish stew, consisting of lamb chops and three veg which had been cooked to within an inch of their lives. The pickled meat was a bit tastier. Mum loved the pressure cooker which used to fill me with dread – I thought the top was going to blow off when it got up steam. On very special occasions – Christmas – we had roast chicken and Mum's roast vegetables were quite delicious accompanied by a pretty good gravy from the meat juices and this new thing called Gravox! She kept a jar next to the stove for the fat and juices from the meat which she would use again for the next meal. She used to tell how as a girl she and her siblings loved eating bread and dripping but thankfully never inflicted it on her own children. While the main courses were nothing to write home about, she excelled at slices, biscuits and cakes, and Saturday mornings were filled with the tantalising aromas of apricot or raspberry slices, coconut ice, pineapple tart, jam-filled sponges, lamingtons and butter biscuits with a cherry on the top.

Dad would call out, 'You beauty!' from where he was mowing the lawn and we'd all look forward to sampling the newly-baked treats. She could also whip up a decent ice-cream which was laid to rest in the freezer and would require some stirring after it froze. Of course when bought ice-cream became available we wouldn't look twice at the home-made stuff!

She also went through a period of worshipping Diane Cilento's recipes and ensured we all ate healthy food. Breakfasts were always cooked – scrambled eggs, omelettes, tuna patties or porridge – we could never get out of the house without a wholesome breakfast – and we often took fruit salad in Vegemite jars to school for lunch. These always looked much better before they had rolled around in our school bags and sat in the warmth of the bag room for a few hours but tasted good if you closed your eyes. If Mum tried to keep us healthy through her cooking, her home-made remedies left something to be desired. Heaven help us if we complained of a sore throat as out of the cupboard would come the jar of yellow sulphur powder into which Mum would insert a straw and then blow the powder directly onto our tonsils. If it did nothing else, it certainly stopped us complaining.

Other memories of Mum are of her at our shack at Moana. When Dad first built it in 1952, we had a meat safe and an ice chest and we got the milk warm and fresh in a billy from the milkman. Mum would heat it on the top of the kerosene heater. I can still smell that burnt milk after it boiled over and inevitably it would have a skin on the top, which not even the Cadbury's Bourneville Cocoa could dispel. Mum was usually happy at the shack. She had decorated the walls with recipes and photos cut out of *Women's Weekly* magazines and these had been varnished. You could spend days reading those walls. Mum would also cook jam and bottle fruit so that we had preserved fruits all year round. We had an orchard of fruit trees – quince, apricot, apple, peach, and nectarine. They all seemed to ripen at once and it was a rush for all of us to wash and slice the fruit for packing into jars and boiling up in the Fowlers Vacola – inevitably during a heatwave. Other fruit was made into jam. One vivid memory features my sister, Jan, sucking on something hard in the ABC (apricot and black currant) jam Mum had just cooked. On closer inspection, what she had been sucking on was a beetle – minus its legs. We didn't throw the jam out but we certainly inspected every mouthful after that!

Days at the shack were spent on the beach with rugs spread out in front of whichever Holden we happened to have at the time. Mum would have packed the Esky for the five-minute drive to the beach and we'd have cheese and Vegemite sandwiches washed down with Woodie's lemonade. But always there was that one-hour wait before we could go back into the water. And she enforced it to the minute, convinced that if we went into the water a minute before the hour was up we'd get a cramp and drown.

I remember having to wear shirts into the water so that we wouldn't burn, a thing I hated at the time, but looking back, should be grateful for. They were shirts that Mum made, too. It must have been 1956 because I remember vividly that they were predominantly green with the Olympic rings on them and we had beach bags to match. Mum was a good sewer – I didn't have any store-bought clothes until I was a few years older and my suitcase was stolen during a trip to Tasmania. Lucky for me I got to buy some bright-pink pedal pushers, a shirt and a dress. I still remember how much I loved those clothes because they weren't home-made!

Mum worked at different jobs while I was growing up. She did secretarial duties for a time-and-motion management consultant whom she disparaged. I think she thought that anything psychological was suspect. She also worked for a real estate agent, and in later years she kept the books for my uncle who owned an importing business. I used to feel quite proud to have a mother who worked although sometimes she would be apologetic about it because she wasn't always home when I got home from school. I loved coming home to an empty house. I'd find the cashews in the cupboard and curl up in one of the oversize lounge chairs in the sun which streamed in the living room through the picture window overlooking the panoramic city and plains. It was heaven!

I could read to my heart's content the *Readers' Digest* hardcover compendiums or bright yellow *National Geographic* magazines lining the bookcases which ran along the walls under the bench seats. If I was proud of the fact that my mother worked, she had been socialised to apologise for it.

Our house was a typical 50s triple-fronted cream-brick veneer with grey tiled roof. Edna Everidge would have had the time of her life with it. One bathroom was predominantly grey with pink basin and bath which highlighted the brown-coloured sludge we called water in those days (it was a long way from the River Murray to Glen Osmond!). The kitchen cupboards were painted grey again which proved a reliable backdrop to the pink-and-grey laminated kitchen table and benchtop. All the doors and runners were varnished timber and we had a state-of-the-art parquetry floor in the entrance hall. I wonder now if she was excited when she chose the colour and furnishings for her new house. Was it what she really wanted? The patio (pronounced 'pashio') was extensive and overlooked the city. We could watch the planes land at West Beach and the sunsets were breathtaking. On warm summer nights we'd gather together with our next-door neighbours, the Janzows, and share the bounty from our kitchens. Mum might bring pickled onions, cheese and slices, Merle would have made some pickled vegetables or a curry, and Dad and Eric would taste test the latest Barossa claret or hock which came in large flagons, allowing us kids to try it as long as it was diluted with lemonade! It was on those nights that I remember Mum being happy and carefree as we all looked to the skies to see who could be the first one to spot the sputnik as it raced overhead.

Mum was an avid gardener. I can see her now with her hands in the dirt as she lovingly tended to her roses. Her rose garden was something to behold and she encouraged a love of them in me, helping me to cut and assemble them in beautiful, blousy arrangements on the walnut table, which I have to this day. And the posies were divine. She taught me to weave tiny pink Cecil Brunner rosebuds with forget-me-nots, violets and 'lambs' tongues' and whatever else was out in the garden at the time. I remember presenting one to Mr Rayson in Grade 5 and being too embarrassed to admit that I had made it myself, although on reflection, it was probably quite obvious. Even today when I am weeding I hear her urging me to shake all the dirt off the roots so as not to waste it!

Mum loved to play cards. Once a month she would get together with the 'Canasta girls' – they would rotate houses so I suppose we only ever saw them a couple of times a year. Dad used to joke that they did more talking than card playing but he liked to see Mum happy with her friends. We girls would all giggle as we tried to keep out of their sight, watching delightedly as Mum served up devils on horseback (grilled prunes and bacon), cheese and cherries or gherkins or pickled onions on toothpicks, a cream cheese French onion dip with Savoy biscuits, and some dainty butterflied cakes with cream, pineapple tart and jubilee cake. We knew there'd be quite a bit left over for us.

Mum and Dad also had a group of friends whom they would see from time to time. They went to each other's houses for dinner – never going out to a restaurant. Once when they were at our house, I remember being so excited that I snuck out of my bedroom window to spy on them on the patio and discovered Mum and Dad having a puff on a cigarette. I must have confessed to them later because I remember them saying they'd never do it again and were only just trying it out. They were quite moral people, Mum and Dad, and both had signed the Presbyterian pledge the year they were married. I believe this was a pledge that they wouldn't drink or smoke or do anything at all that could be considered fun. It's a wonder they managed to have children!

Mum was brought up in a strict religious family – her brother was a Presbyterian minister and her sister's stepson became an Anglican priest. It seemed very strict although it was probably no more or less religious than any other family in those times. It was expected that you would go to church, get confirmed and sign the pledge. Just after Mum married, she had to provide refuge for her younger sister, Ailsa (my Aunty Dookies), who was forced to run away from home because of her intention to marry a divorced man with a child. Incidentally, that marriage lasted over 60 years, and provided a very happy home for my two cousins and their stepbrother but it certainly wasn't considered the 'done' thing at the time.

Edna had a very close relationship with her younger sister. They would spend what seemed like hours chatting on the phone – that big, heavy, clunky, black bakelite phone with the huge silver dial. UX3434 was our phone number, which changed to 793434 when I was at Linden Park. I only have a few memories of Mum in relation to Linden Park. One was sitting with her in an assembly (probably involving one of my older sisters). She had on a hat and gloves and carried a matching handbag. That's what you wore when you went out in those days. The other memory was of her sending long-stemmed roses to school for some occasion which escapes me. We had been asked to take off all but two of the leaves and remove all of the thorns and I remember her being pretty annoyed about that. And rightly so! I was the one who had to take off the thorns! The third memory related to school occurred when I must have been about nine or 10. I took money out of Mum's purse to spend at the tuckshop. I think it was four shillings – a massive amount in those days – and I dreamt that night what I was going to spend it on. Round pink sherbets the size of golf balls which exploded in your mouth when you got through sucking the shiny pink lolly; packets of sherbet with a straw which ended up making your whole mouth, fingers and school jumper sticky with sugar; Liquorice Choo-Choo Bars which could last all day and ended up staining your whole face and mouth a disgusting blue-black. I had such sweet dreams. Until the morning when Mum confronted me with the missing money – said she had been going to put lunch money in my blazer pocket and had found it! Of course I burst into tears of shame which turned into sobs when she asked me if I thought I didn't get enough pocket money. It certainly ensured I never stole money again. A lesson well learned – and well taught!

My memories of my mum are mixed. On the one hand I wish she'd been more of a role model in positive thinking. And she did say to me when she was older and a doting grandmother that she wished she had hugged us more. But I always knew I was loved and well cared for. When I look at the circumstances of her upbringing and understand the hypocrisy, the religious bigotry and the expectations which society had of women in her day, I can imagine that she must have felt quite frustrated and unfulfilled at times. Mrs Ross Macpherson – where was there room for Edna Jean? Even in the years after we kids had moved out she was still very much an appendage to Dad and I only saw her really shine when for the first time ever she went away for a holiday on her own to visit a friend in Melbourne and came back with two new coats – one bright pink A-line with a faux-mink collar and the other pale blue. She laughed as she modelled them for us exclaiming at her own audacity for being talked into two coats because she couldn't decide between them. All her life she gave up things for herself preferring to give to her family – she was generous to a fault – but still very much aware of having to account for all her spending, not just to her accountant husband, but to her Scottish forebears all of whom had known what it was like to suffer through a depression.

As Mum grew into her 90s it was hard to see her struggle to remember things. I would find notes on the stove which said 'Turn off' or she would have documented my movements over the day if I were staying with her, desperately trying to control her memory. No longer able to do her beloved crosswords, she would spend hours rummaging through her precious belongings, packing and repacking them and hiding things. She became fiercely independent after Dad died and resisted going into care until she could no longer look after herself, having fired all the help we had hired to look after her! Resolute to the end she always dressed in her signature red coat and hat.

When I think of what I have learned from her, apart from a love of gardening and cooking, it is that I would never, ever let people address me by my husband's name, that I would never swear 'obedience' to anyone, that I would never be dependent on anyone for my financial wellbeing, that I would question religion, morality and politics and keep questioning rather than accepting, and that I would always have a life and an identity which were independent of husband and family. I also learned that having a cup-half-full approach to life is preferable to the opposite.

Another thing I learned is that it is to these women that the girls of our generation owe our freedom and our independence; what we observed them silently putting up with, we rebelled against. And I thank Mum and her generation of women for making that possible.

Edna's Boiled Fruit Cake

1 cup brown sugar
1 cup water (can be substituted in part with sherry or brandy)
½ cup butter
½ lb seeded raisins and sultanas
A handful of glacé cherries
1 teaspoon bicarb soda
1 teaspoon cloves or mixed spice
½ cup flour

Place all ingredients except the flour into a large saucepan and bring to the boil. Allow to cool and add ½ cup flour to make a thin batter. Stir with a wooden spoon.

Bake in a moderate oven for one hour.

Judy Macpherson Kent

As the youngest of the three Macpherson girls, Judy led a carefree existence growing up in the 50s. While she did well at school – her Grade 3 report shows her having attained first place with 99/100 – she always felt she should be doing just that little bit better! Probably because she also received reviews which stated that she 'would not make a seamstress to the Queen' and 'could do better if she checked her work'. Which is no doubt why she developed a passion for studying and learning, at Linden Park Primary School, then at Unley High School, Flinders and Monash universities, and eventually RMIT University where she attained her doctorate in Organisation (Human Systems and Psychodynamics) in 2010. Her work in organisation dynamics takes her into some of the most interesting industries and she never tires of helping to create positive and productive environments in organisations. In 1967 she was fortunate to be awarded an American Field Service scholarship and she spent an amazing year with an American family in Salt Lake City, Utah, and made lifelong friendships with students from many different nationalities. Judy has been married to Wayne for more years than she cares to remember and is blessed with two delightful sons, Simon and Nathan, the latter of whom, with his lovely wife Emily, has just delivered into the family the first of the next generation.

Nancy SWANSON

née Burgess

(1919–2007)

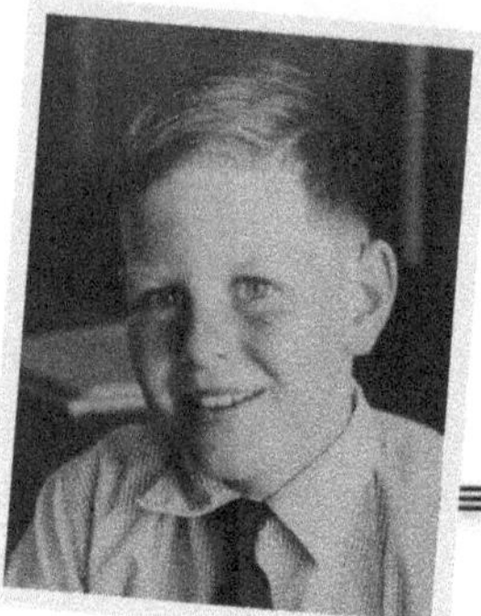

James Swanson

My mother, Nancy Swanson, was born Nancy Burgess in Adelaide on 12 August 1919. She was the second of four children and the oldest girl. Nancy's father, Howard, was a well-to-do accountant and company director, and the large family home, complete with live-in 'help' and a tennis court, was located in Lebanon Avenue, Glenunga. Nancy's mother, Lillie, kept busy with charity work and an active social life.

Nancy and her two younger sisters attended the nearby Presbyterian Girls' College (PGC, now Seymour). Nancy was not very sporty but she did well academically and she was a keen and accomplished pianist. She became Head Prefect in 1937.

Towards the end of her schooling Nancy started to think about a career. This in itself was somewhat unusual for girls in the 1930s but Nancy's family had always valued education for both sexes. Nancy was attracted to medicine but she had the misfortune to overhear a conversation between her mother and the family doctor who expressed the view that medicine was not a suitable career for a girl! A somewhat disappointed Nancy decided to study physiotherapy instead – that was acceptable because it was seen as closer to the traditional female vocation of nursing.

Nancy studied physiotherapy at the University of Adelaide from 1938 to 1940. In her final year she had lengthy placements at the Royal Adelaide Hospital and the Adelaide Children's Hospital, as well as attending lectures. After graduation, Nancy took up a position at the Broken Hill and District Hospital. She was the only physiotherapist on the staff at the time, her predecessor having left to enlist in the army. It must have been a considerable personal challenge for her to begin her career at the age of 21 in a remote city with only minimal professional support. It was also a big cultural change. Broken Hill was very much a man's town. Nancy remembered one occasion when she went to a hotel for a drink with colleagues from the hospital. When she gave her order for a shandy, a shocked silence momentarily fell on the crowded bar (or so she felt).

Nancy gained valuable experience in Broken Hill. Then, in March 1942, with the Japanese on Australia's doorstep, she too joined the army. She was immediately posted to the 109th Australian General Hospital then located in Alice Springs. Later, as the Allies advanced, Nancy moved with her unit to Adelaide River (near Darwin), Port Moresby and then Morotai, a small island in the Moluccas (Indonesia). She treated a variety of patients – civilians, especially in Alice Springs, as well as Australian and American servicemen. She saw the results of the first widespread use of penicillin. On Morotai, towards the end of the war, there were many casualties from the Australian invasion of Borneo. Nancy also treated Allied prisoners of war released from Ambon and was shocked at their emaciated condition. She witnessed a surrender ceremony on Morotai and vividly remembered the Japanese officers, turned out in white silk shirts, solemnly laying down their swords before signing the instrument of surrender.

Despite the suffering she witnessed – the homesickness and the discomfort of army life – it appeared that Nancy's war service was a positive experience, both professionally and personally. She forged her closest friendship during this time with a Sydney physiotherapist, Beth Inglis, who later became my godmother. The tropical climate agreed with Nancy, and after hours there were opportunities for swimming and, from time to time, socialising on visiting hospital ships.

Nancy returned to Adelaide in November 1945. She made the trip in a Catalina flying boat which took several days to fly through the islands and then down the Western Australian coast and across the Bight before landing on the Port River. Nancy greatly enjoyed this leisurely return to peacetime Australia. Her last months of army service were spent at the Northfield Hospital before her discharge in January 1946.

There were many adjustments to be made. Nancy's beloved father had died in 1944 following a heart attack and the family home in Lebanon Avenue had been sold. Nancy lived with her mother and younger sisters in a house on Cross Road (her older brother was now married) and obtained a position at the Adelaide Children's Hospital, working with children with cerebral palsy. This was Nancy's first professional experience of young persons with disabilities and it was to be the beginning of a long association.

At a party in 1946 Nancy met a tall ex-serviceman, Jim Swanson. Jim had served throughout the war in the field ambulance – in the Middle East, New Guinea and Borneo – and had been wounded at El Alamein. He had now returned to his prewar job at the Bank of New South Wales but was also studying accountancy part time at the University of Adelaide. Jim's high spirits and quick-witted sense of humour complemented Nancy's natural reserve.

Nancy and Jim were married in St Peter's College Chapel on 4 October 1947. They honeymooned in Canberra and visited Parliament to hear the bank nationalisation debates (probably Jim's idea). They lived initially in rented accommodation, often short term owing to the acute housing shortage at the time. Later they moved to a house in Alexandra Avenue, Rose Park. Nancy was by now working at the Queen Victoria Hospital nearby. In June

1949 my brother David was born. Soon afterwards, Nancy and Jim bought a block of land at 16 Inverness Avenue, St Georges and built the family home there. It was a two-storey house which took maximum advantage of the view over the city from rising land that was then devoid of both houses and trees. There were still strict postwar restrictions in place so the house was designed to be added onto when circumstances permitted. They moved into their new home in 1950 and were to remain there till 1993.

There were few facilities at first. Nancy and Jim had no car and the bus terminus on Portrush Road was over a kilometre away. To make a phone call, Nancy had to walk up the hill to the nearest public phone situated in Thirkell Avenue. Without surrounding houses, the gully winds all but blew away the garden they were trying to establish, and the winters were cold. One morning Nancy looked out the window to see the hills behind the house covered with a thin sprinkling of snow.

I was born in March 1951. By now Jim, having completed his accountancy studies with distinction, had left the bank and taken up a position with Robern, a family-owned wholesale fruit-marketing company based in Victoria Square. My parents were now in a position to build the planned extension to the house. They were in the midst of building work when, one November night in 1952, life changed for ever for Nancy and the rest of the family.

Jim had been returning to Adelaide from a work trip to the Riverland and Mildura. Past Truro on the Sturt Highway the car, driven by Jim's boss, ploughed at speed into the back of a semi-trailer parked on the side of the road. Asleep in the front passenger seat, Jim suffered shocking head and leg injuries. He was unconscious for over a week and was not expected to live. Once out of immediate danger, he began the long process of recovery. He did not return home for some months and needed to be readmitted to hospital several times for further operations. He managed to return to part-time work in May 1953 but it was years before he was able to work full time. In 1956 the judge who heard Jim's compensation case commented: 'It is nearly four years since the accident, during the greater part of which he has been an invalid. He has had to bear what Dr Barbour describes as great pain, and has undergone repeated painful operations. For much of the time his suffering must have been intense.' Eventually Jim made a substantial recovery though he was left with major leg disabilities. He was able to go on to a successful career as an accountant and management consultant.

I can only imagine my mother's profound shock that November night when she heard that Jim had been badly injured. She was faced with the prospect of widowhood and raising two young children on her own. Although she had good support from family and friends, she must have drawn deeply on her own personal resources to cope with the crisis. Perhaps it was then that she developed the stoicism that I remember as part of her personality.

Nancy and Jim were always a devoted couple. But Jim's accident undoubtedly effected a subtle shift in their relationship. Thereafter, Nancy gave her full support to him in his endeavours and invariably deferred to him, at least overtly. She was protective of him. She recognised the enormous obstacles, both physical and psychological, that he had overcome in his rehabilitation.

I do not remember my father's accident, although it undoubtedly affected me, as it did my brother. My first memory is of a trip I made to Sydney with my mother in 1954. This was a holiday for my mother after several difficult years. We were to stay with her close friend from army days, Beth Inglis. We travelled by train. Jim and David farewelled us at the Adelaide Railway Station. As a consolation to David for being left at home, my parents gave him a model train. When I complained bitterly at the unfairness of it, my mother said, 'But you're going to Sydney,' to which she claims I replied, 'That's not much!'

I have only scattered fragments of memories of the trip. I recall sharing a single sleeping compartment with my mother – what a trial for her to spend the night with a wriggling three-year-old. I also remember riding on a Manly ferry and persuading my mother, against her better judgment, to come out on deck; the stiff harbour breeze almost bowled us over.

I started Grade 1 at Linden Park in February 1956. I was not yet five but my mother was now expecting her third child and no doubt thought that things would be easier if I was settled in school before the birth. The birth of my sister, Mary Alice, in June 1956 was a great joy for my parents after the trauma of Jim's accident. I remember the anticipation that gripped the household in the lead-up to the birth. I was less than impressed when my mother brought a wailing bundle home from hospital!

The ensuing years were, from my point of view, carefree ones. My mother was busy with the household and looking after three young children. My parents had an active social life and went to concerts and adult education classes together. The family attended St Saviour's Anglican Church at Glen Osmond where Jim sang in the choir and became a church warden.

Of course I remember my mother's cooking – what child does not? My mother always cooked a roast for Sunday lunch. Other dishes I especially recall are a delicious curry (before curries were fashionable), crumbed sheep's brains – cheap, nutritious and tasty, but messy to prepare – and bacon and egg pies, which we always ate when we went to the drive-in. But my mother's forte was undoubtedly in the field of desserts, cakes and biscuits. Her best dessert was lemon delicious pudding (see the recipe below). She made wonderful sponge cakes and a rich fruit cake of perfect texture which she called a 'Dundee cake'. In a fundraiser for my Cub pack, my mother baked an extra big Dundee cake as the prize. We Cubs hawked it around the local neighbourhood in a basket and invited people to vie for it by guessing the length of string in a jar.

My mother also made rock buns ('rockies'), various biscuits and lamingtons. She preserved fresh fruit from the back garden in her Fowler's Vacola and she made apricot jam and grapefruit and cumquat marmalade, also from our own fruit trees. My mother liked to see us all eat heartily and we were happy to oblige.

Family holidays were usually at Victor Harbor in the early years. We stayed in a house near the mouth of the Hindmarsh River. In 1961 we went on our first caravan trip, along the coast to

Melbourne and then home via central Victoria and the Riverland. Other caravan trips followed in the ensuing years. These were great holidays for the family (and the dog!). In the evenings we often played 'Quack, quack', an old card game of my mother's which was not unlike Monopoly but involved hen breeding and egg production. As a child, however, I barely appreciated the hard work that my mother put in to ensure that we got away on our trips with everything we needed and to keep us happy and healthy whilst away. Having spent years in tents during the war, a caravanning holiday would not have been my mother's first choice.

The year 1961 also marked the resumption of my mother's professional career. In September of that year she took up a position as the physiotherapist-in-charge of the Activity Centre of Ashford House School at Ashford. Ashford was run by the Crippled Children's Association of South Australia (now Novita Children's Services) for children with cerebral palsy. After formal schooling in the School section, the older students moved on to the Activity Centre to learn self-care and independent living skills. Some continued with their education. Many of the young people needed regular physiotherapy to improve or maintain mobility. Nancy coordinated a team of teachers, physiotherapists, occupational therapists and support staff.

Nancy's job was demanding and she worked long hours. Apart from employing a cleaning lady who came in once or twice a week, I am not aware that my mother scaled back any of her household tasks. She just worked harder and longer.

Jim also worked hard. He had been back in his old employment full time for a number of years now but he was looking to change jobs. He joined a firm of management consultants the year after Nancy started at Ashford. While he maintained the garden and always did the washing up, he was a product of his era and I never recall him doing the cleaning, washing or ironing; cooking was only for special occasions such as my mother's birthday.

We children had to adjust to the change in the family routine that Nancy's new job brought. I did not like coming home from school to an empty house and I was conscious that few other mothers worked. However, I was 10 years old and I was able to understand the situation. It was harder for my sister who had just started school. There was no after-school care in those days and my mother had to make ad hoc arrangements. For some years, Mary Alice was cared for after school by the owner of a dry-cleaning shop on Portrush Road. Nancy would pick her up on her way home from Ashford.

Nancy's busy life meant that she had little time for personal interests outside the family and her work. Her social life was necessarily curtailed but family remained a priority. I do not recall her ever missing an important occasion in my life as I was growing up. She remained close to her two younger sisters and their families and supported her elderly mother who was now in declining health.

Why did Nancy return to work in 1961? My mother gave two motives – financial and professional. My parents had decided that David and I would follow our father to St Peter's College for our secondary education while Mary Alice was destined for PGC for her whole schooling; Nancy's salary was needed to pay the school fees. At the same time, Nancy probably always had in mind to return to physiotherapy at some point; after all she had worked as a physiotherapist for over eight years before David was born. We children obviously benefited from her hard work in helping to finance our education. But equally, she gained immense professional and personal rewards from her involvement with young persons with disabilities. Who knows? – if there had been no financial incentive to return to her career, she might have been tempted to conform to the social mores of the era and continue in her role as wife and mother.

Nancy continued in her career well past the time when it was financially necessary to do so. Her career peaked in the 1970s when we children were largely independent. She continued her professional development. In early 1973 she undertook a course in Sydney to study the new methods for improving movement in patients with cerebral palsy that had been developed in London by Karel and Bertha Bobath. She stayed with her old army friend, Beth Inglis, during this time. In 1976, the Crippled Children's Association amalgamated several of its facilities, including Ashford, at a new purpose-built site at Regency Park. Nancy was appointed the coordinator of the senior section, which was a somewhat expanded version of the Activity Centre at Ashford.

These were busy days but, with reduced family responsibilities, Nancy was able to widen her horizons. She and Jim dined out together once a week and often took weekend breaks in country South Australia. They developed common interests in native birds and flora. In 1975 Nancy visited us (wife Sue and me) in Wewak, Papua New Guinea, where we were then living. It was Nancy's first trip out of Australia since the war. She revelled in the climate, the tropical beauty and the opportunity to reacquaint herself with a culture with which she was familiar from her army days.

In July 1978 Nancy retired as coordinator of the senior section at Regency Park. This was not the end of her working life, however. She worked part-time for a number of years for Heta, an agency that helped people with disabilities find employment. She continued to be involved in a voluntary capacity with groups such as Riding for the Disabled and the Broughton Arts Society and she maintained links, well into her later years, with a number of her former students. In 1983 she was made an honorary life member of the Crippled Children's Association. The work to which she was first introduced at the Adelaide Children's Hospital in the 1940s proved to be a lifelong vocation.

Nancy and Jim's first grandchild was born in 1986 soon after Nancy had retired for good. Four more grandchildren arrived over the next 10 years. Nancy relished her new role as a grandmother. Jim died in 2001 after suffering dementia for some years. This was a heavy blow for Nancy; she had been devoted to him till the end. She never fully adjusted to the loss, but she remained mentally alert and involved with family, friends and the Church. Every Anzac Day she met up with her physiotherapy colleagues from the army.

Nancy died quite suddenly on 17 September 2007 shortly after enjoying a roast dinner with us. Sue knew how much she enjoyed a roast and always cooked one when she came over. It was a happy occasion – the first for some time that both our grown sons had joined us for the meal. Her passing was sad but she had lived a long and fulfilled life.

Lemon Delicious Pudding

Ingredients
1 tablespoon butter (2 ounces)
¾ cup sugar (4 ounces)
2 eggs
Juice of 1 lemon and 1 teaspoon of grated rind
2 tablespoons plain flour
1 cup milk
Salt

Cream butter and sugar. Separate eggs and add yolks to mixture. Add sifted flour and milk. Add juice and rind of lemon. Beat egg whites stiffly and fold into mixture, and place in oven-proof dish standing in a dish of water.

Bake for 1 hour in a moderate oven (350°F gas).

James Swanson

After school, James studied history at Adelaide University and then completed a Diploma of Education in Canberra in 1973. James and Sue married that year and then went to Papua New Guinea for two years where James taught in high schools and Sue did secretarial work for the Catholic missions. Still footloose, James and Sue then spent two years in Europe including a period in the Spanish Basque country during the transition from Francoism to democracy.

In late 1977, James and Sue returned to Adelaide and the reality of establishing their careers. Sue resumed her teaching studies (interrupted by the overseas travel). James, on the other hand, had realised that teaching was not for him and enrolled part-time in a law degree. James qualified as a lawyer in 1984 and then worked in a number of private firms in Adelaide and as a sole practitioner. Meantime, Sue had commenced her career as a primary school teacher. Tom and Sam were born in 1986 and 1988 respectively and Sue took some years out of the work force when they were young.

In 2001 James joined the Crown Solicitor's Office. James's interests are bushwalking and the environment generally, history and Spanish. James and Sue are still working but look forward to an active retirement together.